THE FUTILITARIAN SOCIETY

THE
FUTILITARIAN
SOCIETY

WILLIAM J. NEWMAN

GEORGE BRAZILLER

NEW YORK, 1961

Printed in the United States of America

TO MY PARENTS—

WHO KNOW THE IMPORTANCE

OF FREEDOM

"All activity . . . involves change. The intellect, however, according to traditional doctrine, may grasp universal Being, and Being which is universal is fixed and immutable. Wherever there is practical activity we human beings are involved as partakers in the issue. All the fear, disesteem and lack of confidence which gather about the thought of ourselves, cluster also about the thought of the actions in which we are partners. Man's distrust of himself has caused him to desire to get beyond and above himself; . . . The quest for certainty is a quest for a peace which is assured, an object which is unqualified by risk and the shadow of fear which action casts."

—JOHN DEWEY, *The Quest for Certainty*

CONTENTS

Preface

T HE AIMS OF this book are to study conservative thought in present-day America, to suggest a hypothesis about the nature of American conservatism in general, and to show the relationship between conservatism, freedom, innovation and social change. They are aims which will make it possible to demonstrate that America has its own unique and peculiar conservatism today which is not an offshoot or variation of the European tradition and which has its own particular place in American life.

But to display the distinctive existence of American conservatism does not reveal the real question it poses. This book is written for those who are interested in expanding freedom instead of maintaining stability and a fixed society. It is mainly concerned with the most meaningful aspect of American conservatism today, its attitude toward change and hence its concept of freedom. To examine conservatism in such terms it is necessary, of course, to consider the ideas of American conservatives on specific social and political problems and their

11

general scheme of values. But to understand properly the importance of their attitudes and values and to grasp the element which distinguishes conservatism most significantly from other ideologies, it is even more important to see how those attitudes and values bear on the question of change and freedom. The fundamental project of the conservative is to erect a view of change and freedom; once he has done that he feels relatively secure and knows what to think about the other questions put to him by the outside world.

The rise of conservatism in America in the past decade is sufficient reason for an examination of its meaning for freedom and change. The problems that faced America in the 1950's and the problems that it will face in the 1960's—both those that have been left untouched and unresolved from the past ten years and those that will be new—call for changes and innovation in American life. It is hardly a unique situation for America or any nation. Nor is it unique that this nation faces its tasks in what seems to be at this writing a conservative frame of mind. Other countries, and America, too, have previously faced the future with a deep sense of antipathy toward the problems and changes that await it. But, unique or not, if America looks at itself and the future with a conservative point of view what does this imply for its ability to make the changes that history will suggest to it? Obviously, America will change whether it wills to do so or not. But that fact is exactly the issue. Can it *will* those changes? Can it make them rationally and in freedom? If it does not, then the alternative is to be dragged into the future, complaining each step of the way and generally making the worst of the situation.

It is the thesis of this book that American conservatism can only lead to such an alternative because its attitude to change and innovation is inherently incapable of the sense of possibilities and dynamic development that is required for rational and willed change.

But it will not be just change that will be at issue in the 1960's. What does the American conservative point of view imply for freedom? Will it expand the area of freedom or shrink it? Again, it is not a question of whether or not man is free; misfortune or not, freedom is a fact of human existence. What is at issue is whether or not a society will improve the extent and quality of man's freedom, and make it a rational freedom instead of the freedom to choose between one nonsensical product or another. It is possible to be more free and less free. It is possible for society to produce meaningful possibilities rather than false and ersatz possibilities. There is, after all, one thing that is unique about the situation of America today. Never before has any country possessed a better opportunity to achieve at least a good measure of the freedom which men have always contemplated and for which they have always hoped.

The astounding fact about America today is that it actually has the chance to realize many of the dreams of freedom which up to the present have been dismissed as utopian. Will it throw away that opportunity in favor of a grubby society playing with the shoddy goods, the meaningless images, the disorderly activities, and the endless boredom of the mass society and Madison Avenue? It is the thesis of this book that a conservative society would in fact throw away such an opportunity because conservatism is the refusal of freedom.

In the following pages we shall try to understand and show the nature of present-day American conservatism through an analysis of its ideas. But we may anticipate the results of the investigation by saying here that conservatism in the United States, as a social and political ideology, is an attempt to find the principle and the means of a fixed society, a fixed law, and a fixed man. It is an attempt to fix society, law, and man in the sense that it seeks to bring change, innovation, and therefore freedom to an end. It strives to hold man down, to put him in a position where the desire and ability to change, experiment, and adventure will be suppressed to the greatest possible extent. Like most ideologies it cannot fully realize its aims. It differs from some other ideologies, however, by being far removed from the reality of human existence. But its removal from reality does not mean that it is not a potent ideology. Quite the contrary; in certain circumstances it has a greater appeal than those ideologies which do not promise that the dangers of change and of freedom can be avoided.

It is for these reasons that a conservative society is described here as the Futilitarian Society. It is futilitarian because it cannot expand and develop—*will not* expand and develop—the opportunities for change and freedom. Because it does not and will not do so it is a society which is useless to man because it has nothing to suggest about how man can meet new problems and how he can create new and better ways of living. It can truly be said that a conservative society is one which is trifling, frivolous, and vain. It is all of these because it has no other solutions to the problems of human existence than to keep men quiet.

Conservatism will not allow men to use their freedom for anything that is not trifling, frivolous, and vain because to a conservative the use of human freedom can produce only instability and disorder. It is best, according to conservatism, to keep men restricted, to allow human freedom to operate only in the realm of what does not matter, what is not important. As for those things that do matter and are important, man must be fixed and his freedom must not be allowed to operate on them, because if it did he would only produce disaster. In some cases the conservative will seem to want important change because he wants to transcend that society which already exists by going back to another form of society which once existed in the past. But in such cases his purpose is not to create the conditions for different or better change and freedom, but to seek a stopping point, to bring change and freedom to a halt by fixing society, law, and man. The past for the conservative is a resting place—a permanent resting place—instead of a place from which to move.

Has conservatism anything useful to say on the perpetual problem of a free society, that of establishing structure and order in the midst of freedom? If it has anything to contribute to modern man it is in connection with that question. Certainly it is not to be denied that freedom poses many problems, that its costs are high and that effective freedom can exist only in a system of order. It should be the main function of the conservative in modern society, and particularly in American society, which needs orderly freedom so much, to provide the sense and means of order that can safeguard freedom. But if order is to safeguard freedom it must be directed to freedom as its main concern. The thesis that this book puts forward shows that the attempt to quiet and still freedom makes it impossible for conservatism to work with free men in the pursuit of more and better freedom. Because it is dedicated to futilitarianism, conservatism will not and cannot help create an order that will aid freedom, but only an order that will crush it.

❃ ❃ ❃ ❃ ❃ ❃

Among those who have read parts of the book in manuscript my thanks go first to Professor Murray Levin of Boston University for the time he has given and for the improvement which he made possible in the argument. Others who have kindly given their time to reading various chapters or sections are Professor Scott Miyakawa, Professor John Lavely, Professor John Fletcher, Jr., all of Boston University, Professor Eugene Victor Walter of Brandeis University, and Robert E. Oyer. I am also grateful to Professor Hubert Gibbs, Chairman of the Department of Government at Boston University, for the arrangement which he made of my teaching schedule to enable the book to be finished. I must also thank Mr. Edwin Seaver of George Braziller, Inc., who has helped bring coherence to the presentation and who inspired the subject. My thanks also go to *Dissent* and *The Twentieth Century* for permission to republish the material that appears in chapter VII and to *Commentary* and the American Jewish Committee for permission to republish the material that appears in chapter VIII.

To Mrs. Helena Lothrop, my secretary, I owe an especial debt, not only for the long and difficult hours she spent typing the manuscript, but for her enthusiasm which resolutely refused to flag.

My wife and child both suffered from the demands that a book and writer must make on a family. Their successful effort to organize order make possible my freedom. But their contribution to the book also includes the work my wife has put in on this and many other manuscripts and the urgings of Victoria to "get the book done." She was mild, but persistent and effective.

I alone, of course, am responsible for any errors of fact or interpretation.

WILLIAM J. NEWMAN

Boston, *November, 1960*

THE FUTILITARIAN SOCIETY

1. The Mind and the Face of American Conservatism

THE EXISTENCE, AND indeed the growth, of American conservatism since 1945 raises two questions which this book attempts to answer. The first is, what is the nature of conservatism in America today? The second is, to what extent does it help us or hinder us in solving the problems that face America now and in the future? There are many other questions which might be asked. Why has American conservatism persisted and even grown in the years since 1945? How does it acquire and use the mechanisms of power, both private and governmental? Who are the conservatives, and what is their character, and what social strata do they come from? What are the organs of public opinion through which their convictions or their attitudes are propagated and spread throughout this tolerant land? All of these questions are important, but the basic question, the real problem which conservatism poses for Americans, is the problem of its identity, and the question of what it means for American society and American political life.

Before one can condemn or praise conservatism in America one must know with some certainty what it is, a subject on which most conservatives are rather hazy. They are not given to articulating their opinions, or perhaps one should say their prejudices. Since they mainly spurn the intellectual approach, and prefer to depend not on fluent expositions of their beliefs but rather on bad-tempered or rhapsodic outbursts when the spirit moves them, it is not easy to discover just what is the nature of American conservatism. Indeed, it is so difficult to define that many reputable writers doubt whether there is such a thing at all. It may, of course, be possible that they are correct, that what we have is simply a myth that disguises a vacuum. It will be the object of this study, however, to show that in the 1950's, at least, we possessed a full-blown conservative ideology and point of view.

The problem of identifying conservatism in America should not be—if one may say so—burked. Conservatism has had a long and somewhat honorable tradition in the nations of Western Europe, but even on what both advocates and opponents agree is its home ground it has meant many different things. American conservatism, like British, French, and German, is *sui generis*. It may be possible, after we know its qualities, to come to a proper estimate of its place in the ranks of conservative traditions, but to make such an attempt before acquiring an understanding of its peculiar features would be to distort the inquiry. To put, for example, Dwight D. Eisenhower into the strait jacket of, say, de Maistre, would indeed do a grievous injustice to both.

There are present in America today two currents of conservative ideology. One is the continuation of the older tradition, the tradition of antistate, individualist conservatism which has come down to us from the nineteenth century. The significant feature of this Old Conservatism today is not merely its continuation, but its growing sophistication—sophistication, that is, compared to what it had been before—and its ability to create a potent philosophy of antistatism. Old Conservatism no longer hinges on the rantings and ravings of frustrated politicians—although, as the recent emergence of Barry Goldwater shows, that aspect of it is far from dead. Rather it is able to present a reasoned argument for its belief that the state should shrink to the smallest possible dimensions. The argument is all the more effective, it might be added, in view of the undeniable fact that the state has become increasingly a threat in modern civilization, and that popular opinion even at its most diffident finds itself aware of that threat. For example, those who are anti-McCarthyites and who may have no sympathy with conservatism may nevertheless find themselves listening with a sympathetic nod to the conservative belief that a concentration of political power must open the gates to many dangers.

The second form of conservatism to which we have been witnesses in the 1950's, and which still roams the land in excellent health, is called New Conservatism. It is an idea that has attracted many writers of greater and lesser talents. New Conservatism is not perhaps as unique as its sponsors like to think, but it is an attempt to create an attitude that is more than negative, and a point of view with the attributes of a well-rounded religion. It is immensely conscious of itself, and designed not so much for those who are sure that Franklin D. Roosevelt was a devil as for those who are not sure of anything. New Conservatism deliberately and with forethought intends to establish itself on the basis of certain values and to take conservatism away from the simple belief that if the state would only go away all would be well. We shall see what the values are that the New Conservative tries to establish, but the most significant thing about his viewpoint is that it is concerned with a system of values that extends far beyond the narrow realm of political structure.

What solutions does the conservatism of today have to offer for the problems we face now, and in what ways can it contribute to the improvement of our society? Despite the fact that the future is something the conservative prefers not to think about, we must ask: what hope does conservatism give us that the future can be managed? Does it have a point of view that can grapple in realistic terms with the future? Or is it simply an attempt to avoid the future and its problems?

There are two possible ways of answering these questions. One is to examine the acts of conservatives and conservative governments in the United States in order to establish a pattern of activity in meeting concrete problems of social, economic, and political change. The other way is to examine the ideas of conservatives in order to learn how they think about man and society, and what it is they plan to do with us once they get the opportunity. Neither method is entirely satisfactory. What a conservative, like anyone else, plans to do is not always, if ever, the same as what he really does or can do. But contrariwise, what he or anyone else does is not an accurate representation of what he would like to do.

This book confines itself to the second method for reasons of expediency—a word that may shock conservatives since they are always for principle as against a dangerous and unstable pragmatism. The first method would involve so many socio-logical alleyways and labyrinths of American life that it would lead away from our main concern—the political and social implications of conservative thought for American life today. The study of ideas, on the other hand, will take us into the heart of the questions we wish to put to conservatism, will tell us what the conservative today would like to make of America and of man if he could. Further, such an investigation is, of course, a necessary preliminary to any sociological description of our subject; before one can analyze, say, the Republican party as a conservative party one must know what conservatism is.

In the 1950's conservatism made a comeback in both the political realm and the ideological realm, flourishing in many areas of American life. This was due to more than a mere feeling of political fatigue; the conservatives were no longer on the defensive. Rather, they made an aggressive case for a conservative America.

It is necessary, therefore, to interrogate the ideas of American conservatism in the 1950's. What the conservatives will do if they achieve power will certainly be dictated in a large measure by the facts of American life, but what they will do when they are in power will also be dictated in large part by what they think are the problems of America and what should be done about them. It is often said, for example, that President Eisenhower could not put a conservative ideology into operation because the facts of government and politics in the 1950's prevented him from doing so and made impossible the realization of such ideals. Certainly such a claim holds a measure of truth, but only to a limited extent. Can anyone doubt that Eisenhower and the cabinet he chose were men with a strict and even at times fanatical adherence to the conservative ideology? Or that this ideology had potent effects on the policies of the Eisenhower administration and on the ways in which America developed or did not develop in the 1950's? Mr. Eisenhower and George Humphrey and Robert Anderson may well be disappointed because they could not balance the budget more often than they did. But they did balance the budget more often than anyone had supposed possible and at a heavy cost to American life. Only dedicated ideologues could have flown in the face of the facts so successfully. Balancing the budget is a deeply symbolic act to the American conservative.

It is, however, only one part of his ideal of what society should be. Back of it stands a whole regiment of social and political concepts that go far beyond the problems of government finance. Further, the prevelance of conservatism in the

1950's found expression in acts and thoughts that had little or nothing to do with governmental policy and the Eisenhower administration. If there ever was a conservative era in American life it was the one through which we have just staggered, gladly dropping our obligations to man and the future on the way.

Conservatives in America often complain that they are not taken seriously by liberals and academic writers. They are quite right. It was a defect of liberal and academic thinking, in the 1950's at least, that it did not understand the menace that conservative ideas held for America. This book intends to do the conservatives the honor of taking them very seriously indeed. It will deal not only with their views of society but also with their belief in original sin and the necessity of basing a society on the concept of original sin. It will attempt to show what they think on such questions as class structure, voluntary action, the nature of mass society, the place of the individual in society, and the roles which religion, force, and hierarchy should play in modern society. It will also deal with such political categories as the federal state, the states, the nature of political action, centralization and decentralization of political power, constitutionalism, and the nature and proper position of Congress and the Presidency.

This book is not concerned with the place of conservatives in the social order, or with the politics of conservatism, or with literary or with religious conservatism, or with Southern conservatism (which tells more about the South than about conservatism), although these will be touched on for the light they throw on the terms of reference. It does not include economic conservatism, as represented by Hayek and von Mises, for instance, although both gentlemen have a great deal to say on the questions with which we will be concerned. Actually Hayek and von Mises are exotic creatures who derive their conservatism from non-American roots, although one must admit that they have become well domesticated. However, they are involved with economic problems which must be dealt with in economic terms if one is not to do them an injustice. It is possible, of course, to derive social and political views from their writings, but those views will be better represented by writers who deal in terms of general social and political theory.

Finally, this book will not concern itself with McCarthy and McCarthyism. The question of the relation of conservatism to McCarthy and his gang warfare is a fascinating one, but it is a separate topic. McCarthy was not a conservative, whatever he was, and while he used conservatism, he would also have destroyed it, if he had been successful. It must be said that the flirtation with McCarthy of some conservative politicians, who hoped to use him to get votes, was a shocking display of political greed, and it must also be said that some conservatives could flirt with McCarthy not just because of their lust for votes but also because he appealed to certain aspects of conservative thought. Those aspects, we hope, will be made clear in the following pages. It is only necessary to state here that it is not intended to identify McCarthyism with conservatism, not only because they are not identical—it was, after all, not a liberal but an Old Conservative, Senator Flanders, who brought McCarthy down—but because there is no desire to smear the conservatives. Conservatism must be evaluated on its own premises, not in terms of how it once disgraced itself with a political trollop.[1]

What of the businessman? Is he a conservative, a pseudo-

---

[1] It is for that reason that William Buckley, Jr., will not be considered here. As the professional journalist of right-wing conservatism in America he has contributed nothing to the development of conservative ideas and has merely repeated what others have thought. Further, he is mainly taken up with attacks on those personalities he does not like, and with a defense of McCarthyism. His recent *Up from Liberalism* shows no advance on his earlier *God and Man at Yale*; he is still the undergraduate journalist who is sore at his professors.

conservative, or so wrapped up in his work that he is altogether outside the realm of political and social discussion? As we shall see, he is a perpetual problem to the conservative ideologist. Because the businessman's technological and profit-making functions are so destructive of the old ways of society it is hard for the ideologist to accept his hustle as the manifestation of conservative ways. Yet it is felt that he should be and can be a conservative, that he has the true conservative instinct. Is he not after all a bulwark—somewhat unsteady at times, to be sure—of the established order? True, conservatism is more than free enterprise. But cannot that which is more include that which is less? If business and conservatism are not identical perhaps they are partners with a deep need for each other.

As for the businessman, while this book cannot concern itself with the thought of the business world, it can indicate the logic of the relationship between business and conservatism, once we know what the nature of American conservatism is. Business is certainly not identical with conservatism, if only because it is not a system of ideology, but a system of profit making. It has its own concerns with which this book is not involved. The businessman plays his existentialist role, if he will forgive the term, as a businessman and nothing more. But for reasons that range far beyond the simple question of self-interest and economic motivation, he wants to play another role, that of the conservative. There is a split, in other words, between the businessman as a creator of social change, and the businessman as one who desires the rest of society to stand still while he takes command. More precisely, he is a technological innovator who unwittingly and unwillingly creates vast social developments, but who surveys the world he has himself created with the most conservative of feelings. It is indeed an excruciating position to be in. Yet excruciating or not, it does not prevent the businessman from allying himself with conservatism, from trying to be a conservative.

Thus it will be necessary to give some thought to the nature of business conservatism in America. Our main concern, however, will be with those who have created a consistent political and social theory, who have tried to establish a conservative tradition in America. By studying the ideologues of conservatism and their works, we may hope to define the nature and structure of American conservatism today.

The search for the source of conservatism in America is a difficult one, for unlike American liberalism it is largely a visceral creed and given to short grunts of displeasure at the way the world is going. The liberal and radical is a fine spinner of theories in his own right and he is not hesitant in broadcasting them. One can, indeed, hardly stop the liberal from theorizing, no matter how desperate the situation. He theorizes so much and so often about the nature of his social ideals that he often forgets to think about his enemies. Further, he has had the advantage of a long line of liberal theorists from whom he can draw a basis for his ideas. Bentham can out-theorize Burke any day, while Marx, whom the American liberal has magically brought into the mainstream of liberal thought, gives the liberal a solid, if often contradictory, basis for his social and political beliefs. He also takes pleasure in making theories because he believes in the mind of man, rationality, and the inherent superiority of ideas. If he cannot make a theory of his convictions he feels positively lost, so much so in fact that he even has had to make a theory about not theorizing, i.e., pragmatism.

The liberal wants to look to the future; the conservative does not. The liberal feels that he must have a guide showing what

the future will be like and how he is to get there. He looks to
the past only to give him material for a construct which he can
then throw into the unknown to span the gulf between now and
what is to come. The conservative, being preternaturally nervous about the whole operation of going forward, shrinks from
spanning the gulf that opens up before him. Who knows where
he might land? An ideology that sets him on the high road to
the unknown has absolutely no attractions for him. He has
therefore sworn off ideologies, and to describe a conservative as
an ideologist is one of the worst insults which can be offered to
him. One and all, without exception, the conservatives deny that
they are ideologists.

Does such a denial mean that the conservative cannot be an
ideologist? Hardly. It still remains possible to use an ideology
as a bridge to the past, instead of to the future, or as a way of
standing still in the present. It is difficult, perhaps, to use an
ideology in this fashion, but it can be done, and it has been
done.[2] An ideology is a set of assumptions about the nature of
man-in-society, and about the meaning of change in society.
The conservative should not underrate himself. He, too, can
make an ideology and it is one of the objects of this book to
show that in recent years he has done so.

It is true, of course, that the American conservative has no
great ideological systems—as distinct from beliefs—to look
back upon as his intellectual heritage. There is nothing in the
Anglo-American[3] conservative past quite comparable to the

[2] For a recent criticism of the logical and historical weaknesses of conservatism
from the time of Plato see M. Morton Auerbach, *The Conservative Illusion*
(1960). Although there are important differences between the interpretations
of conservatism put forward by Professor Auerbach and by this book, his work
is a significant and interesting critique.

[3] It is interesting and significant that the writings of American conservatives
in the 1950's ignore the continental European tradition of conservatism, a
tradition of considerable intellectual and systematic power.

ideas and systems of Bentham ["thank heaven", the conservative will mutter], J. S. Mill, or John Locke. He believes, of course, that he has at least one father of doctrine, the bad-tempered Mr. Burke. But the choice of Burke as a father of doctrine simply reveals the problems the conservative faces in making an ideology. Whatever Burke was—turncoat or the first of the modern doomsayers—he was certainly not a systematizer. His fruity prose contains everything but system. Nor is our own John Adams able to provide a system. A comparison of the writings of both of these figures with the writings of John Locke, for example, not to mention Bentham, will show the heavy handicap under which the American conservative has labored so long.

Nevertheless, he is trying today to construct a system. There is even among us a sort of Karl Marx of conservatism. Since 1950, Russell Kirk has endeavored to establish the idea that there is a New Conservatism abroad in the land. Kirk has thought more consistently and written in more sweeping terms about conservatism that any of his fellows, New or Old. If you want to know what conservatism is really about Kirk will tell you. But Kirk is not the only New Conservative. Professor Clinton Rossiter and Walter Lippmann have both felt the urge of the 1950's to write books which embody and advocate the idea of New Conservatism. They also testify to the difficulty of the conservative when he puts his mind to the real problems that face society. Both try to modernize conservatism, to make it a real solvent for the problems of contemporary America, but they both of necessity run into contradictions and conflicts between what they would like conservatism to be and what they see, as realistic observers, to be the needs of present-day society. They are both, so to speak, case studies in the difficulties of being a New Conservative.

One must not forget the Old Conservatives. Indeed, it is necessary to begin this book with that hardy band of true believers who held up the banner of conservatism long before Kirk and his tribe came on the scene. The fact that they are called "Old," however, should not lead one to believe that they are obsolescent. Indeed, the question will be raised, do the Old and New Conservatives really differ as much as their labels seem to signify? Is not the New Conservatism simply the Old Conservatism writ flamboyantly? With this question in mind we will look at W. H. Chamberlin, Felix Morley, and James Burnham. Morley and Burnham especially will give us a true sense of what it is to be conservative about politics, for it is typical of the Old Conservatives to be deeply involved in political theory and hardly involved at all in the cosmos.

Conservatism today includes, however, much more than its ideologists. It includes also a Conservative *Mood* which has come over America and settled here for a long visitation. Like any public mood it is a difficult thing to track down and verify. But it is important to give at least some indication of its nature and its relation to the hard core of conservative ideology. Few persons in America have been left untouched by this mood. Who can deny today that he has acquired a sense of caution from the events of the past fifteen years, that many of the fancy phrases of liberalism and radicalism have shown themselves to be simply fancy phrases, that the sense of rational adventure has weakened—or disappeared—from American public life?

Doubts, confusion, worry, and pessimism have replaced confidence and action in our public life. In such a soil of richly decaying matter conservatism grows and grows well. Those who give way to the Conservative Mood may not be—indeed, usually are not—conservatives in any sense of commitment to cause or ideology. Many of them may feel surprised and even insulted to be made part of the case of conservatism. Yet they reflect the nature of conservatism in America today whether they will it or not. They may not *be* conservative but they *think* to some degree as conservatives think; their ideas give aid and comfort to conservative assumptions. They are people who have responded to the Conservative Mood by adopting it as their own, by accepting it as a basis for their thoughts.

One manifestation of this mood is to be found in certain academic writings—always a bellwether of fashion—in the past decade. All of these writings are concerned in one way or another with the nature of American society and with re-evaluating it from what is essentially a conservative point of view. None intentionally sets out a conservative creed, or is written by a professed conservative, or attempts to apply as such the principles of conservatism to American society. But all of them either describe American society or its problems in ways that show it to be a conservative society as the ideologists would define the phrase, or take a position on the nature of American society that reflects a willingness on the part of the authors to accept certain, if not all, conservative values. Daniel Bell in his *End of Ideology*, Louis Hartz in his *Liberal Tradition in America*, Daniel Boorstin in his *Genius of American Politics*, show how rethinking about the nature of America has led them to conceive of it in terms that are essentially conservative terms. There is no such thing as neutralism in social and political analysis. By repudiating the radical frame of reference, even if they do nothing else—and some of them do a great deal else—they allow themselves to fall into the Conservative Mood. Scientism—the O.K. word for neutrality in the academic profession—in the study of society leads straight into the waiting arms of the conservative. Daniel Bell, for example, tells us that "one's commitment is to one's vocation." If that is the case the scrupulously professional man will find himself being used by the predominant forces in society, forces that have a greater and surer sense of ideological direction than he has. Since those forces were and are conservative, the evidence of the melancholy ruin of the talents—and they are considerable—of these writers is strewn over the pages of their books.

The other manifestation of the Conservative Mood is a more dangerous one than the passive acceptance of the academics. It is the aggressive drive for national purpose proclaimed by those keepers of the American conscience, *Time* and *Life*. Mr. Luce has set out to save us from our follies, come what will, and salvation means to Luce, and the Luce-thinkers surrounding him, a conservative salvation. Luce is a fascinating and frightening example of what happens to a conservative when he faces the facts of present-day life. When he tries to sell us the product he calls national purpose what kind of an American society does he have in mind? The answer is a society so stringently conservative as to make some conservatives blanch.

What is the relation of the Conservative Mood to conservative ideology? To what extent does this ideology represent the true nature of American conservatism? There are those who believe that because the ideology of conservatism is so extreme and so far removed from the normal ways of American life it represents nothing but itself, nothing but an extreme group of futile writers. They therefore conclude that there is no real conservatism in America.

To put the question another way: To what extent is one justified in using conservative ideology as a means of describing the nature of conservatism in America? Conservative ideology is in fact extreme. If we take Russell Kirk as one norm, then certainly there are very few complete conservatives in America. Or if there are, this writer has not met them, and he has met a good many conservatives. It is true that it is very difficult for an American to be a complete conservative on the Kirkean-Burkean pattern. Kirk is tough and his standards are very high; it is doubtful that anyone but he himself could meet them. In this sense he represents no one but himself, and the small group around him. But whom did Bentham represent but Bentham and the small group around him? And, more to the point, what does it prove to show that Kirk's ideology is extreme? Does it prove that there is no such thing as conservatism in America, or that if there is it is not related to the ideas held by Kirk? The fact of the extremeness of an ideology proves nothing either way. An extreme ideology may, of course, belong only to a small, unimportant, and uninfluential group moulding in its own decay. But it may also be an extreme and logical expression of what a large number of people think *in parts, in bits and pieces.* If that possibility is true then it will also be true that an understanding of that extreme ideology will give us a clue to what is a widespread sense of things. The problem is an old one in intellectual history. To what extent do the writers of an epoch mirror the opinions of that epoch? Obviously there is no one-to-one relationship. And obviously there might well be some relationship.

Does our conservative ideology, then, represent widespread conservative opinions in America? Is there evidence that Kirk's extreme thought may give us a clue to the otherwise inarticulate thought of many conservatives in America? Granted that few would believe all of Kirk, and granted even further that they would be repulsed by some of Kirk, can he nevertheless tell us what conservative opinions in America signify if they are brought together and driven to their logical conclusions? Can he give us the quality of American conservative thought? In

33

short, does the nature of conservative thought presented by the ideologists represent the reality—scattered and confused though it may be and always is—of conservative opinion in America?

There are three reasons for thinking so. One is the conservative qualities of American society—some would say simply the conservative quality of America, but such a statement would rouse too many ghosts of American rhetoric. Let us just state the obvious, that there are many strands in American life that are profoundly conservative. If there are few areas of American life that live up to the extreme standards set by the ideologues, there are also few areas that do not embody some part of the ideas of those ideologues.

One must not think that the American avidity for technological change necessarily leads to a radical temper in all other aspects of national existence; technological change may, in fact, be a mask for a profound conservatism in other equally or more important activities—for example, social and political institutions and processes. Certainly the American record in constitutional conservatism can hardly be equalled. It is true that the federal constitution has been changed by constitutional interpretation, but its basic outlines have remained. John Adams could certainly find his way around the corridors of American government today even though he might find some of the characters there somewhat repulsive. Our refusal to discard and our insistence on modifying our original constitution are manifestations of both a conservatism and a radicalism of spirit. It is not necessary in the nonhistorical abstract to say that either is dominant. It is simply necessary to say that America shows as well as a reckless radicalism a canny and even crabbed conservatism in its attitude toward political institutions.

But the case of the constitution is only one example of a conservatism that runs alongside of radicalism in American life.

It is hardly a profound statement, but because American rhetoric so persistently identifies America with radicalism it needs to be said that America is no stranger to conservatism.

Whatever America may be in the abstract and in terms of such truisms (which, like most truisms, are very nearly meaningless) in the actual past decade it has shown a definite conservative trend. True, the Eisenhower regime did not please the ideologues of conservatism, but that displeasure simply proves that ideologues are always unhappy. Why else would they be ideologues?

The second reason, therefore, for thinking that conservative ideology reflects conservative opinion in America is that the 1950's were admittedly a conservative decade. Furthermore, the Truman administration was hardly composed of a red-hot group of radicals. It took a major cataclysm in foreign policy, for example, to force it off its perch of financial orthodoxy. And whatever President Truman may have proposed about a Fair Deal, in fact Congress disposed of a No Deal, and Congress was indisputably elected by the American people. One need only point, thus, to the profoundly conservative nature of American politics since 1945 to indicate the hold of conservatism in the America of here and now.

The third reason for thinking that the conservative ideologues reflect conservative reality in America is the overlap between their ideas, the Conservative Mood, and the ideas of Rossiter and Lippmann, neither of whom is professionally devoted to conservatism in the manner of the other ideologists we will study. Is there a near-coincidence between what the nonprofessional conservatives think and what the ideologues think? If there is, then it is possible to say that those who preach conservatism without being total conservatives show that the ideologue is simply an extreme and logically rigid form of the more relaxed, garden variety. We will be able to point to a wide area of agreement and consensus on basic ideas shared by the most strict conservatives and the luke-warm. It is possible that Rossiter and Lippmann, on the one hand, and the conservative ideologists on the other, may be concerned with something quite different. It is possible, but in fact not the case. As we shall see, a close relationship exists between such protoconservatives as Rossiter and Lippmann, and the more orthodox ideologists.

The three assumptions upon which this book is based are reasonable premises that make it possible to consider the conservative ideologues as significant system makers for a group of ideas that ordinarily are difficult to discover and to relate to one another. The ideologue, of course, is often in conflict with his less extreme fellows, but such conflict should not blind one to the important features they hold in common.

Once the importance and relevance of the conservative ideologists as a symptom of conservative thought is established, it is possible to come to grips with the question: what is the use of conservatism to the United States in facing the problems it must solve today? The significance of conservative ideology and the Conservative Mood, like that of any ideology and mood, is seen in their juxtaposition with the problems a society faces. Ideology is important, among other reasons, because it is a way of looking at problems and a source of solutions to those problems. It is hardly necessary to say that an ideology can be useless and still be widespread, still be even the dominant ideology of a group or nation. Or to add that a useless ideology which is widespread is a positive threat to the ability of a group or a nation to meet its problems.

Before it is possible to answer the question whether con-

servatism is an aid or a threat to the ability of America to meet
its problems, one must ask a further question: What is the attitude of conservatism to change?

The conservative is obsessed with the problem of change, of
innovation in society. Ignoring for the moment the matter of
obsession, it is certainly true that the role and rate of change
and innovation in a society postulates questions that cannot
easily be answered and that modern liberalism sometimes ignores. If conservatism should be capable of dealing with such
problems on a sophisticated and intelligent basis America would
possess a valuable thing, a truly progressive conservatism. It
would be a conservatism that could rise above the level of the
Reader's Digest and come to grips with some of the real problems facing America, that could face the problems inherent in
change and give us some rational and useful guide as to how to
deal with them.

But the question of change involves an attitude toward freedom. The ability to change is the very meaning of freedom; and
the significance of change is the opportunity it gives to innovate, to create something new. It is quite possible, of course, to
change by reverting to what has been. Reversion is one of the
privileges of freedom. But the desire to revert does not tell us
whether or not those who hold such a desire maintain freedom
as one of their main values. As this book hopes to make clear,
whatever desire to revert that conservatism possesses is a manifestation of its effort to find a point of *final* stability, to achieve
once and for all the end of change. The conservative may favor
that change which will end change but he does not glory in it
or in one of the products of change—innovation. Quite the contrary, he fears and detests innovation. He will put up with
innovation only insofar as it leads to a point of rest. Hence his
dislike, his obsession, with change in the society of today. He

sees that society as having an existence of endless innovation and hence a lack of rest. He seeks therefore to bring endless innovation and change to a stop, to bring, indeed, history to a stop. And in doing so he seeks not to expand freedom, or to make it more meaningful, but to bring it also to an end. By using change at best as a means of killing change, conservatism aims to do away with it. It also seeks, therefore, to do away with innovation, which cannot live without ceaseless change. And it seeks, too, and most important, to do away with freedom, which cannot live without change and innovation.

Freedom, change, innovation, are all bound together; one does not exist without the other. That is why it is important to ask what conservatism has to say about them, what it has to offer to make each more fruitful and more tolerable. Certainly there is a profound human and social need for order, even for rest of some kind. But does the conservative view of freedom, change, and innovation help us in the unending attempt to resolve the dilemma of change *vs.* order? It would seem that it should be able to do so, for conservatism has as its main concern the necessity of order in a disorderly civilization. But does his concern for order make possible a better freedom? Or does it threaten freedom? The conservative attitude toward freedom, change, and innovation is the clue to the usefulness of the solutions conservatism offers or can offer to the problems of our society, because a problem postulates change as the necessary step to resolve the deadlock which is at the heart of every problem. Innovation is the way to destroy the deadlock; freedom, the right to think of something new, is the source of innovation.[4]

---

[4] See Hannah Arendt's important "Freedom and Politics: A Lecture," *Chicago Review*, Spring, 1960, for the distinction between freedom (in its relationship to politics) as will and as action. She points out that "freedom as related to politics . . . is the freedom to call something into being which did not exist before, which was not given. . . ." (p. 32).

It is because America faces urgent questions of change and order and because conservatism seems to possess some answer to these questions that it has such an appeal. In a time of bewilderment and frustration, when both the dangers of change and the need for change press so closely upon us, conservatism has its greatest chance to be useful. It also has its greatest temptation to be the means by which the frightened can turn away from reality. The desire to think that one can avoid change when it becomes more risky than usual is a hard one to resist. Perhaps after all the old ways are better; certainly they are easier since they are what is *already known*. Perhaps if we simply stick with our time-honored principles—provided we can find out what they are—everything bad will go away. It takes, one may say, a courageous but perhaps foolhardy man to say that in time of danger we must ignore our old ways and throw away our time-honored principles. He may be right, but it is not certain that he is right, for he talks about the unknown. Does one not feel, therefore, more secure by repudiating the unknown and sticking with the known? Assuredly one does feel more secure, at least for a while.

It is not necessary to point out that such ideas carry especial attractiveness in a period when the issues have become more complex rather than less. A clinging to *order* in the sense of repetition, habit, and avoidance of the new becomes a way of structuring a situation that in itself provides no structure. Liberalism with its emphasis on freedom and free choice of actions, the consequences of which must necessarily be unknown to a degree (otherwise they would not possess the quality of free choice), is at a distinct discount in such a situation, at least in terms of easy and quick approval. Liberalism is based on freedom, and freedom means adventure. Who wants adventure when he has already had more than enough of it, when danger is the very thing he is trying to avoid? Order then becomes the creation of habit to the end of avoiding adventure. It is not a way of meeting a new problem since such order is repetition and hence in itself incapable of the innovation and the original response which is required by a new situation. It may provide the base from which an innovation is created, the infrastructure of originality, so to speak. But it is not itself the possessor or the source of the new.[5]

It is not only danger that can turn a nation into the animal of Kafka's "Burrow," the seeker after total security. When the problem to be faced is one involving the relationship between individuals, groups, classes, mass society, and the nation, conservatism can become an appealing way of avoiding the whole problem. On top of the political fatigue caused America by the aggressiveness of a foreign power there is the consciousness of social alienation that is derived from a mass society. So conscious is America of this phenomenon that it has become a staple product of the organs of mass society itself. Whatever truth there may be in the talk about mass society and social alienation, the result of such talk is too often merely a more or less cheerful, high-income bracket cynicism. Such a cynic is not a natural-born conservative, since to be cynical one must presumably have no ideals at all. But he certainly is a natural convert to conservatism.

Being a cynic he must retire into private life. Once having performed that heroic act he has created the cynic's own peculiar view of politics and society, that since everything is hope-

---

[5] The question may be raised as to how the fixed society in which conservatives believe differs from the fixed societies postulated by utopian thought. It is not, however, a legitimate question, since this book is concerned with thought and attitudes that aim to deal with the social realities of their times and not to construct a utopia. Conservative thought may aim to stop history, but it is not, like utopian thought, out of history. . . . What is so significant about conservative ideas is that they are felt to be appropriate, nonutopian suggestions.

less there is nothing for which to struggle. Therefore things should be left pretty much as they are, give or take a few more mass circulation weeklies. Never has a solution to the world's problems come so easy—and so cheap. Does it matter who is in the White House? Why no, it does not matter because the two parties are the same, one man is as good as another, they both try to imitate each other, etc., etc.; the clichés roll on into the night. The word *engagement* is a relic from a French past. Why commit oneself? What we have will continue to be what we have. Thus the cynic argues, and thus he shows that social alienation is the meat he feeds upon. And because he is both a product and a producer of social alienation he is in a very profound sense the truest conservative of them all. With the cynic no act becomes possible—except, of course, the act of making money.

The appeal of conservatism today, therefore, is not to the gentleman of slender means but good upbringing, but to those who have been affected by a widespread bewilderment, cynicism, and apathy. There are few who have escaped being touched by this bewilderment and cynicism to at least some extent, and few who have not felt that perhaps conservatism might after all be the easier and even better way. Needless to say there are some in high political office who have been more positive about the virtues of conservatism. The significance of conservatism in the past ten years is its appeal to groups who formerly would never have conceived of themelves as conservative and may not even do so now. The bewildered and the cynical may know nothing about conservatism except that they want a rest. But this passivity is conservatism's greatest strength because it reduces the thrust for innovation.

Social passivity is composed not merely of a sort of generalized hopeless feeling, but also of a quite specific feeling of hopelessness. It is hopeless about the possibility of change in the sense that it does not believe that new ways of doing things, new ways of living, can be attained. Such a passivity can be illustrated by William Whyte's best seller, *The Organization Man.* After describing the horrors of being alive, if that is what one can call it, in an organization and a suburb, what does Mr. Whyte suggest we do? He suggests we cheat on the corporation's personality tests. Obviously, for Mr. Whyte petty cheating is the only possible solution. It is the only possible solution because he refuses to contemplate alternatives to the kind of society that already exists. And he refuses to contemplate alternatives because the only frame of thought he has is a memory of better days in the past when the horrible problem of the gargantuan corporation did not arise. He is forced to accept the thing he so cordially dislikes because he cannot conceive of anything different. One hastens to add that Mr. Whyte's predicament is common to us all today and that this very fact gives him his importance. It is precisely the lack of a set of new values different from those of the corporation that makes significant criticism impossible. Mr. Whyte would answer, no doubt, with statements about the impossibility of reforming or doing away with the corporation. But he would find it as hard to prove that it is impossible to reform or do away with the corporation as the conservatives have always found it impossible to prove that what is must always be.

Since bewilderment and cynicism are by their very nature incapable of embodying new values, they are the prime breeders of a certain type of conservatism. But bewilderment and cynicism may only be a stage in the development of a conservative. Some people, it is true, will stop there. But others will begin to feel the value vacuum and begin to look at alternative values that fit their already-existing mood of disenchantment and apathy. Liberal values certainly do not fit such a mood, but the values of conservatism can fit, and very nicely, too.

The appeal of conservatism today, then, lies not only in its attitude toward change and innovation, but also in the specific nature of its system of values. The conservative has certain ways of looking at social phenomena such as class, hierarchy, the state, power, decentralization and centralization, voluntary activity, pluralism, and, of course, tradition, which possess an appeal as a value structure, as well as an appeal based on an attitude towards innovation. These two aspects of conservatism —its general approach to change and innovation, and its specific values on social problems—make up the whole that is conservatism. It is important to realize that this system of values appeals not only to the bewildered in search of an answer, but also to a profoundly deep set of convictions held by the American people—their liberal instincts.

It will be objected that such an assertion is paradoxical, that if Americans possess deep liberal instincts, if America is by its very nature a liberal society, then it is in a fundamental sense impossible for a real conservatism to exist among us. But the seeming paradox of the assertion expresses the most important truth about conservatism in America today.

Much of modern conservatism appeals to the classical liberal ideals of the nineteenth century, ideals which the conservative invokes to distract himself (and us) from the future, not to mention the present. It is precisely because the conservative adopts nineteenth-century liberal principles as his own and considers them to be an unchanged essence that he is a conservative. It is precisely because he conceives modern society,

the society of today, in terms of nineteenth-century liberal society that he is a conservative. He is a conservative because he is
a nineteenth-century liberal (more or less) in the twentieth
century. He adopts nineteenth-century liberalism most obviously in his espousal of individualism. By postulating nineteenth-century individualism as an ultimate value in an age in
which, at the very least, it must be rethought the conservative
attempts to face the problems of today with a social system
that has been, not with one that is or might be. Whatever the
idea of individualism may mean today, and there is little evidence that the conservative has given much real thought to the
question, what he means by it is what it meant in the nineteenth
century.

The appeal of such atavistic thought is obvious. Who, to
carry on the example of individualism, in America, or anywhere
else in the West, is against the individual? Not the modern
liberal of the left, not the modern radical certainly. No one in
fact is against the individual. And those who think they are
liberals but who are fuzzy in their minds about what liberalism
is, and have not yet discovered that there are various ways of
looking at the individual, obviously can find the solicitude of
the conservative for the poor old battered individual a touching
one. And so it is with most of the values of conservatism. They
call up images of basic American doctrines that as generalized
doctrines no one would think of disputing. Who, for example,
is against constitutionalism? Yet the conservative claims that
he is the true constitutionalist because only the conservative
wants to go back to the constitution as it was in 1787. It certainly is an intriguing thought.

Does such slavish worship of the eternal essence of nine-
teenth- and eighteenth-century liberal principles mean that the
conservative is really a liberal? Does it mean that We Are All

Liberals? There are those, like Professor Louis Hartz, who would convince us that such is the case, who would convince us that there is no ideological difference of opinion in America because this country is a country with only one political theory, the Lockian, liberal theory. Such a belief is manifest nonsense, but it is plausible nonsense.

It is plausible because obviously any country must have a certain set of basic political principles with which to operate. If it does not, the country dissolves; it ceases to be a country. Great Britain, too, has certain basic political principles within which it operates, as do most nations if they are not the victims of revolution. Such facts would seem to be too elementary to need discussion, except that Professor Louis Hartz and his followers insist on confusing national consensus on basic principles with ideological conformity on all principles. Thus, for example, there is in America a general agreement on constitutionalism. (There is such an agreement in Britain, too, for that matter, though Hartz considers Britain to be the non-Lockian antithesis of Lockian America; but that problem may be allowed to pass.) Does such a national consensus mean, therefore, that there is no ideological division in America? It hardly follows in either logic or fact. It can follow if one is eager to smear out all the conflicts of American history and concentrate only on the fact that one nation indivisible has been able to exist since 1776. But such an act of historical vandalism makes American history unintelligible, not to say dull. The past conflicts of America cannot be forgotten without making the American past meaningless, something, we are sure, Professor Hartz does not want to do. But for those who wish to think, as the conservative does, only of essence and not of the fact and variety of reality, the idea that there is only one happy family in America certainly is attractive.

The doctrine is nonsense as well as plausible because history is not made up of essence but of existence. Given the fact of national consensus there is also the fact of conflict in America, conflict that has gone far beyond that of interest groups striving for cash returns. We are all Lockian constitutionalists, no doubt, but what is the Constitution? There seems to be some disagreement on the question even in this foam-rubber age. The South has rather sharp opinions on the question, and the Supreme Court has equally sharp opinions leaning the other way. (We will notice in this book, it might be said here, that the conservative of the North has rather tender feelings toward the South of both yesterday and today. Russell Kirk, for example, is not altogether sure that the slave issue was worth all the fuss made about it. And almost all the conservative ideologues feel that Calhoun's concurrent majority is just what the country needs today.) Constitutionalism as a basic principle may be acceptable to all Americans, but not all Americans agree on what is meant by constitutionalism. Some people think that constitutionalism today should mean something quite different from what it meant in 1787. Others think that what was meant in 1787 is quite good enough for today. Are not such divisions of opinions serious? Are they not based on ideological differences that may be comprehended within the national consensus, but that nevertheless are serious conflicts involving serious human interests?

There is today, as there has been in the past, a conflict between liberal and conservative points of view. The content of those points of view may, of course, change. But the fact of conflict can hardly be ignored. As for the divisions of opinion today, it seems wondrous weird to have to prove that America is not exclusively a liberal nation after the past decade.

The fact that such an endeavor is necessary, however, is evidence of the confused state of opinion about the differences between liberalism and conservatism, a confusion that helps make it possible for conservatism to batten on the body politic. If we believe that We Are All Liberals then the ideas of conservatism not only will not hurt us, but they are not even conservative ideas at all! What could be better? It is no longer necessary to make the effort to discriminate between one idea and another.

Alas, but it is. It is necessary, for example, to see that a nineteenth-century liberal in 1960 is not the same thing as a twentieth-century liberal in 1960. It is necessary to see that someone who wants to bring original sin back into politics is not a liberal.

One of the objects of this book is to describe conservatism in such a way as to make possible an accurate discrimination between conservatism and other ideas today. It therefore goes against the grain of American thought in the past decade. It is in basic disagreement with those who assert that all there is in America is Lockian liberalism and with those who claim that ideological differences are no longer significant, that there is an "end of ideology." It asserts to the contrary that there are ideological differences in America today and that conservatism is one of the ideologies abroad in the land. Those who prefer not to recognize the existence of an effective conservatism because of their own ideological fatigue are wrong. They are making a sad and painful and expensive mistake.

This book does not discuss the state of the modern, twentieth-century liberal mind in America, but it does hope to speak to that mind by showing the liberal the meaning and nature of conservatism and by making it possible for him to know what to think about it. Daniel Bell has written: "Today, intellectually, emotionally, who is the enemy that one can fight?" The sense of shock one has in realizing that Daniel Bell does not know the identity of the enemy one can fight is equalled by a sense of the flatulence that the liberal mind can demonstrate. Is it so hard today to know who the enemy is? Or is it that one has only the enemies one deserves? Are so many liberals-cum-men-of-good-will without an enemy today because they, as good middle-class intellectuals, wish to strip themselves of enemies in obedience to the dictates of the soft-soap society they have helped to create? Whatever the case, it is hoped that this book will convince some liberals intellectually that there is at least one enemy and that its name is conservatism. While their emotional convictions can best be left to themselves, their intellectual convictions should recognize the fact that conservatism is an ideology in full bloom today, and that a mood of acceptance on the part of those who are not conservatives aids the growth of conservatism. There are other enemies, of course, besides conservatism. But conservatism is the one we are dealing with here.

Who is the enemy one can fight? The conservative is the enemy one can fight and for a very good reason. Conservatism in America today is fundamentally and essentially an ideology dedicated to stripping man of freedom. Behind all its talk of essences, higher truth, religion, individualism, hierarchy, concurrent majorities, and the constitutional state, is a search for a fixed society, not a search for freedom. It is a search for a society in which innovation will have come to an end, so that what exists may continue to exist; a society in which there will be no problems and no danger because no one will be allowed to repudiate the past and venture into the unknown; a society in which rational, scientific, and inquiring man will be replaced by traditional, obedient, and placid man. It is a search for a society in which essence will replace the excitement of concrete reality, and everyone will have his fixed place, and freedom will have come to an end.

Is such a society an impossible dream? By all means. But it is not the first impossible dream to appear on the political scene. And as an impossible dream it can have unhappy consequences. The search itself, impossible though it may be, can do much damage to a nation that has brutal problems to face and must face them with intelligence and innovation—with freedom. For those who hope to avoid freedom, who seek to flee the freedom that is the unique offer of liberalism, conservatism is a way of ending their condemnation to freedom.

2. Old Conservatism: William H. Chamberlin, Felix Morley, James Burnham and Senator Goldwater

William Henry Chamberlin, Felix Morley, and James Burnham introduce us to an important problem of Old Conservatism, one that often confuses both the observer of American conservatism and the practitioners themselves, Old or New. It is the problem of the liberal-as-conservative, the conservative who clings to the nineteenth-century form of liberalism. Is he a case of a liberal sheep in wolf's clothing? Or is he just a wolf who should be identified as such? It is not always easy to know, for these men sometimes call themselves liberal and sometimes conservative. Some, like Chamberlin, are liberals at one point in their lives but then evolve, as Chamberlin himself puts it, into conservatives. Others refuse the conservative label while possessing all its traits. But whatever the case, they have one thing in common—a belief that the nineteenth-century liberal past should be restored.

It is not a past of which they are ashamed. Quite the contrary, they glory in it. And it is the glorification of that past and not their liberalism which marks them as true, perhaps the truest, conservatives.

When is a liberal in fact a conservative? When he is a conservative liberal; i.e., when he is intent on preserving or recreating the liberal society of nineteenth-century America. He is one who clings, as a good conservative should, to the only past America has, to the pure liberal life as it was lived in the time of American "innocence," when there was no other ideology to create doubts. In doing so he is at least more realistic than the New Conservative who fixes on a Burkean past that never existed in America. But however that may be, the unique trait of this particular type of Old Conservative is the Garden of Eden complex.

The hallowing of ground which has reverted to the silence of history is a trait that the conservative shares with other types of ideologues, but of which he is particularly fond. It is inherent in the logic of conservatism, for to be a conservative it is necessary to begin with something to conserve. A Garden of Eden must be fabricated to serve both as a standard by which to measure later degeneracy and to serve as assurance that at least once in man's history troubles were stilled. The past thus becomes a club with which to beat the present, to shame the present. The conservative is a past master—if the pun will be forgiven—at shaming modern man, at demonstrating the awful depth of his Fall. One of his characteristics is his inability to be at home in the present, his profound sense of loss, his refusal to come to terms with the present and work with it. There are many nonconservatives, of course, who have the same repugnance for the present, but at least some of them think of the present in terms of innovation, of what new things the human mind can create. It is only when present possibilities are spurned in terms of the past that a conservative is in the making.

It is from this sense of loss in the present that the other function of the Garden of Eden complex comes. The conservative is one who, for whatever reason, cannot believe that if the present is bad the human mind can create a better future that would be different from the past. He cannot believe it because the venture would be too uncertain. Indeed, it would be an adventure, and if there is one thing a conservative dislikes more than any other it is adventure. It is precisely man's ability to adventure that he wants to avoid. And it is the possibility of avoiding it that the Garden of Eden gives. Man has at least once known peace; peace can be achieved. There is after all a Home of which we may at least dream even if we have been expelled from it. Once things were right and good. Why then experiment, adventure into the future? Having known goodness one need only return to it. To experiment is to spurn and repudiate the past. No more terrifying thought can occur to the conservative for it robs him of a Home.

Many American liberals, especially in the years after 1933, were victims of this type of atavism. In making that statement one does not doubt their fidelity to liberal principles. Quite the contrary, it was that very fidelity, that deep ideological commitment, that caused them to become conservatives. When British liberalism went on the rocks after 1919, it became conservative in the political sense; i.e., many British liberals joined the Conservative Party or voted Conservative, without the development of the same Garden of Eden complex found among the stranded American liberals. British Liberals retained at least some ability to move with the times even if moving with the times meant turning away from liberalism (there are, of course, still those who believe that history stopped with the death of Gladstone). Has the American liberal turned classical liberalism into conservatism because the pure milk of nineteenth-century liberalism was more pure in America than it was in Britain? In part. But more important, the American liberal, finding himself afraid of the present, refused to change and clung with might and main to nineteenth-century liberalism because there was no where else to go but back to the nineteenth century. The British liberal who disliked the present and feared the future could turn into a full-blooded conservative, ripe and overripe with Burkean wisdom. The American liberal, however, turned nineteenth-century liberalism into a conservative doctrine because it was the only idea in America that had a past, that could be imagined as an unchangeable essence.

Is this particular type of liberal simply a delightful but irrelevant figure from the past? Is he nothing more than that moaning sound one sometimes hears in the noise of American politics? By no means. The Conservative liberal has been a veritable powerhouse in the domestic politics of America since the end of the war. It is he, not the New Conservative, who provided the ideological wherewithal of the Eisenhower administration, the compulsive drive of the Eisenhower cabinet to stand pat by going back to the simple government of the nineteenth century. When President Eisenhower called his administration a conservative and liberal government he was not, improbable though it may seem, making a joke or trying to get votes from everyone. The utopianism of his administration lay precisely in the fact that it was based on the desire to get back to the liberalism of the nineteenth century. The President, it is true, not uncharacteristically got his terms mixed, when he said that his administration would be conservative in economics and liberal in human welfare, but in doing so he demonstrated the nineteenth-century basis of his thought by showing that he saw no conflict between conservatism and liberalism. The two ideas in his happy-go-lucky view would co-exist neatly side by side. He was correct except for failing to point out that they can do so because liberalism has become conservative. Never has the

White House seen a more conservative liberal regime, for the Humphreys and the Andersons were men dedicated to the principle, as Secretary of the Treasury Anderson said, that "all that is required of us is that we manage our affairs prudently and abide by the disciplines of economics that the past has proved sound."[1] Which past? The New Deal past? One does not think so.

The conservative liberal is no joking matter not only because he runs our economy but also because his atavistic myth is particularly attractive to many Americans. For it makes it possible to claim that all of us, right as well as left, are liberals. The fact that the liberalism of the conservative is the liberalism of the nineteenth century does not prevent the claim being made that Americans are a singularly united people because there really is no conservatism in this happy land. There are, it is said, simply varieties of liberalism. Sir William Harcourt once remarked of British politics that "we are all Socialists now." The Americans like to say that we are all Lockian liberals now and, even better, always have been. The fact that the argument is both fallacious and a piece of special pleading does not destroy the myth for it enables those who wish to do so—and they are many—to ignore the profoundly conservative ideas of those who believe that a Garden of Eden really does exist and that it is possible to get back to it. But just because such men have been in charge of the government since 1953, and even before that under the Truman administration with its fanaticism about ceilings on defense expenditure, it is important to dispense with myth and see present-day nineteenth-century liberals for what they are—conservatives.

[1] Douglass Cater, "The 'Little America' of Robert B. Anderson," *The Reporter*, January 21, 1960. Cf. W. W. Rostow, *America in the Arena of World Affairs* (1960).

Further, the conservative liberal is confused about the nature of liberalism itself. He may not have changed since the end of the nineteenth century but liberalism has. He makes a mighty effort to freeze liberalism in a stance that discredits the very ideas of liberalism. He uses, very often, although not always, liberal means to conservative ends.

Most significant of all, conservative liberalism is one way— only one; there are others—in which the conservative forecloses the future. It is a way of not facing the fact that there is a future, of grasping the future by hypostatizing it as the past. By so doing he makes a valiant and even convulsive effort to prevent what is to come from happening except as it has already happened in the past. Thus he is able to destroy unique and new possibilities, unique and new alternatives. He allows no break in the seamless web of history because the future must not contain adventure.

Are these men reactionaries? It is often claimed that they are and one may call them reactionaries if one wishes to do so. But it is not only an unfair smear word; it is a word that obscures the nature of conservatism, since its use to mean one-who-would-go-back holds the unstated assumption that there are conservatives who-would-stand-still. Such an assumption confuses the true nature of political thought in general and conservatism in particular. All political thought postulates social and political movement as possible and desirable; by its very nature it sets goals and values to be attained. From this point of view, therefore, the only real difference between conservatism and, say, liberalism or socialism, is the *direction* which social and political movement should take. The conservative hopes to *restore* a society or a system of values, to conserve the essence of a past epoch. The liberal or socialist wants to create a new and different society, one which has not yet appeared.

Such a conclusion does not assert that liberalism and socialism may not become stagnant or undynamic, and that conservatism may not be dynamic and purposeful. It is the *nature* of the ideological movement, not political potency that is in question. The word *reactionary*, in short, is a red herring that many persons, liberals and conservatives alike, use to distract themselves from the possible dynamism that *conservatism* may have.

The conservatives themselves do not doubt that conservatism seeks to go back. Thus, *The Modern Age: A Conservative Review*, scorns those who think conservatism is a philosophy of the status quo.

Neither from the standpoint of history nor from that of theory can conservatism be depicted as a set of principles aimed at the preservation of the status quo. On the contrary, . . . conservatives have upon many occasions worked for great changes in the world about them . . . We would not preserve the status quo insofar as it manifests collectivism. We seek, rather, to remove collectivism and all its works from the human scene. . . . Conservatism is not wedded to the status quo as such but only to the extent that the status quo gives effect to time-tested principles. . . . It is to the preservation of . . . use-tested institutions that conservatives are dedicated, opposing themselves to those foolish experimenters who cannot see into the future because they will not first school themselves by an examination of history.[2]

Conservatism, in other words, resolutely walks into the future facing backwards.

WILLIAM H. CHAMBERLIN

One does not look to William Henry Chamberlin for political theory but one can derive from him a sense of how it feels to be

[2] *Modern Age*, Spring, 1960, pp. 115-17.

a conservative liberal. Felix Morley and James Burnham will provide the ideology of that particular form of conservatism. But Chamberlin will give us something that is just as valuable in understanding conservatism as the constructions of the ideologues. It is the sense of shock at what the twentieth century has done, the sense of hurt, that Chamberlin demonstrates and that explains how a common garden-variety radical of the early 1920's "evolved"—to use Chamberlin's own phrase—into a conservative in the 1950's. We are familiar with how shock at the horrors of the twentieth century has transformed liberals into radicals and communists. But it is also true that the reverse process has taken place. Chamberlin is not in a sense a "true" conservative; his name does not appear on the lengthy list of editorial advisors of *The Modern Age,* although he has been published recently by Henry Regnery Company and thus has gained at least partial acceptance. He came to conservatism slowly. But he came surely.

His reaction to the terrors of Leninism and Stalinism, which he watched as a Moscow correspondent of *The Christian Science Monitor,* was to seek a refuge in individualism as the only secure place in a world turning to totalitarianism. The *only* secure place. With war and revolution on the rampage Chamberlin came to feel that it was the individual person alone who could be trusted with power, that anything collective could not, and that security could be found only within the individual personality. As he put it in 1940, in the immediate pre-World War II years he could not suppress a "feeling of helpless, bitter disgust with the age in which I lived . . . . I tried to take refuge in an increased sense of individual personality." Of all the conservatives we shall discuss, Chamberlin has the best case for our sympathy, for few of the others have actually witnessed the horrors of this century.

But while Chamberlin's reactions to totalitarianism deserve
only sympathy and respect it is necessary to say that this emotional response accompanied the development of a historical
scheme of the rise and fall of Western civilization which
landed Chamberlin eventually in the ranks of the conservatives.

It was not ideology that brought forth his scheme of history,
but the search for a point of stability. Chamberlin discovered
in Russia not merely the brutality and boorishness of Soviet
officials but also an intellectual elite surviving from prerevolu-
tionary days, which, compared with the former, appeared to
him in a very good light. Here in this old elite was humanity
poised against barbarism, and he thought "how young and
fresh Russia was in the nineteenth century." By 1940 his discovery had instilled in him a belief that the nineteenth century
held the keys of the kingdom, that the year 1914 was the turning point after which general decline set in.

With 1914, according to this view, came the end of a road
which had begun with the French Revolution; whatever one
might say of the abuses of the French Revolution it had led to
an epoch of "mighty progress," an epoch of individualism.
Chamberlin lays his cards on the table: Was there any European country that was not better off,

. . . on any reasonable standard of comparison, in 1900 than it had
been in 1800? . . . Who . . . could predict with confidence that in
the year 2000 there could be a similar verdict of progress in relation to 1900?[3]

"Dare we look ahead?" Chamberlin asks sepulchrally in 1940
and his answer is clear. No, we must only look back.

It is high time, I think, to put aside hopeful illusions. European

[3] W. H. Chamberlin, *The Confessions of an Individualist* (1940), p. 280.

civilization is in an unmistakable process of deterioration and decay . . .[4]

It would be an infinite blessing to restore the world of 1913, Chamberlin concludes.

Such was the shriveled vision in 1940 of a liberal—and Chamberlin not only said he was a liberal but in 1940 was one in fact—who had seen too much. What he called "the world's iron age" had set in and salvation was too far off to even contemplate. Since he was not a noticeably logical thinker, he was able to escape the consequences of another of his conclusions— that the root cause of the twentieth-century collapse lay in what had happened in the nineteenth century itself. The principles of pure nineteenth-century liberalism were stuck fast in his mind.

Those were (as he stated them in 1940): belief in liberty; belief in the "absolute right of the individual human personality to full and free expression (subject always to the reservation that the rights of other personalities are not infringed)"; belief in the validity of reason against dogma; belief that "power is the most evil thing in the world" and thereby (since it is necessary in the modern world) belief in the necessity of restraining it as much as possible; belief in civil liberties; and belief "that individual man's instinct is to create, while collective man's instinct is to destroy." He believed, in other words, "in a kind of mild anarchism as the ideal state" with a stress on the adjective "mild," for the state should be strong enough to protect internal peace but not carry on wars.

All these beliefs are honorable except the operative one, the idea that collective man destroys. But this was the idea that acted to catapult him from the liberalism of 1940 to the con-

[4] *Ibid.*, p. 288.

servatism of 1959. Once the grudge against collective action had set in there was no other road to follow except the one to the never-never land of utopian liberalism.

Chamberlin's rejection of collectivism was a root-and-branch affair because he identified collectivism with totalitarianism.[5] When he made that identification in 1941, he was doing so in the name of liberal democracy, not in the name of conservatism. Yet the logic of his position drove him on, and he could therefore write in 1959 of his "evolution" into a conservative. Individualism in his view was no longer strong enough to protect liberty against collectivism. What had happened after 1941 to cause him to look to conservatism as the only way to realize a limited government of checks and balances and a competitive economic system, to realize, that is, the liberal utopia?

What had happened was that classical liberalism had faded as a reality and therefore could be preserved only as a dream of the Garden of Eden. Chamberlin was simply recognizing the failure of classical liberalism to be relevant and the consequent necessity of becoming a conservative—a Conservative liberal. He discusses what he calls "the strange death of Anglo-American liberalism" as a death brought about by the New Deal and those liberals who supported it. We are on old and tiresome ground—conservatives are nothing if not repetitive—but it is important to see the part played by the New Deal in the mythology of conservatism. It is not just the actions and attack of the New Deal on the liberal principles of the conservative liberals that made them conservative, and it is not just that it gave a convenient date for the Fall—1933. Much more significantly the New Deal was the means for those Americans who were predisposed to do so, who *wanted* to do so, of turning liberalism into conservatism. It provided what they were look-

[5] W. H. Chamberlin, *Collectivism—A False Utopia*, (1937), *passim*.

ing for, what they hoped and expected to find—*proof* that they were out of the Garden, that only by going backward could they keep liberalism pure, that only by an act of conservatism could liberalism be kept alive as a memory. The New Deal and the Welfare State were a godsend to those liberals who feared the future, for it gave them the excuse of no longer having to look at the future.

What was tragic for Chamberlin in 1940 and 1941, therefore, became corrupt in 1959. In 1940 and 1941 the liberal had seen the orderly civilization of the nineteenth century finally destroyed. But by 1959 he could claim that since man had been given another chance and had refused to rebuild that civilization, he had deserted the faith, had become, in other words, corrupt. Such is the story told by Chamberlin in his official declaration of the conservative faith.

What kind of a conservative is the nineteenth-century liberal? Chamberlin tries hard to mouth all the sentiments that are proper to a conservative. He talks about the ideas of Burke, Adam Smith, Calhoun, John Adams, and de Tocqueville as now being the best shield for liberty, but he spends as little time on them as possible and fails to convince the reader that he either knows anything about these heroes of the conservative conscience or cares anything about them. Certainly he makes a case for conservatism but it is a case for "Conservatism: Shield of Liberty," or, in other words, conservatism as a means of protecting nineteenth-century liberal values and indissolubly fused with liberal values *in this day and age*. Chamberlin in publishing his *Evolution of a Conservative* had—as he always had—the courage of his convictions. And his conviction was that liberalism was now conservatism.

He makes this claim by postulating that conservatism is not outmoded for the twentieth century but, quite the contrary, is just what is needed for the age of the masses. Why is conservatism so successful as a means of protecting the individual against the many? Because Burke, John Adams, Calhoun, Tocqueville, Burckhardt, had all described what has really happened, the rise of the Leviathan state. Once, Chamberlin admits, it was true that conservatism was identified with a strong state, but that fact is no longer true today. Further, conservatism has always been identified with a belief in private property. But most of all and best of all, conservatism is the bulwark of freedom today because it has taken up the struggle for the positions which liberalism had abandoned. Since man has been so foolish as to turn away from classical liberalism, manifestly it is necessary for a liberal to turn to conservatism; as Chamberlin remarks, conservatism dispells many of the now impossible illusions of the liberals and particularly their optimism, and shows that the good society is the creation not of theoreticians but of organic growth. Modern liberalism has gone statist; it has failed to see that individual liberties go hand in hand with an individualistic economic system; it has failed to support liberty under law and the rights of the individual. It has in short become so corrupt that it is now necessary to become a conservative.

When Chamberlin, like other conservative liberals, takes the position that what is conservatism is liberalism and *vice versa,* and that both are required for this day and age, he exposes several of the underlying ironies and absurdities of the conservative liberal. First, he adopts as his heroes a heterogeneous group of eighteenth- and nineteenth-century thinkers most of whom did not have much if any faith in the liberalism of their time, in that very liberalism which Chamberlin is so anxious to preserve. Second, and more significant, when he postulates that conservatism is not outmoded for this era because it protects liberal values in the present he makes two indefensible claims. One is the claim that there is an ideological reality which is a thing called conservatism and which as such is distinct from liberalism. But that claim is never substantiated and cannot be substantiated because the very nature of the conservatism postulated for today by the conservative liberal is the liberalism of the nineteenth century.

The other claim is that conservatism is what we need today. But that cannot be true, for what the conservative liberal means is that what we need today is nineteenth-century liberalism and that conservatism is only a means to that end. The absurdity of this claim becomes even more confounded when we realize that the real reason why the conservative liberal has turned to conservatism is that he realizes that classical liberalism cannot stand by itself. Hence his situation reaches a point of total absurdity. On the one hand he postulates a conservatism that he identifies with nineteenth-century liberalism; on the other hand he realizes that nineteenth-century liberalism cannot stand by itself and therefore must rely on the aid of conservatism. But conservatism in his eyes *is* nineteenth-century liberalism!

Chamberlin, it is clear, is not a powerful thinker; his bits and pieces of conservative ideology do not signify as much as the more orderly ideological thinking of a Burnham or a Morley. Perhaps the most interesting aspects of Chamberlin as a conservative are the prejudices that he expresses in his *Evolution of a Conservative*. They do not represent an ideology, but taken together they give a sense of the conservative tone that is absent from more rigid thought. Since there is no consecutive framework of these attitudes one can only list them:

There is very little difference between socialism and communism because their long-range objects are the same. Socialists and liberals of the modern variety are often soft on communists.

63

The Federalist Papers and the American constitution show the quality of individual self-reliance on which America's subsequent growth and well-being were based.

There are two forms of democracy. One means equality of opportunity, the other means leveling. The first has made America great, the second has done her great harm.

Senator McCarthy and the Congressional committees investigating communism performed a "job that had been long neglected."

The Supreme Court hardly deserves the title of Shield of the Republic since its decisions seem to be calculated to make conditions easier for the communists in America.

The advantages of social mobility in America are that it prevents revolution and makes it easy to make money.

"Many things that might be stigmatized as conformity are entirely voluntary. Babbitt had his moments of doubt, even revolt. But in the end, he felt better about shouting as loud as his neighbor at the Boosters' Club luncheon."

There has been a general decline in individual moral responsibility as a result of the influence of Freud and Marx. Their ideas are "not unrelated" to the high crime rate in America.

"Government by its very nature, does not create wealth. All it can do when it goes into the business of subsidization of special group interests is to rob Peter to pay Paul, to pillage the thrifty for the benefit of the thriftless."

Spengler and Burckhardt were more accurate in forseeing the future than Marx.

"Baseball is the American character in action." Ty Cobb was the greatest baseball player; "he was a mean, tough, hard competitor."

Switzerland is very close to utopia. "One reason for my instinctive fondness of Switzerland is that this country . . . has changed little in spirit since the nineteenth century."[6]

Not all conservatives would agree with all the opinions expressed by Chamberlin but most of them would agree with most of them. He is a compendium of the sour prejudices of modern American conservatism.

We have already seen that regardless of the ideas postulated, the addiction of the conservative liberal to a vision of a liberal Garden of Eden turns him into a true-blue conservative. But now we can go one step further in estimating the conservative quality of this brand of liberalism. It is in the nature of conservative liberalism that it should result in an inability to have useful, feasible, or tolerable ways of looking at the future.

Its most frightening and dismaying feature is the fact that it has no ideas with which to face new problems, problems which did not exist in the nineteenth century. If we accept their grounds for dislike of this age and their arguments about the loss of freedom, all the conservative liberals can tell us with a sickly smile is that they too are trapped. They are trapped because the only ideal they can suggest is one that has been inoperative for some sixty years and in fact may never have existed at all as they imagine it. They put themselves in a box and then ask us to come in with them. Because they cling to a set of attitudes which they know are irrelevant they have no alternatives to offer to a world which they admit and indeed insist is tottering on the edge of ruin. They have no alternatives

---

[6] These opinions are scattered through Chamberlin's *Evolution of a Conservative.*

to offer because their ideas prevent them from conceiving of new ways of doing things. In an era which on their own proof and submission needs new methods of dealing with its problems they can only primly point to the past and say "wasn't it good?" But that inability to conceive of new alternatives *is* conservatism.

The quality that makes conservatism stand paralyzed in the face of the terrible future it has created out of its own mind can be seen in the problem posed by Chamberlin's well-known isolationism in the 1930's and after. His isolationism has certain puzzling aspects that cannot be explained by the logic of his career. Here was a sophisticated foreign correspondent who had seen the worst that Lenin, Stalin, and Hitler had had to offer and yet could only suggest as a solution to the crisis the prescription that America should stay out of it all. Although he felt deeply the collapse of European civilization—and he had spent most of his working life in Europe—the best thing he could say was that it was doomed and that America should not try to save it. Undoubtedly the war required to save Europe was a terrible one. But does that explain his attitude?

In part, of course. But another part of the explanation lay in the box he had built for himself with his faith that the nineteenth century was the good century and the twentieth century the bad. That badness seemed to him to be so deeply ingrained that nothing could be done about it. Once having postulated a Garden of Eden there was nothing he could suggest except a return to the past, which is precisely what he did suggest—a return to nineteenth-century America when it was protected (so the myth goes) from the facts of life. His mind had stripped itself of the possibilities that might exist in the future because he had destroyed the future as a possibility.

Chamberlin's isolationism is simply one example of how the

conservative, although he is willing to move, looks to movement as repetition, not as the invention of something new. It is also an example of how classical liberalism has come today to be inherently conservative, and thus used to close off the future, to prevent freedom.

Not all Old Conservatives choose 1914 beyond which neither their imagination nor their wits can pass, but whatever the date chosen, they share with Chamberlin his inability to adapt not merely to the society in which he lives but to the future society in which he will have to live. Chamberlin could not in 1940 and 1941 and cannot today see the possibility of a culture or civilization that is at the same time decent and yet different from that of the nineteenth century. He is one of many conservatives who, by seeking to identify civilization with a particular past moment of time, are trying to *fix* history so that they may forbid the emergence of civilizations different from those already known. Indeed, they are trying to forbid the very possibility of a new civilization.

FELIX MORLEY

Conservatism has propagated the idea that the state can do no good. J. K. Galbraith's *The Affluent Society* has shown what a high cost in social neglect flows from state-hatred. What are the roots of this idea? Is it the result of some neurotic aspects of the conservative personality? Or does it rest on some philosophical foundations that transcend neuroticism? Here the discussion will be confined to the former, but it should be understood that the existence of a philosophy of state-hatred does not preclude the possibility that there is in fact a neurotic temper at work.

There is no doubt that the conservative in his conservative-liberal guise has developed a consistent and even persuasive political philosophy based on state-hatred. It reminds one of a religion not only in the fervor with which it is preached but also in the impressive results that flow from several simple assumptions. Once those are accepted the opponent is lost. But more important is the very fact of a thought-out political philosophy at all. The American conservative has his chapbook to turn to if he wants reassurance for his strong feelings about the state and its misdeeds. He also has the self assurance that the possession of any doctrine gives and which makes an excellent propagandist. Unfortunately, along with these advantages of doctrine there is a concomitant disadvantage. The conservative may have his doctrine, but what does it tell him? Does it tell him where he is going or does it only tell him where he is *not* going? Does it give him possible lines of action for the future, possible ways of meeting unique problems? Or does it instead simply turn him to the past?

We have seen how one conservative liberal has reacted to his existence in the twentieth century—his reaction being to act as if he existed in the nineteenth century. How are such attitudes justified? The answer is, in brief, that by playing upon old liberal myths the conservative liberal creates the belief that the state corrupts and destroys and that only nineteenth-century liberalism can fend off such corruption and destruction. Is it surprising that President Eisenhower could see no reason for federal aid to schools? That President Truman could believe that a severe budget limit must be put on defense expenditure? The dislike of the conservative liberal for the state is not just some secret mumbo-jumbo whispered by conservatives in secret conclave; it is the mother's milk of most political figures in American life even today.

Felix Morley gives us the clearest and most up-to-date version of a philosophy that has, of course, a long tradition in American life. His ideas are expressed in two books, *The Power in the People,* published in 1949, and *Federalism and Freedom,* published in 1959, the latter of which represents a significant toughening of his line rather than a weakening. That is to say that we have, in the case of Morley, a generalized expression of ideas that are accepted more widely in America today than they were in 1945. No wonder Morley toughened his line.

Not that Morley was satisfied with the Eisenhower administration, for it had not, after all, reduced the state to nineteenth-century proportions. That is essentially what Morley wants, and this desire is based on a hymn of state-hatred that has to be heard to be believed.

The State . . . subjects people; whereas Society associates them voluntarily. . . . State and Society are naturally and continuously in opposition. . . . The inclusive discrimination of the State is tyrannical. The exclusive discrimination of a social group is merely offensive. . . . There were implications to [the] creation of the State that, as we look backward, are horrifying. . . . The State moves consistently to augment its power. . . . Power in the hands of the State is less inhibited morally and more destructive physically than in Society. . . . State power, no matter how well disguised by seductive words, is in the last analysis always coercive physical power. . . . As we come to recognize that the State is the repository of coercive power, and by its nature works ceaselessly to enlarge that power, much that seems shameful and senseless in the world today becomes intelligible, though not for that reason cheerful.[7]

The state, in this noncheerful view, cannot hold the balance between the forces in society because it is itself the main force and as a force is always tending to aggrandizement. Dunning's motion is once again in order. The problem as the conservative

---

[7] Felix Morley, *The Power in the People* (1949), Chapter 5, passim.

liberal sees it, harking back to the The Founding Fathers and
all that, is not to use the state for whatever good purposes it
might be used, but to hem it in as one would hem in a rampag-
ing lion.

It must not be thought, however, that such an approach is
necessarily sterile—not yet at least. For this antistatism is part
of a dualism of state and society that makes society into the
only creative force. The key, in fact, of this particular brand of
conservatism is the posited antitheses of state and society that
enables the conservative to answer all questions about What
Shall be Done with a generalized reference to the fructifying
powers of society. The problems that men face are not answered
with a plan of action, but with a faith in society qua society, a
belief that if society is only left alone it will solve problems by
itself. Thus the important conclusion is reached that the particular problem that is under discussion *need not be discussed.*

What is this "Society" that Morley talks about with such
glibness? He describes it as voluntary companionship in contrast with the state that is involuntary association based not on
free contract but on status. As an example of voluntary companionship, he points out that society cannot ostracize people
while the state can. However, society as voluntary association
does limit freedom. Thus it is necessary to make a distinction
between freedom and liberty, freedom being the indulgence in
carnal appetites, and liberty the cultivation of spiritual qualities. In this way it can be said that voluntary association increases liberty while it decreases freedom since it operates to
increase the individual's spiritual qualities, i.e., his skills, ambitions, self-development. Hence the individual finds liberty in
society while he finds freedom-servitude in the state since the
state serves only carnal needs; i.e., the lust for security. Undoubtedly, Morley admits, there is a need for a state since it is

necessary to have an agency that can draw together the multi-
farious activities of a society. But the boundary line between
the two should be drawn as precisely as possible, and in America
they have been so drawn because by happy chance the origins
of the American state were distinctly placed in time. But
alas, even here the state has followed its usual course of
aggrandizement.

Such is Morley's justification of society as against the state.
Some of the terms are a little odd; e.g., freedom *vs.* liberty,
although one sees what he means. But does he answer what is
after all a crucial question? Are there grounds other than faith
for believing that society will solve its problems with no state
help? A Samuel Smiles view of society is what his theory means
—or it means nothing, a possibility which should not be ignored.
Does he present evidence—factual, concrete evidence—for his
claim that a free society will find its way? No, he does not, a
curious omission for one so eager to make that very point.[8] He
simply assumes its truth.

But the apotheosis of society is only part of a larger attack on
democracy, and of an argument that freedom can be found only
in a federalism that is so strictly conceived as to be almost unimaginable—almost unimaginable, that is, to anyone but a
conservative. But whatever may be true of anyone else the
argument against democracy and for a really potent liberal
federalism is fundamental to the conservative liberals and to
American conservatism in general. Something of those ideas
will appear in the writings of conservatives of any description.

---

[8] It should be stated that the investigations of the American frontier by
Professor Scott Miyakawa of Boston University cast some curious light on
Morley's concept of voluntary activity in "society." Professor Miyakawa has
shown that, contrary to Turner's thesis, the American frontier established not
only forms of voluntary action but also stringent forms of social regimentation.
Freedom and/or liberty was not necessarily a conspicuous element of the frontier.

The form that these ideas take varies, of course, from conservative to conservative. In the case of Morley they take the
form of an attack on Rousseau and his idea of the general will.
For the concept of democracy to Morley is the concept of the
general will as it is stated in its most extreme form. Having hit
upon the happy idea of attacking democracy by slandering it,
Morley, and other conservatives too, are thus provided with a
devil and a myth of the devil's deeds. Not only does the reader
become fascinated by this tale of Good *vs.* Evil, and the way
the fortunes of battle sway back and forth—the metaphors are
not too extreme—but one feels that the author of the myth becomes fascinated, too—indeed, so fascinated as eventually to
lose all touch with the reality of what he is trying to present.

The story starts on a bright day in the eighteenth century—
just the kind of day the devil would pick for his nefarious deeds
—when one ne'er-do-well, would-be philosopher conceived of
the idea of the general will. From that point on one might say
that the history of all henceforth existing societies is the history
of the struggle between the ideas of the general will and the
ideas of (a) Burke, (b) Locke, and (c) Madison. The nineteenth century saw the struggle intensified because Karl Marx,
a bitter man of notorious fame, weighed in as subordinate of
the devil (or has he taken over the position?) in order to make
Rousseau's ideas more effective. Or, as Morley says, "Marx im-
plements Rousseau." Other unfortunate developments took
place also: parliamentary socialism put on a good face but it
was and is "a direct offshoot from the theories of Rousseau and
Marx, differing from communism not in basic theory but in
application." The result of both the ideas of Rousseau and the
developments that stemmed from them is that democracy and
dictatorship do not differ. For democracy is the use of centralized power in which "the political sovereignty necessary to

make the general will effective must be both indivisible and unquestionable . . . . Since the general will must come to a precise conclusion in any particular issue, and if this single conclusion alone is 'right,' then there can be no justification for political opposition."[9] We all know, of course, what happened in the French Revolution.

Thus we have a definition of political democracy: "Political democracy is actually a form of government in which the executive can successfully assert that its direction is in accord with the general will . . ."[10]

Such is the world-wide drama that has been played out in most areas of the globe and that has come to a sorry end in practically all of those areas. But not in America. Thanks to good luck, John Locke and especially The Founding Fathers— and we shall be meeting The Founding Fathers many, many times before we are through; indeed, we shall have a surfeit of their company—political democracy was not allowed to raise its misbegotten head in this land. And we must all, the whole world, be thankful for such foresight, since the American Republic is a "beacon unique in history." Or, more exactly, we must not "abandon the American in favor of the European political philosophy."

Is the conservative antidemocratic because he is against political democracy? In ordinary logic it might seem so and in fact it is so, but ordinary logic does not work in the technical complexities of nuclear physics, and it does not work in the technical complexities of American conservatism. Hence a conservative such as Morley is able to claim that he is not really antidemocratic, because he believes in "social democracy." We have already seen the roots of this bifurcation of the concept

[9] Morley, *Freedom and Federalism* (1959), pp. 29-30; p. 34.
[10] *Ibid.*, p. 93.

73

of democracy in Morley's distinction between the state (bad) and society (good). Social democracy is, insofar as one can work it out from Morley's prose, evidently the democracy of the people as they operate in their ordinary affairs, their voluntary groups; e.g., Babbitt at the Boosters Club was performing an act of social democracy. It is unfortunate, to say the least, that Morley does not give a more precise definition of what he means by social democracy. The result is that the key to his thought is left airily suspended. It is a key concept because social democracy is what he poses against both the state and political democracy defined as majority will.

However, we can come closer to what he means by social democracy if we juxtapose it with his definition of political democracy as majority will and with his faith in federalism. Social democracy is a socio-political system that operates to frustrate the majority will through the concurrent majority of Calhoun and through the federal structure, which makes the concurrent majority possible. Morley describes one aspect of this democracy in discussing the election of the president. He says that "the farther we get from the local community, the more gaudy and less democratic our politics become."[11] The federal system of the United States is, and quite deliberately so, incompatible with the nationwide enforcement of Rousseau's general will. Yet federalism allows democracy in the states: the "failure to realize that democracy functions best when localized, and worst when centralized, accounts for much of the confusion which surrounds the term."[12] It certainly does, for in lieu of the fact that Morley does not discuss at all how democracy functions in the states one may beg to differ with him about the superiority of state democracy over national democracy. But

[11] *Ibid.*, p. 158.
[12] *Ibid.*, p. 47.

Morley ignores such problems and goes on to claim that owing to the foresight of The Founding Fathers the American constitution is undemocratic and a very good thing too. Hence Morley's concern to show that the Federal Republic is not a centralized democracy. "We are proposing to demonstrate that it is incorrect, and therefore injurious, to call our Federal Union a political democracy. In so doing we shall also consider whether Soviet Russia has a better claim to that description."[13]

Given these ideas it is no surprise to find that Morley is pleased to see Interposition come back into its own. "The word inherent may properly be used for the associations of the doctrine of Interposition with the federal form of government."[14] Its revival in America is greeted by Morley with great satisfaction since it is testimony to the abiding faith of America in federalism. In this way Morley strips it of any racialist taint for, as he says, its connection with the race issue is strictly fortuitous. Instead it has been revived to protect the states from the centralizing trend apparent in the decisions of the Supreme Court, and to protect the citizen from the government in Washington. We are witnessing, in the revival of Interposition, another chapter in the long saga of federalism *vs.* the Rousseauean general will. An earlier chapter in that story was the Civil War, in which the cause of the South was morally valid because it was based on the American belief in home rule.

The fact that the South was defeated brings up the possibility that federalism as defined by Morley may not have been in the best of health since 1861 despite the revived and gallant resistance of the South. And so it appears. One purpose of Morley's insistence on the vital distinction between local democracy on the one hand, and Rousseauean general will, majority rule, and

[13] *Ibid.*, p. 11.
[14] *Ibid.*, p. 187.

centralized government on the other hand, is to show that since
1861 federalism and democracy have come into conflict so
severe that reconciliation between the two has become impossible. Actually the threat of democracy began even earlier, with
the election of 1824, at which time the nominating convention
replaced the Congressional caucus. After 1824 those who were
in favor of democracy were against federalism and those who
were against it were in favor of federalism. The rot really set in,
however, with the fourteenth amendment, for it embodied the
Rousseauean, leveling, centralizing spirit of Thaddeus Stevens.
It goes without saying, of course, that Franklin D. Roosevelt
was also a disciple of Rousseau and that his goal was totalitarian
democracy and socialism. But we have the South; we can depend on it at least.

The positive faith of the South clearly favors something quite different from and antagonistic to totalitarian democracy. It favors
the federal principle. . . .[15]

It is apparent that Morley's fear of the federal government
rests on an assumption of individual virtue that is quite stag-
gering in one who has such a suspicion of what men will do
once they hold centralized power.

Whenever we seek for the real sources of American strength we
find them, in the last analysis, resting on the belief that the individual
is at least potentially important, and fulfills himself through voluntary cooperation in a free society. . . . The condition of freedom . . .
is maintained only by the individual love of liberty.[16]

Federalism as a conservative ideology assumes not only that the
individual wants liberty but that he is "interested in, and for the

[15] *Ibid.*, Chapter 14.
[16] Morley, *The Power in the People*, pp. 83-4.

most part competent to handle, local problems." (Nothing is said about national problems, but presumably they do not exist.) But this faith is only a part of a view of man as free enterpriser.

To assert that men should have equal opportunity is to imply that with this opportunity they will become unequal. Some will push ahead and others will fall behind. . . . That biological fact . . . cannot be denied.[17]

Hierarchy flows naturally from such a "biological" fact and no society can avoid it; the attempts of democracy to avoid it only lead to more and more centralization of power; by now we know to what that centralization in turn leads.

Morley, however, sees the issue that is raised by individualism, free enterprise, and the resulting hierarchy; as he says, "the problem is the control of privilege as such."[18] But given his absolute refusal to consider centralized government as a way of controlling privilege, what solutions for the problem does he have? We are now at the crux of the question that conservative liberalism poses. For it is plain that much of what they propose is attractive. Who would not like to live in local pockets of social brotherhood? As a matter of fact, there are some who would not; still, no one can deny the appeal of this archaic form of liberalism to many. But what can Morley's conservative liberalism do to face this crucial problem of the control of privilege? For Morley himself is aware that centralized, nationally organized power—big business, for example—is just as destructive of liberty as centralized, nationally organized big government, and he has harsh words for the actions of big business after the Civil War.

[17] Morley, *Freedom and Federalism,* p. 44.
[18] *Ibid.,* p. 81.

His words may be harsh but the net result of his thoughts on free enterprise will hardly cause General Motors to worry over the possibility that their conviction, that what is good for them is good for everyone, will be threatened as a viable policy. Morley as a true believer in local freedom is also and of necessity a true believer in open access to an open market. Yet two doubts remain.

State intervention destroys the freedom of the market. But the mere absence of State intervention does not mean that the free market will be preserved. Those who cannot compete are also men.[19]

"Those who cannot compete are also men"—the warmest words spoken by Morley. But what is one to do about those who cannot compete?

The demands of freedom, we are told, are stern and call for sacrifice. Who is to do the sacrificing? The businessmen, voluntarily and spiritually.

To the extent that Society disclaims responsibility for them, the State, always impinging on the market, will enlarge its paternalistic role. Thus it becomes axiomatic that the less significant the spiritual element in business, the greater will be political intervention in the economic sphere.[20]

The remedy must come from within. From within what? From within the soul of the businessman? In part. But what if his soul is, so to speak, somewhat shriveled, a possibility that has not been altogether unsuspected, as even Morley admits. Then we must rely on the forces that operate within the economic sphere itself. Bigness in economic matters, we are told, carries the seeds of its own disintegration. Thus, whatever happens, it is

[19] Morley, *The Power in the People*, p. 200.
[20] *Ibid.*, p. 200.

not necessary for either business, or those harmed by business
—"those who cannot compete are also men"—ever to depend
on the national government to help them out. Morley's final
words are that free enterprise must balance material output
with moral output—it must be directed to the service that man
owes his Creator.

The daring quality of such a solution to the problem of the
"control of privilege as such" cannot be denied. But Morley
does not give any reasons to believe that economic bigness
carries the seeds of its own disintegration, or that there is a
spiritual element in business. One may wonder therefore
whether or not his approach to the whole question is not more
foolhardy than bold. But whatever it is, it is at least logical, for
it is written from the self-confident viewpoint of a nineteenth-
century liberal.

As we have seen, Morley is no believer in political democracy.
How does he square that attitude with the liberalism he pro-
fesses in his earlier book, *The Power in the People?* The answer
will show another of the ways in which liberalism through a
process of metamorphosis becomes conservativism.

Undoubtedly, Morley tells us, it is easy to make the mistaken
assumption that liberalism and democracy have something in
common, but in fact liberalism is dead set against democracy.
"There will always be a latent conflict between democracy and
liberalism."[21] It is through such reasoning that Morley is able to
present himself as a liberal in 1949, can praise John Locke and
can claim that "the liberal mind [reached] its highest political
attainment in the writing of the Constitution of the United
States."[22] Yet even he evidently had to recognize eventually
that this liberalism was a conservative liberalism, for by 1959

[21] *Ibid.*, pp. 146-54.
[22] *Ibid.*, p. 254.

he was an editorial advisor to *Modern Age* and parts of his
Freedom and Federalism, published in book form in 1959, had
appeared in *Nation's Business* and *Barron's Weekly.* But perhaps these affiliations do not matter, for, as he put it in 1949,
"The American system of government is based on principles
that are eternal."[23]

The word that summarizes this type of conservative-liberal
opposition to democracy is the word "republic" as defined in
Madison's formula (quoted by Morley as the motto to his
Freedom and Federalism):

The error . . . seems to owe its rise and prevalence chiefly to the
confounding of a republic with a democracy. . . . A democracy . . .
will be confined to a small spot. A republic may be extended over a
large region.

The word *republic* connotes to a conservative not the freedom
that is derived from loss of a king, nor the right of the majority
to rule, but rather a dispersal of power to the point where the
national government is only negative. The American republic
was designed solely to protect the individual from the state. Or,
to quote the jargon of the conservatives, a republic "is designed
to provide a people who are instinctively democratic with a
government calculated to safeguard them from the excess of
democracy as a political system." Or, the republic is designed
"to make it easier for every resident to advance himself, in the
sense of moving from lower to higher standards."[24] Or, "the
Constitution represents an unprecedented and unparalleled
effort to integrate a system of government with an individualistic code of personal conduct . . . To attack the principles
underlying free enterprise is to impugn the traditional morality

[23] *Ibid.,* p. 213.
[24] Cf. *Ibid.,* Ch. I.

of the American people."[25] The Founding Fathers really *did* think of everything.

Everything? According to the conservative liberals, yes, everything. Certainly no primitive tribe could show an ancestor worship more profound than that accorded to The Founding Fathers by the conservative liberals. That is how we know they are *conservative* liberals and not just liberals.

But we know they are conservatives for other reasons, too. In the case of Felix Morley in particular and for example, the conservative roots of his attitude go much deeper than veneration for The Founding Fathers. We have passed in review many of his attitudes on government and society and have seen them as reflections of authentic nineteenth-century liberal doctrine. They all turn about the central idea of balance in the constitution as a way of protecting the individual and society from— from what? Oddly, Morley is not really very clear on that vital point except to equate the "State" with totalitarianism, a position so ridiculous and childish that one wonders exactly what he is up to.

He is not really interested in liberalism qua liberalism; he is interested in defeating the majority will, state action, collective activity, in order to prevent change from taking place. A John Stuart Mill—the greatest liberal of them all—could contemplate the use of state action to serve liberal ends. But a Felix Morley cannot. And he cannot because he uses and manipulates liberalism as a means to the end of stopping innovation.

The clearest revelation of what Morley is getting at is his failure to handle the vital problem that he sets himself and that he must solve if his ideas are to be viable. A solution is also

[25] *Ibid.*, p. 30.

necessary to those of us who live in the twentieth century. How
does his philosophy of democracy "confined to a small spot"
deal with the brutal fact that local concerns no longer are self-
sufficient—if they ever were—and are subordinate to the affairs
of larger units? We have seen that Morley is aware of the problem but has no answer to it except to cry that big business
should become spiritual. (One may ask, by the way, if it is
possible for big business to be spiritual, why it is not possible
for big government to be spiritual? But that possibility is not
even raised.) Is Morley cheating us? Or does he really think he
has given an answer? Neither. He is simply incapable of seeing
that he has cheated his reader, that he has failed to give an
answer. And he is incapable of doing so because he has erected
nineteenth-century liberalism as a blind between himself and
the society he lives in. Since he takes nineteenth-century liberalism in its purest form as the only attitude which is feasible, he
is thereby prevented from coming to grips with the problems
of his day because nineteenth-century liberalism did not conceive of those problems. If he tried to apply his "liberalism" to
current problems it would collapse, since it is irrelevant. To
preserve his attitudes he must avoid answers to the problems of
present-day society. And thus it can truly be said that he neither
thinks he has given an answer nor is he cheating. The whole
question of an answer is beyond the scope of his thought and
quite deliberately so.

Why has Morley turned away from the society of today to
talk about local groups operating in terms of concurrent majorities when all the facts indicate that if local life is to be made
significant in the United States it will have to be done by national action, by the "State"? With Morley we see another aspect
of that same dislike of the twentieth century which drove W. H.
Chamberlin back to the nineteenth century and which also

drives Morley to the same place. In the case of Morley, however, because his thought is somewhat more sophisticated, his
opposition to the society and time in which he lives takes the
form of opposition to bigness, or centralization. Does this opposition mean that such conservatives as Morley have a significant approach to, and understanding of, at least the problem of
centralized power that modern society certainly does in fact
pose? If they do they would be well worth listening to, for the
problem is not one which can be treated lightly. But they do
not have a significant approach to the question because they are
not capable of understanding that the drive for centralized
power is more than an accident or the result of evil temper. In
fact they cannot explain that drive at all; they are simply
baffled by it. And since they have no means of analysis they
cannot provide possible solutions to the problem; they can only
cry "back, back before it is too late." But one can push the
analysis of their attitudes one step further. Their inability to
analyze power in modern society, their failure to cope with the
problem in any significant way has its roots in their instinctive
antipathy to a large society, a society composed of big units, to
what Graham Wallas called the Great Society.

It is this antipathy, amounting very often to hatred, that lies
behind so much of the chatter about the "State," for the modern
state to the mind of the conservative represents bigness carried
to its ultimate and most frightening extreme. But this antipathy
to the "State" is only one facet of a larger inability to accept the
very nature and basic characteristics of the modern Great
Society in which the conservative lives. It is a society marked
by rootlessness, hugeness, bureaucracy, impersonality, and
many other things too numerous to mention at this point. We
all know what the society is like because we live in it. But the
conservative liberal prefers not to live in it. He has in fact with-

drawn from it, opted out, turned his back on it, and gone to roost with The Founding Fathers in a green suburbia. One can sympathize with him; from this distance The Founding Fathers look quite comfortable. But one must point out that as a result of his choice a conservative such as Morley has nothing to say to those simple-minded persons who have not opted out but still find it necessary to sweat in the muck of present-day reality.

A conservative liberal, therefore, is someone who represents one type of hatred for the Great Society. There are others who hate it with a different ideology, but this form of hatred is one which reacts by turning back to better days in the past rather than by trying to present new alternatives for the future of that society. His hatred and disgust are so great that he does not even attempt to apply nineteenth-century liberal principles to the problems of the society in which he lives but simply prefers to reiterate those principles while pointing out how far everyone else has fallen from them.

Morley shows clearly the political ideology that results from the conservative fear of the Great Society. Dedicated as he is to an image of society that is derived from the early nineteenth century, he must of necessity postulate a simple governmental structure in which the national state exists only as the federal state of a group of republics and in which even the fourteenth amendment has not yet been written. This devolution of power and dispersal of power is the conservative's political reply to the facts of the Great Society. In one sense it is not only an effective reply but perhaps the only root-and-branch reply, since it would destroy the Great Society. But a nagging doubt must remain even in the minds of the conservatives. What if such a society will not easily yield up its life? What relevance then has the reply of the conservative liberal to hugeness? For the nonconservative the question will occur, is there no new way of dealing with the problems of such a society? Must we always depend on The Fathers? But the conservative liberal considers such questions and such doubts an impertinence, because the facts of the Great Society are so awful, because his despair at hugeness is so great, that it is only through dreams of a return to the known security of past political systems rather than by the invention of new and therefore unknown expedients that he can bear his existence in that society.

JAMES BURNHAM

Not all conservative liberals agree with each other in every respect. While they have in common a devotion to the political system of nineteenth-century liberalism, they often disagree about the exact epoch and years when the Golden Age may be said to have existed. Morley thinks it existed in the years before the Civil War and the fourteenth amendment, although he feels that even as early as 1824 certain unpleasant signs of degeneration had occurred. Certainly by 1900 the Fall from grace had come. James Burnham on the other hand takes a slightly different bead on history, and finds his Golden Age in the years after 1865 when, in his view, the liberal political system and the liberal economic system flourished with healthy vigor. The result of this disagreement is not fundamental but it does display two different facets of conservative liberalism. Where Morley, as a result of his placing of the Golden Age, looks to federalism as the savior of America, Burnham sees Congress as the key element in the return to virtue and propriety. Where Morley sees something he calls the "State" as the enemy, Burnham sees the executive branch of the national government as the enemy. His formula for political happiness is therefore a strong legislature and weak executive, a president who does not hold the reins but simply rides. In this view the executive is literally the executor of the tasks given him by Congress; a series of weak presidents does not spell danger but, as they say, Peace and Prosperity. The significance of this point of view after some years of President Eisenhower is obvious.

The significance of Burnham's conservative attitude, however, is more than that of a mere description of institutional rights and duties. It also displays another aspect of the way the conservative liberals look at constitutional balance and shows another method by which liberal principles and theory have been taken over to provide a nesting ground for conservatives.

Liberal political theory has always been concerned with the problem of political balance, this concern usually taking the form of a simple discussion of the proper role of institutions in a political system. Behind the institutions, however, certain basic political forces were understood to be operating. Thus, even though liberal political theory has often been too naïve to support an accurate description of the political, social, and economic forces that operate in a society, it has nevertheless been able to encompass the significance of those forces by virtue of its institutional analysis, since it was through institutions that the forces were expected to express themselves. Despite our more sophisticated techniques of social analysis today we are in no position to deny the significance of this liberal insight.

Hence the importance of institutions in liberal political analysis. And hence, too, the balance motif that runs through that analysis. To the classical liberal, institutions not only exist to perform their functions but also, so to speak, to prevent social forces from following the logic of their ideals or desires; i.e., institutions not only express the socio-economic forces at work in a society but they also can *contain* those forces and prevent any one of them from dominating the others. Liberalism believes that if political institutions are in balance (and their balance has a certain visibility that can be seen on paper) then the forces that operate through them will also be in balance.

These institutions-as-constraining-devices were supposed to work in two ways. First, they would constitute the arena in which what the eighteenth century called the passions of men would find expression, the place where conflict between men would and should occur. Second, they were the arena where conflicts between men would and should take place because methods had been devised by which *limits* on conflict had been placed *previous* to the conflict, so that when passions erupted the stage was already set and set in such a way that the actors had to stay within it. Exactly the opposite would be true if the conflict took place in the wild and amorphous realm of society where anything was possible. What were those limits? The very nature of an institution was one limit. An institution is, by virtue of its existence, the embodiment of limits, for in order to establish it one has to draw lines and say: this is what the institution is concerned with and that is what it is not concerned with. Hence the crucial importance of institutions to the maintenance of social balance. Further, rules, i.e., law, would provide the means by which the conflict was to be fought.

This type of political system has often been described as a system in which the state "held the ring." In fact, however, the metaphor is incorrect. The State and its various institutions are the ring. It is inside that particular ring that the struggle takes place. And it can take place safely because the boxing match— the metaphor is certainly irresistible—is fought according to certain lawful rules and because the ring was set up before the match started. The state is not a referee; it is the arena itself.

One could go on for some time spinning out the metaphor or developing others; liberal political theory lends itself to that activity because it has a neat mechanistic character. But the real problem of liberal theory is not susceptible to eighteenth-century mechanics. The problem is that of getting action out of a system that is in balance. Is stasis the only possibility for such a system? If there is balance how can decisions be made by passionate men? (It must not be forgotten that the important questions are those men are passionate about.) Is this political system a model for a dynamic society or an agricultural-pastoral dream in which the annual round of the seasons is the only evidence of change? Taken on its own terms, is there any reason to think that it can work in the simple sense of getting things done? Or is it merely a system for preventing things from being done?

A discussion of conservatism raises such questions because conservatives love stasis; they are so to speak, stasis-seekers. But it is necessary to point out that stasis is a very real problem of the liberal political system. It is also necessary to point out that it can overcome its built-in tendency to stasis only with great difficulty and only after what is often an extrainstitutional effort, only because of a force that operates outside the explicit framework of the system. One such force is, of course, a personality. Another such force is a crisis. But when these forces do not exist stasis becomes the main fact of such a system.

The significance of liberal balance for a discussion of conservatism is the appeal which the built-in stasis of the liberal political system holds for the American conservative who aims, as we have seen, at *not* changing except to change backwards. Or to be more exact, he aims to prevent innovation, an aim for which the liberal political system is admirably designed. Although it may be true that such a system need not necessarily prevent innovation, it is also easy to make such a system arrive at a point of stasis. That is why the American conservative is so fond of it. Being in a condition of near-stasis himself he desires —insofar as he has desires—only a political system devoted to an unending round of the same maneuvers, a system that is in perfect and *perpetual balance.* If one has such a system then one is *insured* against change. It spins and spins and spins with great and vigorous energy and it never moves— it just spins and spins and spins on into infinity.

To achieve such a state of bliss a perfect liberal system must be created. No part of it must be allowed to get out of balance. No one part of it must be allowed an ascendency for then the whole system will be disarranged and it is well known what happens to perpetual motion machines once their delicate systems are jarred. If the system can be disarranged once, it can be disarranged again. The innocent nonconservative may ask, how then will a crisis or in fact anything else be managed? But we have already answered that question. Felix Morley has told us that it is society that will make arrangements. Just trust society and its voluntary methods and all will be taken care of in due course. As we have seen, the problems of big business will be solved by a spirit of voluntary goodwill and self-restraint. It should be pointed out in all fairness that the conservative is sometimes skeptical of the effectiveness of this voluntary spirit but since he has nothing else to suggest he is stuck with it. He has nothing else to suggest because the liberal political system must not under any circumstances be disarranged.

Unfortunately for the conservative, the problem of defining exactly what the balance of the Constitution is or should be is a knotty one. It is easier to talk about stasis and balance than to define them because the methods of measuring the power of one institution vis-a-vis another are so inexact. Nevertheless the conservative plunges ahead, and when he looks at the American system today what he finds is that the balance is decidedly off center. Indeed, he discovers that the American political system has virtually lost all semblance of balance between the various institutions of government because Congress has been so degraded. Or at least one conservative, James Burnham, has made that discovery, and he can be taken to stand for most, although not all, conservative opinions on the subject.

The heart of Burnham's concern over Congress[26] is his statement of the needs and virtues of constitutionalism and conservatism and his consequent fear of democracy, majority rule, and modern (i.e., post-1933 New Deal) liberalism. He starts out from the basic assumption that constitutionalism and therefore liberty require some standard of law other than the conduct and will of the sovereign. The sovereign power in his view must of necessity be checked for if it is not, then there will no longer be a balance. Constitutionalism means to Burnham a system in which government is restricted in its powers and also a system in which the sovereign is restricted. He is afraid of government itself. But he is more fearful of the sovereign power, of a democratic government in which the "people" would be sovereign. He dislikes and is afraid of democracy and that is why he is so eager to have a constitution. For in a democratic age, the conservative thinks, and rightly too, that the majority will *act* unless their sovereign power is restricted.

Burnham's devotion to constitutionalism is not, therefore, without a taint of special pleading. It is not devotion to a constitutionalism that would enable democracy to function by pre-

[26] James Burnham has written many books stating his conservative views. See his famous *The Managerial Revolution,* and *The Machiavellians.* The discussion here, however, will be confined to his *Congress and the American Tradition* (1959).

venting minority control. Instead it is a devotion to constitutionalism in order to so restrict democracy that it will cease to
be effective and troublesome, or even better, simply cease to be.
In Burnham's view The Founding Fathers (he too is an addict)
had a place for democracy in the Constitution but not for democratic ideology. He means that a little bit of democracy never
hurt anyone but it should not be allowed to be the ruling
principle.

Burnham's attitude towards democracy is thus the touch-
stone of his approach to constitutionalism and Congress. He
makes a sharp and absolute distinction between constitutionalism and democracy, refusing to consider any possibility that
they might not only co-exist but actually fructify each other.

Between the democratic formula and constitutional principle there
is no logical relation whatever.[27]

Why can the two not aid each other? The answer comes from
his concept of democracy, which is, like that of Felix Morley,
based on the idea that democracy is the General Will. The
people who are the General Will have no obligation to conduct
themselves in a constitutional manner. And in empirical fact,
Burnham thinks, they do not so conduct themselves. If one
wonders how democracy and constitutional government came
to be so easily and so often confused as Burnham admits they
have been, he has a ready answer. Democracy was once used
by the middle class as a means of combating the privileges of
aristocracy and kingship, but it was adopted by the middle class
"without any expectation that it would ever be carried out fully
in practice." Yet, alas, the myth proved attractive to those who
were left outside of the middle class, and therefore the middle

[27] Burnham, *Congress,* chap. XXI.

class had to erect constitutionalism to prevent such naïveté from gaining ground. This charming admission of middle-class hypocrisy does have a certain ring of truth about it.[28]

The American conservative is nothing if not logical. The problem that democracy presents to Burnham is, that while it seems to be tolerable on the surface, in fact it is utterly intolerable because it means unanimous opinion or it means nothing. In this sense law is hopeless and of no use because it simply becomes an expression of the general will. In the happy, happy eighteenth and nineteenth centuries government and politics were dominated by the "sober" middle classes. (It is worth noting here that Burnham regrets the ending of voting restrictions based on color of skin.[29]) But what he calls the "logic of democratism" cannot tolerate sobriety and/or middle-class control; instead it heads straight for Caesar. Thus Caesarism is not the ruin of democracy or its perversion but simply its logical realization. For only Caesar can realize the general will.

Once again we have a conservative securely tied in knots of his own making. Once again we are back in Calhoun-land where there are two kinds of majorities, those which arise from a vote for or against a leader, and those which arise from a majority of majorities in different parts of the land; i.e., a concurrent majority. The latter is, to the conservative if he uses the word at all, real democracy, for it comes from voluntary agreement and consensus rather than from a plebiscite. It follows therefore that real democracy can exist only in small communities since only in small communities can real political equality exist. We have been here before, but Burnham goes one step further than Morley.

[28] See David Spitz, *Patterns of Anti-Democratic Thought* (1949), for an analysis of the authoritarianism of Burnham's *Managerial Revolution*.
[29] Burnham, *op. cit.*, p. 295.

Democratism-Caesarism-the masses: all three are elements of the same political equation.[30]

The antithesis of the masses on the one hand and the people snug and secure in their different local communities on the other hand, is an important one for Burnham and the conservatives. For it enables him to say that the masses can and must be represented by a single leader while the people in their multitudinous differentiation cannot. It also enables him to make the basic distinction on which his argument for Congress depends, that the President has emerged as the "primary democratist institution," as the representative and Caesar of the masses who acts best when unimpeded by constitutional niceties, while Congress—one is not surprised by this conclusion—represents the people in their manifold variety. Congress is the embodiment of the concurrent majority. Once the states were able to perform that function. But Burnham obviously thinks things have gone much further than Morley does and thus he finds that only Congress is left from the wreck which That Man made of the constitution. It should be pointed out that Burnham believes that the wreck of the Constitution has even included the Supreme Court, since the appointment of Mr. Warren to the Supreme Court is a clear case of putting the democratic ideology into practice.

More concretely, what is Burnham's view of the proper role of Congress? In a society threatened by democracy what exactly can it do to stem the tide, man the bulwarks? As we shall see Burnham prophesies the final deluge. Yet Congress does have certain functions that give it an important role, at least in that ideal constitution of which he dreams. As he points out, although The Founding Fathers divided the government into

[30] *Ibid.*, p. 319.

three branches they did not necessarily intend them to possess equal power. "The Founding Fathers believed that in a republican and representative system the preponderant share of power was held and exercised by the legislature."[31] And, of course, if that idea was the idea held by The Founding Fathers . . . well, then.

Knowing conservative ways of thought one does not expect Burnham to attempt a precise definition of the role of Congress vis-a-vis the other branches of the government. And not expecting such an attempt one is not disappointed. How much power should be in the hands of Congress? Burnham says that The Founding Fathers felt that no government can exist without the confidence of the people—a sound enough statement—and that that confidence can be achieved only if sovereignty is in the legislative branch. What does such a claim mean? Does it mean that Burnham is looking to a parliamentary system such as the British have created out of the concept of parliamentary sovereignty? Hardly, for the parliamentary system of Britain is seen by Burnham and most conservatives as a sign of senile ruin. Burnham, of course, as a devotee of the dispersal-of-power doctrine, could not advocate such a system. What does he mean then? What is the proper role of Congress?

To say that such a question is a crucial one for conservative ideology is to put it mildly indeed. If they cannot give some precision to their notion that Congress has a certain significant role to play in a system of dispersed powers, then such intellectual concoctions as Burnham's and Felix Morley's fall to the ground. It is a fine thing to say, as Burnham says, that Congress has priority at the same time that there is a diffusion of power. It is indeed a splendid idea but does it get us anywhere?

Burnham's attempt to make an evaluation of the proper role

[31] *Ibid.*, p. 92.

of Congress is weak not only because he depends on rhetoric to take the place of homework but also because his standard of the proper role of Congress involves him in an absurdity. He faces, of course, the knotty problem of deciding how one determines what is the proper role of Congress. He is not prepared to accept the results of political pressures and say that when Congress is strong it is fulfilling its function in one era and when it is weak it is fulfilling its function in another era. He cannot accept that view because he must find a fixed place for Congress in his system of stasis and because such a view would open up the possibility that a weak Congress might be useful and proper. No, there must be some transcendent proof of the real role of Congress. And what better and more transcendent proof is there than tradition? Does one want to know what the proper role of Congress should be? Look back to history and see how Congress behaved at the height of its history. That role will be its proper role.

When Burnham looks at the history of Congress' law-making power it is clear to him that for nearly a century and a half Congress has kept the control of law making in its own hands. Even the Supreme Court, that currently aggressive and unpleasant body, respected Congress' law-making powers in the past. As for the President, he was literally the executor of Congress' will. But then, of course, came the beginning of the end, i.e., Franklin D. Roosevelt. Many things happened after 1933 but one of the most significant was the loss of Congressional law-making powers to the President. This shift of power has made Congress merely an approving or disapproving institution, has made it into a replica of the British parliament. Burnham wishes to be fair; the shift of power which started under Roosevelt has continued under his successors; Eisenhower after all is a Caesar, too. But the point of calling attention to this shift is to show that it is contrary to the traditional concepts of the American political system. (That the welfare of America might have suffered if the shift had not taken place is not even considered as a possibility.) Thus, one can see what the proper role of Congress vis-a-vis the President should be by looking at the history of America, during most of which Congress has dominated the presidency. And if it dominated the presidency in the past it should do so today. Does Burnham consider the possibility of innovation in that relationship? He does not.

The results of his consideration of other Congressional powers are the same. In regard to the power of the purse Congress is in theory, and was in practice, supreme, yet while Congress has not lost all of its power in this respect—not even Burnham would make that claim—it has lost a good deal of its power. It has lost it because the legislature cannot control expenditure if there is a huge government bureaucracy under the control of the president. (Again it is legitimate to ask if Burnham considers whether or not this bureaucracy may not possibly fulfill some function and again the answer is No, he does not.) The same sorry history can be observed in the case of the treaty power— a long period of Congressional domination followed by the decline of its power as centralized, statist government arose to take the place of the traditional government. And of course the same is true of war-making powers and military affairs in which it was the intent of The Founding Fathers that Congress dominate.

So it goes, a melancholy tale of ruin and degradation, of decline from the high standards The Founding Fathers set for us. One sometimes wonders why these conservative liberals keep up the fight at all. But there is one hopeful aspect of the situation of Congress and that is its power to investigate, which has indeed grown in effectiveness. Burnham is somewhat embarrassed by the fact that the only really effective power that remains in the hands of Congress is not mentioned in the Constitution, but the conservatives have faced this embarrassment before and have triumphantly overcome it. Their technique is to say that the Constitution, and of course The Founding Fathers, took such a power for granted. And that is just what Burnham says here. Certainly, Burnham stoutly maintains, the failure to mention it in the Constitution was not due to an oversight. One is inclined to agree, for by now one is accustomed to the idea that The Founding Fathers were omniscient men who saw to the end of time. Burnham is not without some criticism of the actual way the investigatory power is used; e.g., when it results in the firing of people from their jobs, it improperly becomes a judicial power rather than a legislative power. But that conclusion does not lead him to ask whether this improper use is not perhaps a result of at least some aspects of the system itself. Congressional investigations are simply a "vital" aspect of the proper role of Congress, and since they are, in Burnham's view, the only real power left to Congress they must be protected all the more carefully. Thus in regard to the McCarthy affair Burnham is less concerned with any possible erosion of individual rights—although he makes a general admission that investigations can have such an effect—than with the weakening of the essential investigatory powers by those who attacked McCarthy. The McCarthy affair to Burnham is significant only as another attempt on the part of modern liberals and statists to break the power of Congress.

Burnham is desperate about Congress for the same reason that Morley is desperate about Federalism. "Can Congress Survive?" Burnham asks, and answers that it is possible but not probable that Congress will survive. Since the meaning of the word *survive* is not made explicit—does he mean literally, or in reference to certain powers?—the statement is less significant than he would like it to be. He sees little future for Congress, unless there is a sharp reversal of the historical trend, if only because of the existence of what he calls the "theoretical grave-diggers" who attack Congress as an institution. But behind them lies a deeper cause of Congressional decline, a world trend, a trend of strengthening the executive as against the legislature. Hence the "traditional balance" has been upset, a balance maintained throughout the nineteenth century in which Congress had priority. Woodrow Wilson recognized that fact although he was one of those theoretical gravediggers responsible for the ultimate fall.

It is clear that this particular form of delight in things past and fear of things to come is based on a severe dichotomy between modern liberalism and conservatism. We are once again faced with a problem of conservative terminology and definition. What is Burnham? He calls himself a conservative, and he hates liberals. But is not his whole system of values one of nineteenth-century liberalism? We have a real catch in Burnham for here is a nineteenth-century liberal who not only admits to being a present-day conservative but who brags about it as the mark which sets him off against the modern-day, post-flood liberals. Burnham has no doubts that ideological differences exist in America: "Conservatism and liberalism . . . are social facts in contemporary America." Indeed he draws up a summary of the differences between conservative and liberal which he calls "The Conservative Syndrome" and "The Liberal Syndrome."[32] And like all syndromes these give a clue to the health of the patient; "Conservatives tend to be for Congress . . . Liberals . . . tend to be against Congress. . . ."[33] Burnham, how-

[32] See Burnham, *op. cit.*, pp. 121-23.
[33] *Ibid.*, p. 123.

ever, is a flexible or perhaps one might say a slippery sort of
conservative, for he does not want to be tied to the defense of
Congress forever and, as he points out, in fact there have been
periods when conservatives were not defenders of Congress.
But such a point is academic, he thinks, for the present division
of opinion is "not likely to change for some while to come."

This flexibility should not lead one to believe that Burnham
is lukewarm in his conservatism. The exact opposite is true, for
his whole approach to politics, political systems, and Congress
flows from his conservatism. But what is the nature of that conservatism? What does it tell us about the qualities of the modern
conservative liberal? His own particular syndrome will give
added detail to a description of conservative liberalism.

While Burnham is more deeply conservative than Chamberlin and Morley, he has all the basic attitudes of the conservative liberal. He believes with Morley that the localization of
power in America should break the power of central government. Limited government is the great thing in his view, and
he denies that the American experience before 1933 demonstrated any lack of whatever governmental power was needed.
We are not, however, given a definition of need. Political parties in America, too, aid the diffusion of power by their decentralization and that is their glory. Burnham is so taken by the
theory of diffusion, in fact, that he gets quite carried away by
it and even includes an independent bureaucracy and the system of lobbying as a part of the traditional diffusion of power
in America. But essentially he and Morley see eye to eye. Social
power should be divided among as many groups as possible because that is the American tradition. We are back to Morley's
concept of social democracy, although once again the statement
is simply made that such pluralism is a good thing, without
proof or evidence to show whether it exists or ever did exist in

fact and if so in what form, or whether such a system even as an ideal is sufficient to meet the problems of today. But as Burnham says, the "Americans are fortunate in knowing the purpose of government. . . ."[34] Is it necessary to say how and why we are so uniquely blessed? What other nation has had The Founding Fathers? Besides, the purpose of government is stated in the preamble to the Constitution.

It is this avowal of tradition that demonstrates that a belief in nineteenth-century liberalism and a belief in conservatism are not incompatible with each other but, on the contrary, are essential to each other. For how can one justify clinging to nineteenth-century liberalism in 1959 (the year Burnham's study of Congress was published) if one does not appeal to tradition? It is, moreover, the openness with which Burnham makes his appeal to tradition that makes him a significant example of conservative liberalism. Most conservative liberals try to hide at least some of their conservatism by appealing not to tradition but to eternal principles of government and society. Burnham will have none of such chicanery. He goes with tradition all the way. Indeed, he begins his book on Congress with the sentence: "In ancient times, before the illusions of science had corrupted traditional wisdom. . . ."[35]

Burnham's devotion to tradition takes several forms, one of which is its opposition to rationalism. Rationalism, according to Burnham, presents itself with various political problems which it cannot solve. One such problem concerns sovereignty; i.e., rationalism claims that sovereignty cannot be divided, but in many nations it is in fact divided. Such a division of sovereignty is, to Burnham as it is to many other conservatives, a triumph of "existence, time, and tradition [over] a paradox of abstract

[34] *Ibid.*, p. 16.
[35] *Ibid.*, p. 3.

reason."[36] It is apparent already and will become more so as we consider the even more romantic thoughts of the New Conservatives that the conservative postulates tradition against reason because he is fearful of reason and science as such. To him they represent abstractions that contain a devastating threat. It is the threat of unknown possibilities. How much better to trust what is known because it has already existed! How much warmer tradition is than science! How much *safer!*

But Burnham and other conservatives not only try to destroy reason because it opens immense responsibilities but also because reliance on tradition instead of reason makes it possible to prove anything whereas with reason one must use logic. In the rag-bag of history one can find whatever one wants to find and that being so the problems of politics at once become soluble whereas with reason they do not.

The miracle of government, like other miracles, occurs in time. In and through time, the paradox is resolved, reason merges with what is beyond or outside of reason, the word is made flesh. If we translate into political and historical terms: the problem of government, insoluble by abstract reason alone, by ideology, becomes solved by social experience acting through time—that is, by tradition.[37]

The unfortunate aspect, however, of relying on tradition as a solution to political problems is that it poses a pretty problem itself. When does a series of actions become a tradition? It is an ugly question, for it immediately puts the conservative back into the open field again with no sure guide or choice of roads. Burnham says that a "new nation . . . creates and confirms its own traditions. Its own way of living as a nation becomes estab-

[36] *Ibid.*, p. 34.
[37] *Ibid.*, p. 25.

lished; . . . the rational gulf is bridged."[38] But is it bridged? Do such statements mean that everything that has happened to a nation immediately becomes a part of its tradition? And if not, how does one know how to pick and choose? Surely one does not have to create a rational principle to be able to discriminate between what is traditional and what is not? Burnham, having raised the question, finds himself forced to face it. For the awful possibility—and for a conservative it is an awful possibility—is raised that the New Deal may now be a part of the American tradition. Face to face with that result of his non-reasoning efforts, any conservative is likely to feel giddy and somewhat cheated. Burnham tries to put on a good face, but the best he can do is to say that what is a part of tradition and what is not is an arbitrary choice, an answer that destroys the conservative position at one blow.

Since the choice is arbitrary, Burnham finds it possible to establish his theory of recent history, which is that the New Deal was a violation of the traditions of American life and that "the government of the United States that existed in 1933 was recognizably the same government that came into existence in 1739."[39] Since the government that came into existence after 1933 was not recognizably the same government as existed in 1933, Q.E.D. the New Deal destroyed tradition. The Constitution, therefore, to someone like Burnham, is not a frame of government which is to be filled or to be changed if necessary, but rather the government established complete and once and for all. The Constitution to Burnham is a tradition which solves the rational dilemmas of government simply because it is a tradition. Indeed, it is a tradition not only because it has been with us for so long, but because government as such requires

[38] *Ibid.*, cf. ch. II.
[39] *Ibid.*, p. 65.

that there be a tradition. Burnham insists that the ancient tales of how the gods brought government and civilization to man instead of man creating his own government hold much validity because they are a recognition that "government is . . . in part, though only in part, non-rational. Neither the source nor the justification of government can be put in wholly rational terms. . . . The central truth [of the old tales] is the insight that there is no adequate rational explanation for the existence and effective working of government, much less for good or fairly good government."[40] Tradition, in short, covers the abyss. And because it covers the abyss such aspects of American government as, for example, the localization of power must be accepted and not questioned. For to question it might be to destroy its tradition. As Burnham points out, the localization of power is irrational, especially from the point of view of democracy. It is, therefore, supported only by tradition and not by reasoned argument from a set of principles. Hence the point of view that Burnham takes toward Congress in particular and American government in general.

I am defining "conservatism" and "conservatives" in "traditionalist" terms, and am concerned specifically with the "American system" as developed through the history and tradition of the United States as an independent nation based on the 1789 Constitution. . . .[41]

Sound though this statement may be, it still does not get rid of the question of when a tradition is a tradition, for Burnham has to admit that there could not be a conservatism in the early period of American history because there was no tradition to conserve. But then, one wonders, how can Burnham treat The Founding Fathers as conservatives if they were not conserva-

[40] *Ibid.*, p. 6.
[41] *Ibid.*, p. 119, n. 18.

tives? Even worse, a conservative is evidently a person who must *make* a tradition out of whole cloth.

BARRY GOLDWATER

One hesitates to mix an active propagandist with the conservatives we have so far considered by including Barry Goldwater, the Senator from Arizona, and his *Conscience of a Conservative*, as representative of their beliefs. Chamberlin, Morley, and Burnham are serious men in the philosophical sense of the word; Goldwater is not. They have thought about conservatism in terms that extend beyond the complaints of a politician who hopes to hold and gain office; they have produced books while Goldwater has handed us, as he says, his speeches, broadcasts, and notes. But not only is Goldwater our best-known conservative today, the man who battled for the true faith at the Republican National Convention and who fought against John Kenneth Galbraith on the weekly best-seller list.[42] He is also a right-wing conservative who shows that while Old Conservatives may differ and while some may be thoughtful and others not, the ideas that they hold in common are greater than those that separate them. Goldwater in his raving way is no less an Old Conservative than those we have discussed. He is not as capable as they are of knowing what he is or why, but that is a defect of Goldwater's mind, not of his conservatism. Nevertheless, it is sad to have to bring Old Conservatism down to his brawling level.

It would be easy to say that Goldwater's book proves that the conservative has no conscience. Yet his book is more significant than a mere demonstration of how far a conservative can

---

[42] By September, 1960, over 170,000 copies of *The Conscience of a Conservative* had been sold.

go with his eyes closed, and how impossible it is for Goldwater to move beyond Herbert Spencer. It also shows that the frustrations of the Old Conservatives—Goldwater's book had more accurately been called "The Frustrations of a Conservative Conscience"—are deeply involved in the nature of Old Conservatism itself.

Goldwater, like all conservatives, is insistent that conservatism is a political and spiritual theory, not a shallow and materialistic economic creed; it is the liberals who are materalistic. Conservatism, he tells us with round-eyed solemnity, deals with the whole man. He does not develop his theme, nor are we ever quite sure what he means by such a statement although he does inform us that the failure to cut taxes in America is a prime example of the failure to take into account the whole man.[43] As he says, you cannot divorce spiritual from economic matters.

More important, neither can you divorce the spiritual from the eternal. Conservatism, in Goldwater's view as in the view of every conservative, New, Old, Wild, or Mild, has the exclusive franchise on the laws of God and nature. One can fairly hear the lectern shake as he cries:

Conservatism, we are told, is out-of-date. The charge is preposterous and we ought boldly to say so. The laws of God, and of nature, have no dateline.[44]

One must not think that Goldwater is merely making a passing bow to the time-honored axioms of conservatism. By no means. The assumption that he and others of his kind know eternal truth, or at the very minimum semieternal truth, is necessary if he is to prove the validity of his specific views on American society and politics. One may wonder, indeed, how he can talk

[43] Barry Goldwater, *The Conscience of a Conservative* (1960), p. 59.
[44] *Ibid.*, Foreword.

about the conscience of a conservative in view of some of his proposals, but the answer is clear. He can talk about his conscience because his conscience is responsible not to humanity and the welfare of humanity, but to eternal law and principle. And not just responsible, but responsible in a total, rigid, and absolute manner. Thus, what is the issue of civil rights in America as far as Goldwater is concerned? He tells us that personally he is in favor of desegregation of schools in the South but that he is against the decision of the Supreme Court. His conscience will not allow him to give way to his sense of humanity because if he did he would be infringing the Constitution, which is a body of eternal law if there ever was one. As he puts it, ignoring all complexities and standing strong for What is Right, "the Constitution is what its authors intended it to be and said it was—not what the Supreme Court says it is."[45] So much for that question. The same conscience appears in his discussion of states rights. It is not expediency that makes Goldwater act the role of a states-righter. It is principle; in this case again the principle that the Constitution is the True Guide to What is Right. There may be those in both parties who think that the federal government should intervene if the states fail to fulfill their obligation but they have not reckoned with Barry Goldwater. He is there to fling his body between such seducers—like Arthur Larson—and the virtue of the Constitution. No, the argument of those who would rob the states of their rights is wrong. It is wrong because the Constitution is a document that prohibits federal intervention; the Constitution is not to be treated as a "kind of handbook in political theory," one that can be interpreted as contemporary federal officials wish to interpret it. And that is the end of *that* question too.

Almost any issue can be made to yield similar moral divi-

[45] *Ibid.*, p. 36.

dends on the basis of the appeal to eternal principle; the Right to Work Laws, for example, are derived from natural law, according to Goldwater. But the principles involved include more than the Constitution of the United States, grand and glorious structure though it be. They include a view of man which is in accord with "nature." Each man differs absolutely from any other and a philosophy that ignores that fact is not in "accord" with nature. Goldwater never explains what society is about if such is the case, but perhaps nature is silent on that question. Further, the economic and spiritual aspects of man are "inextricably" intermixed. We have already seen the results of that principle; taxes should be lower. Finally, each individual man is responsible for his own development; it "is not something that can be directed by outside forces."[46] This belief is so much at variance with the usual role and experience of mothers and fathers, not to mention school teachers and political leaders, that one can only visualize Goldwater's universe as more akin to that of the early dinosaurs than to a society. Perhaps, after all, he does not have to answer the question of what society is.

But whether he should consider the nature of society or not, Goldwater certainly will not do so because society is already too much with us. He grouchily admits that we must have a social order, but as far as he and his conscience is concerned there is already too much order and not enough freedom. The political power "on which order is based is a self-aggrandizing force; . . . its appetite grows with eating." Thus,

. . . in our day, order is pretty well taken care of. The delicate balance that ideally exists between freedom and order has long since tipped against freedom practically everywhere on earth.[47]

[46] *Ibid.*, p. 12.
[47] *Ibid.*, p. 14.

One wonders why freedom has not been lost everywhere instead of practically everywhere; perhaps Arizona has held out to the last. But what does Goldwater mean by freedom? The answer is clear. By freedom he means simply the absence of government control. And absence of government control is *all* that he means by freedom. No other issues are raised. No other problems occur. If you stop "state paternalism," stop federal spending, stop centralizing government, and stop the Soviet Union, then you will have freedom, Q.E.D. It is simple, neat, and even appealing. But is it freedom?

No, it is not freedom. It sounds like freedom. It might be freedom in some other time and place. But it is not freedom today. It is simply irrelevant. It is simply an avoidance of the issue.

Goldwater's attempt to think about freedom fails for the same reason his book fails. It is pathetic but true that he is baffled about the failure of the American people to rally to his standard and tear down the welfare state.

Though we Conservatives are deeply persuaded that our society is ailing, and know that Conservatism holds the key to national salvation—and feel sure the country agrees with us—we seem unable to demonstrate the practical relevance of Conservative principles to the needs of the day. We sit by impotently. . . .[48]

Why such impotence in a creed that is so aggressive and so manly and which is based on eternal truth—the laws of God and nature which have no dateline? Let Goldwater himself unwittingly answer the question.

The principles on which the Conservative political position is based have been established by a process that has nothing to do with the

[48] Barry Goldwater, *The Conscience of a Conservative*, p. 4.

social, economic and political landscape that changes from decade to decade and from century to century.[49]

In the face of such an admission of futility and irrelevance the critic of conservatism is silenced.

In conclusion, it is necessary to say that the frustration of Goldwater's conscience reveals to us in lurid colors the epitome of Old Conservatism. He is a parody of Old Conservatism, but like most parodies he reveals the real nature of his subject. The search for eternal principles upon which to base a society, the discovery of those principles in the American Constitution as it "is" and not as it is interpreted, the simplistic idea that if only the problems of today would go away we could all get back, back, back—these beliefs are the very stuff of Old Conservatism. One may indeed feel that it deserves better than Goldwater, but the fact is that he represents in a crude and plebian way the faith of the Old Conservatives as it does battle in the everyday world. Granted Goldwater's public pre-eminence as a futilitarian, it is still necessary to recognize that his futilitarianism arises not from his peculiar views but from the very nature of Old Conservatism itself.

The logical difficulties with which conservative liberalism is beset do not prevent the conservative from maintaining it as an ideology. Since he has little use for logic and reason, he has no cause for disgruntlement at the existence of logical problems in his ideology. More important, however, is the fact that his traditionalism is an absolute necessity for the conservative. Burnham makes it quite clear that it is his attitude toward tradition that separates the conservative from the modern, twentieth-century

[49] *Ibid.*, p. 5.

liberal, a point on which both will be in agreement. For clarity on that point one must be grateful to Burnham.

Chamberlin and Morley obscured the issue—from themselves at least—by claiming until recently to be simple liberals because they believed in nineteenth- and eighteenth-century liberalism and because they believed in The Founding Fathers who, it is necessary to recall, were mainly and with only a few exceptions like that deplorable Hamilton, Lockian liberals of one variety or another. Burnham makes it clear that when nineteenth-century liberalism is postulated as the proper frame of society, the attempt is being made to establish tradition as a way of politics. The conservative liberal, like African tribes, is tradition-minded. He not only accepts tradition as a guide but eagerly searches for a tradition to maintain. It is the fact of tradition as much as its content that is important to him. Burnham does not differ from Chamberlin or Morley in his view of what is a proper political system, or in his view that the nineteenth century was the best of all possible centuries, or in his view that one must look back in order to stand still. The only difference between them is that Burnham comes into the open and says that tradition is the thing and that he therefore is a conservative and not a liberal.

Old Conservatism is well named. What of New Conservatism? Because it is New does that mean that it finds another basis for conservatism than tradition? Or that it has found another tradition than that of eighteenth- and nineteenth-century liberalism? Does whatever thought the business world gives to the question of conservatism differ from the thought of the Old Conservatism? Has the conservative mood created different grounds for conservatism?

These questions are important because behind them is the larger and most significant question: is conservatism able to face the need for innovation, not just change, but innovation, new ways of social activity? The Old Conservatives are not capable of facing the task of innovation as they themselves admit. Are the other varieties of conservatism any better placed for creating the new? Or are they too so tied to tradition as a way of thought that they cannot find a basis for integrating innovation into conservative ideology?

The conservatives today more than at any time since 1933 claim to have the solution to our social ills. Does that claim mean that these other varieties of conservatism have been able to break free of the paralysis that tradition has put on the Old Conservatives, that they have found some way to make innovation and conservatism compatible? If New Conservatism achieves that significant and unique synthesis then indeed it is New and presents a feasible ideology. If it does not, the New Conservatism like Old Conservatism will be a potent force in preventing innovation.

3. New Conservatism: Peter Viereck and His Metternich

FROM THE POINT of view of conservatism in general the Old Conservatives have important weaknesses, certain disadvantages that cripple them in the stern fight which good conservatives must wage all the time and everywhere. These disadvantages stem not just from the fact that they have a rather quaint and even charming air of faded gentility, or from their refusal to acknowledge the world around them. The sense that they have really let down the cause is due rather to a feeling that this day and age needs something besides complaints, something more positive than anti-New Dealism. In a peculiar way the New Conservatism has repudiated its own past; it thinks the Old Conservatives are simply too old to tolerate. What the New Conservatism wants is a modern brand, one with push and drive and not simply a sterile hanging on to old hatreds.

The Old Conservative, somewhat bewildered that he now be asked to live by Burke and repudiate some of his heroes, might ask what has he done that is so wrong? The answer is that he has been too exclusive in his preoccupations with the particular crisis that has excited his instincts for revenge and that he has not been able, therefore, to focus his attention on larger issues, bigger ideas. He has been much too much concerned with a particular tradition, and not enough—definitely not enough—concerned with tradition as tradition. And his almost Machiavellian obsession with sin as it was exemplified by Franklin D. Roosevelt has led him to neglect sin as it is exemplified by man in general. The Old Conservative is terribly weak on Original Sin. Indeed it is not even clear that he has a sense of sin at all as a general phenomenon. Certainly he has a clear sense of the sin of other people, but the New Conservatives click their tongues in disapproval and give him low marks for not thinking more about sin in general and too much about particular sins. That is what comes, they say as they pace the cathedral close, of concentrating on the rights and wrongs of the American past. One must take a broader view; one must also see where other nations went wrong. In fact, they say, taking another sip of camomile tea, one must see where man in general went wrong. If we know that man is sinful, why then it follows as the night follows the day that American man is sinful. In the face of this profundity the Old Conservative turns away, abashed by the new and wider learning of the new and wider conservative. All he had known was that he did not want to be interfered with, and now such knowledge is no longer enough.

The concentration on one particular national tradition has therefore both narrowed the content of American conservatism and caused it to ignore metaphysical concepts, not to mention the value of old and ruined buildings, which, of course, are in such short supply in America. Even worse, it can be said that the Old Conservative was in great doubt not only about the metaphysics of his ideas but even about the vital and necessary distinction between a conservative and a liberal. We have seen that in fact the Old Conservatives were conservative liberals who postulated nineteenth-century liberalism as the best of all possible worlds even though it has been dead and gone these past sixty years. To someone who is less interested in defending a past system of government and economics than in creating an ideology, such a postulate is simply a failure to think through the problem of what it is to be a conservative. It is a failure to create an ideology in which this obsession with a liberal past would take its place as simply one facet of a conservative belief by which all men can live, not just the nineteenth-century liberal. The proper ideology should act as a general guide for the conservative life; it should, as all true ideologies do, act as a total explanation of the world. There should be no more guess work about the proper conservative attitude on any subject. There should be no such deplorable differences as exist between Felix Morley and James Burnham for example, with the former writing Congress down and the latter writing Congress up. No more looseness of thought should be permitted. The test should be as strict as it is for any order, but having passed it, one would be on the inside, sustained by all the comforts which ideological assurance can provide. As an old revivalist song has it:

> There is one door and only one,
> Though its sides are two;
> I'm on the inside,
> Which side are you?

Those who had thought that they were conservative simply because they liked to collect antiques to place beside their electric dishwasher must now learn to make their choice in this world as in the next. And if they chose antiques then they must know that that choice is only the first step, that they must go on for an intensive course of study, which might even involve them in a reading of all twenty-seven volumes of W. H. Mallock. As for those businessmen who think they are conservative because they support the status quo, i.e., their profits, they have a shock in store. While the Old Conservative had some doubts about the propriety of their behavior in its more crude aspects he nevertheless saw the businessman as a true blue conservative liberal—which he often is. But the New Conservative will have none of such weak-minded efforts to find allies. The business-man and his antique-hunting wife as well, will have to give long and anxious hours to meditations on the texts of the new ideology. A mere devotion to the status quo is not enough. As for devotion to profits—the New Conservative turns away in horror and disgust, his teacup trembling violently as he strives to master his emotions. He has no particular grudge against profits, it should be understood, but he prefers that they be kept out of sight and certainly that they should not be made the base of an ideology. Besides, look what happens to men of money. Some of them, Averill Harriman for example, have become Welfare State men. No, profits are not all there is to conservatism although they must, of course, be protected, for without them the ancient and venerable institutions which are the real base of conservative ideology would be even more ruined than they are now—and one may go too far with ruins. Whether or not such *sub-rosa* use of profits does not have a certain corrupting effect on the ideological purity of conservatism is not, naturally, a discreet question.

An "ism" must be made. Made? Does it not lie already fully made and embedded in the silt of the past? Surely a tradition cannot be made, but must simply be excavated? Perhaps so, but a good deal of work has gone into the excavation or fabrication of New Conservatism. It required a good deal of work because to make or discover a conservative ideology in modern society and America is not an easy thing to do. Certainly it is not impossible, for the heroes are all lined up, ready to be given their certificates of worthiness. But certain problems must be faced.

The first problem is the lack of an Anthony Trollope in America. Antiques in the United States appreciate in monetary value in strict ratio to the number of millionaires, a fact that means that antiques are seldom loved for themselves alone in a sort of Trollope-ish way. Tea in the vicarage, if one can find a vicarage in America, tends to make the millionaire's wife nervous. It is not her habitat and though she can talk well as an expert on antiques, the sad fact is that she talks as an expert and not as one who has dwelt among antiques—except as one who fled the ancient midwestern farmhouse to get East. The whole atmosphere is wrong. It takes more than a millionaire's wife clutching a steadily appreciating antique to her well-tailored bosom to create a tradition—a fact of which the New Conservatives are only too aware.

But the lack of a Trollope is only one of their worries. To create an ideology of conservatism one must go beyond the shores of America. The failure to do so is in fact one of the main faults of the Old Conservatives in the far-seeing eyes of the New. But when they leave America certain difficulties appear. It is all very well to seek a conservative tradition in, say, the Trollope country of Britain but, as we have seen, Trollope does not really apply back home. What relevance, to leave Trollope to a well-deserved rest, does the archpriest of conservatism, Burke, have in America? Is it possible that after all the Old Conservatives in their bumbling, irascible way had a sort of intuitive sense that if one is to found a conservatism for America it must be done with American materials? Chamberlin, Morley, and Burnham and almost all the Old Conservatives are strong for America First, Last, and Always. They are, not to put too fine a point on it, nationalists and even isolationists. America to them represents not one country among others but the only country. It is the best and last hope of man, nothing less. Other nations may have been worthy once, but the whole point of the panegyrics of the Old Conservatives is that other nations have quite palpably and literally degenerated. They have gone the way of all flesh, and it is only in America that conservatism can find itself. How, then, can one excavate a conservative tradition in other lands? This question, which the Old Conservative implicitly poses to the New, is a serious one, for there are many besides conservatives who see America as unique. If America is unique, then it follows that one need not, indeed must not, look to Burke and Canning and Coleridge and others to create a conservative ideology for America. To try to bring America into a world picture, to look at it as only one exponent of a belief—that is heresy indeed.

However, the New Conservatives will reply, what is a tradition if it applies to only one state? It may be useful but it is not an ideology to live by and for. An ideology must be world comprehensive or it is nothing, a fact that is characteristic of ideologies in general. Thus the New Conservative sets out on a quest that will take him to many strange lands in search of a way in which he can be conservative in America.

But how many lands? How wide does he sweep? Does he look into France? Into Asia? Certainly he will look into Britain. But if an ideology is to be an ideology it must include more than two nations. How many then? The answer in practice is that the New Conservative confines himself to British and American tradition in his search for an ideology. He does not deny that other countries have their mite to contribute, but the crumbling walls of British mansions hold a fascination that no other nation can match.

It is, however, not only the reek of decaying matter in Britain that draws him there. Britain is the conservative state par excellence. The New Conservative is not disrespectful of France, say, but France, he tells us, has suffered from not just war and unstable government but above all from the French Revolution. And Britain, as we know, is what it is because it did not have the French Revolution. In fact, the failure of the French Revolution is what is so good about Britain as a source of conservative ideology; tradition had its greatest victory in Britain when it was able to contain and then extinguish the threat of the French Revolution both within and outside of Britain. If one can explain that wonderful act of Providence— and the conservatives, as we shall see, are very, very strong on Providence—then we need not seek further for that quality that makes conservatism great. The history of France, after all, is the history of the failures of conservatism, de Gaulle notwith-standing, while the history of Britain is of its success. It would be asking too much of any conservative, New or Old, to ex-amine the former in order to draw lessons from it. It might even lead to moments of depression about the future.

Yet one must ask if the New Conservative is correct in assum-ing that what is good for Britain is good for America and what is good for both Britain and America is good for everyone else. For what exactly do the ruins of Britain, which please a New Conservative like Russell Kirk so much, mean to America? Harken to Kirk on British ruins:

Close by the wreck of St. Andrews cathedral, we talked of the inundation which only here and there has spared an island of humane learning like St. Andrews town. . . . These chapters have been written in a variety of places: in a but-and-ben snuggled under the cliffs of Eigg; in one of the ancient towers of Kellie Castle, looking out to the Forth; in my great-grandfather's house in the stump-country of Michigan; among the bogs of Sligo in the west of Ireland; upon the steps of Ara Coeli, in Rome; at Balcarres House, where what Burke calls "the unbought grace of life" still abides.[1]

One is awed by the ability of this rootless intellectual to write on the run. But with the somewhat dubious exception of the stump country of Michigan, dubious because Michigan is not a place one normally thinks of when one thinks of tradition, these ruins have little to say to an American battling today in an attempt to prevent his own life from being ruined in a superorganized society. Those ruins have little to say today even to the European who lives in their shadow, and shadow is the word.

But the relevance of ruins is the case they aim to prove. For the New Conservatism plans to take the world by the scruff of the neck and force it back into venerable ways, into ways of religion, class, order, hierarchy, and aristocracy. Do such aims mean that the New Conservatives are simply a group of delightful eccentrics? If it is true that their attempt to shore up Europe's ruins against the stresses of modern society is not relevant to those stresses, can we therefore ignore the New Conservatives as a factor in the public life of America? Is their faith merely an off-beat whine over the lack of "unbought grace" in America?

The New Conservatism does have an off-beat quality to it; one would expect its practitioners to revive Edwardian clothes. But regardless of the slightly mauve quality about it, New Conservatism is not a joke. The years of its birth alone indicate that it has a serious quality about it, for they were the years after 1949 when conservatism in fact came to American life not only in the person of the President, but in the very quality of American life itself. Certainly the New Conservatives did not bring

[1] Russell Kirk, *The Conservative Mind* (1953), p. V.

about such a change. But can one deny importance to a movement of opinion that coincides so well with the movement of the times in other areas of national life? One cannot deny that New Conservatism was an accompanist to history because in fact the years after 1949 demonstrated an urge, a desire to find a point of rest, i.e., of conservatism. New Conservatism is an important set of ideas because it represents a need, because it is the public and printed announcement of that need.

What was the need? For social quietism, for social placidity. There was a public figure who attempted to provide placidity; is it so odd that the need should also provide an ideology of placidity? In this light the New Conservatives are even more significant than they themselves would claim. They represent the logical conclusions and aims of what was the most powerful current of events in the 1950's. Since there were other forces at work in those years, and since history is anything but logical, the logical results of the ideology of New Conservatism were not attained and could not be attained in the form they had been postulated. But the thought of the New Conservatives gives us a clue to at least some of the meaning of the past decade. They are decidedly children of that decade. If they are interrogated we may find that social quietism has some unexpected nuances. No ideology has a one-to-one relation with reality and the ideology of New Conservatism is certainly no exception. But romantic Burkean dreams aside, the "solution" to the problems of our society which New Conservatism proffers is more likely to be accepted by those who run society than other proffered solutions.

To provide answers for the postwar years, and more specifically for the years after 1949, it was necessary for conservatism to search through history in order to provide an ideology and a view of man that would justify social quietism. It would be an ideology proving the necessity of relying on tradition and showing that such a reliance was based neither on the self-interest of a few, nor on fatigued and bad-tempered cynicism. The age of ideology may have been over for the liberals, but for the conservatives it was just beginning. It is not easy to argue against innovation in this day and age but it would be possible, the New Conservatives hoped, if certain ideological postulates were laid down which, once accepted, would lead straight to a rejection of innovation. Further, Conservatism should cease to be an instinct and become a thought process. Hence, the seriousness of the New Conservatives is different from the seriousness of the Old. Where the latter were concerned with a situation, a threat to stability, and were committed to a political position as a consequence, the New Conservatives are seriously concerned with ideas. Certainly they, too, are concerned with a situation and with a political position, but even that concern is on the higher level of general ideas.

The situation they deplore is seen as a part of a trend of history, of a world-developing social change. Partly, this sense of the drama of history comes from their involvement—the word is not too strong—with the French Revolution, a cosmic event in their eyes. Partly, it is due to their belief that man is a sinful animal and has a long record of transgression and misbehavior for which to account. But whatever the cause, their texts are marked by an effort to deal with political and social theory at a high level of abstract ideas. They try to teach Americans in general and conservatives in particular that they must learn to think broadly and deeply and to move out from parochial concerns into the dark places of history, political theory, and human sin. Rule of thumb conservatism must go by the boards and a *Weltanschauung* be created to take its place. No one is to have any doubts any longer as to who is a conservative and who is not, for there are tests to be applied and they will not be the easy ones which have enabled so many to slip by so often in the past.

Whether the New Conservatism is successful in this stringent task, whether it really strikes the profundity at which it aims, and especially whether it is so different after all from Old Conservatism are questions we shall have to discuss. But if it is not successful it is not because it lacks a Karl Marx.

New Conservatism is a fancy term, but what it actually means is the thought of Russell Kirk. Coming on the scene of American life in the 1950's it was Kirk who established the whole idea that there was a new kind of conservatism abroad in the land and who created, by his own writings, its basic shape and inner content. Others, even some Old Conservatives, followed the dynamic and aggressive propaganda of Kirk by grouping themselves around the periodical he founded and edited, *The Modern Age: a Conservative Review.* But they have little to contribute that is not already inherent in or stated by Kirk's writings. Still others, who cannot be described as followers of Kirk but who thought out the new problems and perspectives of conservatism by their own efforts, differ from the master in some significant respects while nevertheless reproducing most of his basic ideas. The coincidence between the conservatism of Clinton Rossiter and Walter Lippmann in the 1950's, and the ideas of Kirk, is an important indication of the quality conservatism in fact acquired in those years. Was an alternative possible? Alternatives are always possible. But what is so significant is that another type of conservatism did not appear, that it was fundamentally the ideas of Kirk that dominated the thoughts of conservatives in the past decade. When two such independent and intelligent thinkers as Rossiter and Lippmann come to fundamentally the same conclusions as Kirk we know that the latter is not a lonely genius but the gushing fountainhead of conservatism.

Before turning to Kirk, however, it will be useful to glance for a moment at Peter Viereck, who quietly but perceptively anticipated in 1949 some of Kirk's New Conservatism on a small scale with his *Conservatism Revisited.*

PETER VIERECK

Mr. Viereck affords us a genial and rationally humane introduction to New Conservatism. His is not the conservatism of pomposity, Burkean teeth-chattering, and romantic thunderstorms. Quite the contrary, what characterizes Viereck is his modesty, his willingness to believe that those who oppose him are not sinners—although he has the true New Conservative belief in original sin—and his attempt not to be romantic. It is against romanticism that he battles; as one who not only survived but remembers the '30's—most New Conservatives survived those years but most of them have forgotten what the crisis was about—he knows only too well what romanticism can do in politics.

But how can one hope to revive Metternich if one is not a romantic? For that, no less, is Peter Viereck's aim. He presents Metternich to us as a true and proper guide for the troubled world of today, and also as a source for the New Conservatism that we need. Metternich will answer the question: what are the values we can live by in the face of revolutionary movements? Metternich has his faults, as Viereck admits. But he is less worried about those faults than he is concerned to extract what is valid from Metternich's political analysis. It is a heavy burden that is borne by Viereck's small book, *Conservatism Re-*

visited: The Revolt Against Revolt. Every New Conservative has his hero from the past, but Viereck is the only one who tries to bring Metternich back to life. It is, in its way, an impressive effort.

Why Metternich of all people? The answer in part lies in one of the most important facts about *Conservatism Revisited,* the fact that it was published in 1949. Its attempt to resurrect Metternich is an attempt to find a principle both of international and domestic order at the time when it was first becoming apparent to post-World War II Americans that the crisis years of 1948–49 were years in which they faced a revolutionary threat to order of all kinds. There was a conservative job to be done; it was suddenly necessary to protect peace and tranquillity within America. Viereck's point is plain; since America must now do what Metternich once had to do why not turn back and study some history lessons from "Professor" Metternich. The proposal may seem startling at first but undoubtedly there is a certain logic about it, especially if one is willing to accept Viereck's claim that the failures of the Old Professor were due less to his principles than to his execution of them. (It may be hard, however, to accept that claim, for Viereck never argues his case—a weakness often found in conservative writings). Unfortunately the choice of Metternich as a symbol of American policy still leaves one uneasy. Viereck admits that his hero's activities lacked a popular base. Was not his lack of popularity inherent in what he was doing, namely conserving the old order?

But of course Viereck does not intend Metternich to be taken as a guide to policy as such. Rather he is to be a preceptor, a professor, to teach us basic principles. Metternich can provide the conservative principles necessary for a civilization grown weary of revolt. The phrase, "the revolt against revolt" means what it says; we are at the terminal point of a struggle which began when Metternich failed in 1848 and when, therefore, the polarization of Europe took place. Metternich fell prey to two forces—the feudal rulers of Europe who were blind to "his Burkean kind of conservatism, which would reconcile through free institutions 'the monarchist principle and the democratic,' "[2] and the new middle class which gave up its liberalism for nationalism. There has never been a political force of the "center" as a result of this tragic failure, for it was a center position that Metternich tried and failed to establish. But now the time has come to put an end to revolt, to establish a center. Hence it is necessary to re-create Metternich in order to find a principle of rest. The age of revolution is over and Metternich is the man to tell us how to live in the middle without revolution.

This center principle, in Viereck's eyes, is not based, as is so often thought, on sterile do-nothingism or on pure negation but on important ideas which are applicable to the problems of today. The most basic of those principles is the restriction of the ego of individuals and states. In a sentence that might seem to come from an Existentialist text, Metternich said (as quoted by Viereck) that "the cultivation of the ego must recognize bounds in the lives of the states as in private life, in order not to be reduced to absurdity."[3] Metternich evidently not only had a keen sense of the absurd but, going the modern Existentialist one better, he had an answer to it: conservatism.

Viereck's view of conservatism (and of Metternich's idea of conservatism) is not that it should be a philosophy in support of ruling princes but rather that it should support law. It is law

[2] Peter Viereck, *Conservatism Revisited: The Revolt Against Revolt*, (1950), p. 140.
[3] *Ibid.*, p. 59.

which restrains the boundless ego of man and state, which
fends off the absurd, and creates peace and society itself. These
laws must be "outside" laws, i.e., outside of the group that sub-
mits. Thus the self-determination of a force is forbidden by
external discipline. Such a discipline would forbid both the
orgies of, say, German nationalism and the orgies of mass politics, since both repudiate limits to their actions.

Thus Metternich the great constitutionalist—not a pose in
which one has often seen him. The effort to present him as a
constitutionalist makes heavy demands on the imagination but
Viereck does not lack imagination. Metternich, he points out,
fought to get a constitution accepted in Austria and failed, a
failure that caused the explosion of 1848. Did Metternich desire
a constitution because he was a liberal? By no means. He
wanted a constitution because he was a conservative, because
he saw that only a constitution could avert revolution, that
only law could provide the necessary discipline for the new
forces of middle-class business, democratic liberalism, and
nationalism. Viereck goes even further. While denying that
Metternich was a socialist in the Marxist sense of the word—
a sound observation—Metternich did see, like Marx, that business needed restraint and that the industrial revolution should
be controlled from above.

Unfortunately no one understood him. But in these ways
Metternich was, in Viereck's eyes, a true descendant from
Burke and the English parliamentary system, in the true line
of conservatism as distinct from reaction. Constitutionalism
meant to Metternich, or perhaps one should say to Metternich-
Viereck, a "sober, rigorously rational appeal of liberty" as distinct from the "romantic, emotional appeal of its enemies."[4]

⁴ *Ibid.*, p. VII.

Freedom is the thing, and "whether the rulers be the aristocracy or demos, it is essential to limit their rule by a constitution and by just laws."

Viereck confuses his case for Metternich as the great constitutionalist, however, by dropping hints that his hero not only depended on law but also on tradition to act as a backstop to revolution. Metternich, it seems, went beyond the mechanical analysis of rootless liberals to build on the solid groundwork and reality of tradition. What tradition? Viereck is not at all clear on this question, but he does imply that law is a part of that tradition and that

. . . every stable society has certain traditional institutions acting as brakes on precipitous mass action.[5]

The American Bill of Rights, for example, performs an aristocratic and conservative function.

Is Viereck as unaware of his confusion between law and tradition as Metternich was? Perhaps he is, for the real delight that Viereck takes in Metternich and his constitutionalism is not a delight in law as law but law as a rock of order.

Metternich as rock: . . . this role met the emotional needs of a repose-craving and revolution-shocked generation.[6]

It is this search for a rocklike existence that causes Metternich-Viereck to praise constitutionalism, for in his eyes it holds the secret of movement without disorder; i.e., without the overthrow of tradition.

By their saints you shall know them, and the choice of Metternich and the way he is portrayed has given us some sense

[5] *Ibid.*, p. 35.
[6] *Ibid.*, p. 17.

of the conservatism that Viereck is putting forward as the need of our times. Conservatism is a principle of order in a confusing and whirling world; it is a rock—a principle of stability. Or:

Conservatism is a social and cultural cement, holding together what western man has built and by that very fact providing a base for orderly change and improvement.[7]

Conservatism creates freedom, too, while having rocklike qualities, because it makes possible orderly change, that is, change which does not destroy tradition. It also creates freedom by preserving the individual as opposed to mass man. The conservative, or at least Viereck-Metternich, is not against democracy but only against democracy when it crushes the individual. He is quite touching in this devotion to the individual, and although we have already seen some aspects of that devotion it is proper to let Viereck speak on the subject.

What we need, and what a humanistic, non-utilitarian education will foster, is a century of the individual man. Such a century would no longer change persons into masses but masses into persons, each with an individuality and a sense of personal responsibility, each with a sense of his ethical duties to balance his material rights.[8]

No one, certainly, could disagree with that statement—as it stands.

And since no one could, the question arises: what distinguishes the way the conservative approaches that platitude from the way others approach it? The answer is that he approaches it by claiming that only conservatism can preserve the individual. A century of individual man can exist only if civilization is not destroyed. But what is civilization if it is not

[7] *Ibid.*, p. 21.
[8] *Ibid.*, p. 24.

the traditions of civilization? And who attempts to preserve
the traditions of civilization except the conservative? Just as a
rock is an accumulation of the debris of the past in hardened
and frozen form, so is conservatism. Accumulation is the glory
of conservatism, the reason why it and no other creed can preserve the individual. It preserves him by preventing him from
running amok, from indulging in his appetites, one of which
is an appetite for unlimited freedom. The accumulations from
the past will weigh man down. Viereck asks: what prevents
man from being a cave man today? It is the "conservative force
of law and tradition, that slow accumulation of civilized
habits. . . ."[9] There is, of course, much that is bad from the
past, but it is the conservative's duty to reject the bad and conserve the good. The trouble comes, however, when the good
and bad are mixed, for then the "liberal" often destroys "some
minor abuse within a good tradition." In lieu of any statement
to the contrary by Viereck, is one justified in assuming that the
conservative will almost always think that an abuse is minor and
tradition is always good? Viereck would deny such an interpretation, for he quotes Metternich to the effect that " 'stability is
not immobility.' " What then is the distinction between the
conservative view of tradition and the view of nonconservatives? The answer is that

the conservative evolves change peacefully and gradually from
above instead of by unhistorical haste or by mob methods from
below.[10]

The century of individual man will be brought about by the
aristocrat, British-type of course, who will be replenished from
below but who will nevertheless follow the elite, tricke-down

[9] *Ibid.*, p. 20.
[10] *Ibid.*, p. 29.

theory of social change. As for possible disagreement between those above and those below, it will be solved by the Constitution. Quoting Maine, Viereck tells us that "by a wise constitution, democracy may be made nearly as calm as water in a great artificial reservoir. . . . Democracy can be made tolerable."[11] Such is the function of the American Constitution: to make democracy tolerable. The individual will be saved from the masses by civilization, by, that is, tradition. But how does tradition square with change? Are tradition and change as easily compatible as Viereck seems to imply? His discussion of the role of the state, for example, indicates that he finds it difficult to accept at least one change, a change in the role of the state.

Seemingly, Viereck is not opposed to the modern welfare state. He will not have conservatism tied to the privileges of an economic group or to the doctrine of *laissez-faire*; like almost all conservatives he is cruel to his best friend, the businessman. But he evidently does not consider him to be his best friend, for in his opinion the businessman has done a great deal to harm the cause of conservatism. The role of conservatism, he feels, is to conserve the humane and ethical values of the West, not the economic interests of a fraction of the West. Nor is he impressed with the argument sometimes used by businessmen that a suggested reform is socialistic. But in the end the conclusion he reaches is not very different from that of, say, the late Senator Taft. The problem of social reform arises, he thinks, when the welfare laws cross the line between welfare and a superstate. Beyond that line the loss of freedom is more than the gain in security. Whose freedom and whose security is in question he does not discuss. Therefore, although he says that

[11] *Ibid.*, p. 37.

welfare as welfare is not to be rejected by the conservative and that the conservative should fight statism from the right as well as the left, he also says that social reform should not be confused with equalitarianism. Since most people insist on making that confusion, and since equalitarianism is in fact what social reform is usually about, it is not clear that his acceptance of welfare measures in the abstract will help change society very much.

But it is because of such reasoning that Viereck is able to say he is an advocate of English conservatism as distinct from the conservatism of Eastern and Central Europe. English conservatism is evolutionary, Eastern conservatism is rigid, reactionary, inclined to an "irrational anti-radical panic" rather than a "rational anti-radical alertness."[12] To a reader unversed in the subtle metaphysics of conservatism the difference sounds quantitative—and only slightly quantitative—rather than qualitative. But the New Conservative is a worshipper of the successful ways of his English cousin, whose ability not only to survive but to flourish offers proof that conservatism can work. England has, of course, another attraction for him. The place reeks of the past; the past, as they say, "lives" in England. All those old stones . . . ! But England also allows Viereck to dream of a conservatism with "roots in the factories and trade unions," for was it not the Tories under the Earl of Shaftesbury who brought the first factory laws? It is through such means that the mass man, the "barbarian invasion from below," will be tamed.

But it is not just Tory democracy that will save the masses from the consequences of democracy. Conservatism, Viereck tells us, is "the political secularization of the doctrine of original sin." In contrast to the faith of Rousseau in the natural good-

[12] *Ibid.*, p. 28.

ness of man, a faith that leads straight to radicalism as we know well by now, the conservative postulates a sturdy sense of sin. In place of the lawlessness of mass man will be the calculating care of religious and conservative man. Religion in fact will even protect man against amoral statism. It is a dike erected to protect the fragile standards that civilization has managed to create over the centuries.

Viereck does not make as much of original sin, however, as does Russell Kirk. And for a good reason. He hopes to make some appeal to disenchanted liberals, and even disenchanted liberals are likely to shy at original sin.

As we have seen, the attitude of the Old Conservatives toward liberalism was somewhat ambiguous; there is liberalism and liberalism. Viereck too, is bothered by the liberals, whom he identifies with mob rule. The liberal is one who lives on the moral capital accumulated by the conservatives; he is also a relativist with no "tradition of moral restraints" to guide him. Obviously, one cannot expect too much from him in the way of defending freedom. Yet Viereck begins and ends his book with an appeal to the liberal to coalesce with the conservatives, to end the breach caused by the split of 1848 and to bring an end to revolt. Which liberal is Viereck talking about, the old nineteenth-century liberal or the modern anticapitalist liberal? He refuses to make a distinction, considering merely that liberals in general are confused. Yet it is clear that he is thinking in terms of nineteenth-century liberalism, because he wants to wipe out 1848, the gulf between the nineteenth-century liberal and the Metternichs of that century which, in Viereck's view, destroyed the restful center he now hopes can be restored. Thus he can see no real reason why the two sides should now come into conflict; in the face of the police state of today the conservatives and liberals must come together. By ignoring, therefore, the possibility that liberalism may have changed Viereck is able to conclude his book with his plea that, taking progress at a "judicious pace" (as Goethe said) the liberal today will recognize the necessity of a "deep-rooted center" or third force of all the forces of moderation, "broad enough to include parliamentary socialists and parliamentary capitalists."[13] Viereck's faith in the virtue and necessity of balance is the point to which he returns as he ends his book.

> In the centrifugal epoch, only an outlook of inner balance can resist this pull toward extremes and restore the magnetism of the center. . . . The dynamism . . . of unprincipled men-of-action is no solution to the crisis but one of its causes.[14]

Viereck, as was pointed out at the beginning of our discussion, possesses a certain geniality and even a certain faith in man that are lacking in the other conservatives, New or Old. But geniality can sometimes overwhelm the facts of a situation. Viereck is never so conservative as when he assumes that liberalism can be taken in by the timeworn call for moderation, mediation, conciliation, compromise, etc., etc. Perhaps, after all, 1848 was about an important issue.

Peter Viereck's book represents a transition; it attempts to found conservatism as an ideology in its own right and at the same time to retain the assumption of the Old Conservatives that the divorce between the nineteenth-century liberal and the conservative is simply a blunder. On his showing, it was not only the men of 1848 who blundered but those who came after them and interpreted the events incorrectly. One wonders, after reading Viereck, whether there was an 1848 after all and if so just what all the fuss was about, for his history tries to

[13] *Ibid.,* pp. 138, 139.
[14] *Ibid.,* p. 142.

demonstrate that there really was nothing to shout about—
Metternich and the German liberals really had the same fundamental aims. But perhaps the question of the treatment or mis-
treatment of history is not at issue. What is obviously more
important to Viereck than the facts or meaning of history is his
bold attempt to prove that the conservatism of Metternich is not
incompatible with the needs of today and with what the liberal
should do today because the conservatism of Metternich is an
ideology of the revolt against revolt, of the restful center. Viereck is a New Conservative because he postulates an ideology
as an answer to this time of menace. He is an Old Conservative
because he cannot see why the split between nineteenth-century
liberalism and conservatism should have occurred.

Seldom has anyone called his shots so well. What has American foreign policy been since 1950 if not the policy of Metternich with his ideas of a grand alliance against the revolutionary
forces of the world? Just as Metternich became committed to
reactionary princelings so have we become committed to reactionary semidictators. Maybe Metternich was not such a bad
fellow after all! We can begin to see that he really did have his
problems! For just as Metternich became known for the up-
holding of a social system which, whatever its virtues, was
identified with a past epoch, so has America since 1950.

The unfortunate and superficial resemblances—and of course
they are only superficial—between Metternich's policies and
America's policies demonstrate not so much Viereck's ability
to foretell history as the fact that New Conservatism even at
its most *outré*—who would *ever* have thought of Metternich
as a guide for American life!—is in tune with the times. It has
an ear for what is going on, it vibrates in sympathy with the
trend of events. Can one laugh at Viereck after our embarrassments, to put it no higher, in Korea, Iraq, Japan, Turkey, Cuba,
and our no doubt coming embarrassments in Iran, South Viet-

Nam, and Africa? But the sympathy of Viereck's sensitivities goes well beyond the realm of foreign policy. It extends to the domestic affairs of America in which Metternich's principles have also been put into practice.

Metternich, as we know, had certain peculiar attitudes and policies on domestic affairs, too. Viereck gladly acknowledges that he went too far in some of his ideas—press laws for example. But the unhappy thought occurs—have we not had our loyalty purges, our Senator McCarthy? What would Metternich have thought of those events? The impression of Metternich we get from Viereck indicates that he would have pursed his lips with disapproval. Viereck tells us that the real concept of domestic politics held by Metternich was that of constitutionalism. But why was he a constitutionalist? Because he believed in the liberal theory of constitutions, that a constitution provides freedom and order together? Hardly. Metternich was, it is now apparent, a good fellow, but not even Viereck tries to make him a modern liberal. No, constitutions meant a great deal to Metternich because they were a means of *preservation*. A constitution in the eyes of Metternich, Viereck, or any conservative, New or Old, is not designed to provide orderly ways of action. It is designed to prevent orderly ways of action or, simply, to prevent action of any kind. We know that Viereck conceives of constitutions as a counterthrust against change because at no time does he give a criterion to distinguish orderly from disorderly change, proper from improper change, except to say, as Metternich said, that change should not disrupt tradition and civilization. But what is tradition and civilization in the eyes of Metternich-Viereck except the accumulated dust heap of history, that which has been and is?

We are never told that man can create civilization by innovation, by making something new. Despite Viereck's claim that the conservative looks to orderly change, in fact his discussion of Metternich demonstrates that his brand of conservatism is no more capable of facing the problem of change than that of Old Conservatives. Why was Metternich a constitutionalist? Because in his mind a constitution and its laws would prevent disorder. And what is disorder to Viereck-Metternich? Disorder is that which is against the already established ways of government and society, against, that is, tradition and civilization. Metternich favored a constitution because, Viereck tells us, he knew if he did not have one there would be revolution—a thing no conservative likes to contemplate, given though conservatives are to contemplation.

Viereck refers to conservatism as a cement; he also refers with approval to Metternich's description of himself as a rock. What then is a constitution but a rock or a cement for the conservative to use in defense of established tradition? A conservative like Metternich, whether in his true disreputable guise or his new disarming guise, will use any tool to do the job of preserving what Is, of preventing innovation. Metternich in a sense was forced to be more radical than say, President Eisenhower, for he had to contemplate using new constitutions to stop change while the President found one ready at hand. But this difference does not negate the fact that then as now, for New as well as Old Conservatives, constitutionalism is a mighty instrument for the preservation of a traditional society. When we find Metternich portrayed as an advocate of constitutions we can no longer doubt that it is not the existence of a constitution but who uses the constitution, and for what ends, that determines whether freedom shall be expanded in the name of democracy or be contracted in the name of tradition.

Thus the facile belief, that if a man believes in a constitution he is therefore a liberal to some considerable degree, receives another blow.

4. Russell Kirk or Burking the Issue

WITH THE COMING of Russell Kirk conservatism ceases to be a catch-as-catch-can affair, a matter of odd bits of historical lore, of a simple but intense yearning for a Garden of Eden. It becomes instead a full-blown ideology. But Russell Kirk does more than convert conservatism into an ideology. He transforms its style, the very quality of its thought. Kirk not only modernizes American conservatism by going back to Burke—a considerable feat in itself; he also gives it a temper—a bad temper.

The Old Conservatives as we have seen had something of a temper themselves, but it was a choleric temper, one which tended to beet-red faces and stuttered exclamations of anger at the way the world was going. There was a sort of Union Club, after-dinner indigestion about it all, and one felt that once the fit of expletives had passed reason would reassert its sovereign sway. The temper was not, so to speak, based on a thoroughgoing commitment.

Russell Kirk is not having any such milktoast beliefs. To Kirk conservatism is the best and last hope of man. He makes no pretense, as Viereck does, about a jolly get-together with other ideas. Nor does he make any pretense as to the nature of conservatism. As he spoons conservatism out to us he tells us that it is nasty stuff but that we have to swallow it if we want to survive. He is certainly correct about its being nasty stuff. This evil-tasting medicine is, we feel, authentic, the real thing. This is how conservatism should taste. It is a shocking experience, for in Kirk's hands conservatism suddenly displays its ruthless and brutal nature. "You there! In your place!" No more benign talk about a balanced constitution or the sweetness of life in the nineteenth century. Tradition ceases to be a mask for economic *laissez-faire* or for nineteenth-century liberalism; it becomes a way of keeping in their proper order *(read* class) those who might want to step out of it for a breath of free air, or those who might want to play. The Golden Days are done. The Iron Age is here and here for good and always. The best we can do is suffer through it as quietly as possible. "You there! No noise!"

The significance of this new temper lies in the fact that Kirk is the most important figure of American conservatism to appear since 1945 and probably during the twentieth century. With the publication of *The Conservative Mind* in 1953 and *A Program for Conservatives* in 1954, and with the establishment of *Modern Age: A Conservative Journal* in 1957, which he edited, Kirk created an ideology, a canon, for conservatism for the first time in the twentieth century. No one before had been so bold; no one before had been so thorough. The 1950's were the great chance for conservatism and Kirk struck and struck hard to make it good.

The temper of his conservatism comes not, however, from the appearance of the great chance. It comes instead from his wildly romantic prose and from his intolerant and arrogant religious convictions which are so vital and so indistinguishable from his conservatism. He is a political Calvinist who offers us damnation or salvation; those who choose the latter are the elect and those who choose the former—why, they are the damned. And now, brother, now is the time for choice! Liberalism and liberals are, frankly, loathsome. They are loathsome because they are the damned. Kirk is very fond of Scotland; certainly it is his spiritual home, for he has more than a hint of the wild gloom of the Scotch ethos. He is also fond of some aspects of the eighteenth century and he has more than a hint of that century's Gothic madness about him.

Great civilizations do not fall at a single blow. Our civilization has sustained several terrible assaults already, and still it lives; but that does not mean that it can live forever, or even endure through another generation. Like a neglected old house, a society whose members have forgot the ends of society's being and of their own lives sinks by degrees almost imperceptible toward its ruin. The rain comes in at the broken pane; the dry-rot spreads like the corpse of a tree with the wall; the plaster drops upon the sodden floor; the joists groan with every wind; and the rat, creeping down the stair at midnight, gnaws his dirty way from the desolate kitchen to the mildewed satins of the parlor. We men of the twentieth century have this house only, and no other: the storm outside, in the winter of our discontent, will allow of no idle building of dream-castles; the summer indolence of the age of optimism is long gone by. The conservative, if he knows his own tradition, understands that his appointed part, in the present forlorn state of society, is to save man from fading into a ghost condemned to linger hopeless in a rotten tenement.[1]

Kirk's conservatism is the conservatism of nightmare, of an obsession with decadence and decay. It is worth noting that this necrophilic quality is nothing new, for Kirk mentions with evident approval that Burke gave orders for his burial to be secret in order to prevent the Jacobins from disturbing his bones.

Russell Kirk is a young man from Michigan, or as he likes to

[1] Russell Kirk, *A Program for Conservatives* (1954), p. 312.

139

say, from the stump country of Michigan. It is a state which has produced many odd things, including the modern automobile. Both the modern automobile and Kirk have a great deal in common, for each in its own way is flamboyant and rococo in style. They are also each supercharged with a reckless energy. And they are each more than slightly insulting.

Immersed in the present by the deliberate policy of the Deweyites, both the school-children and the university students nowadays are what a friend of mine, a parent, calls "bird-brained"—not that they are stupid, but that, birdlike they cannot bear to keep at any one occupation for more than a few moments; they hurry from one amusement to another, unable really to work or to contemplate.[2]

But why not insult the damned? And especially why not insult liberalism? Liberalism is doubly damned for it hopes to get rid of damnation by getting rid of the idea of sin.

Emerson, discarding with the forms of Calvinism the very essence of its creed, never admitted the idea of sin into his system. . . . Recognition of the abiding power of sin is a cardinal tenet in conservatism.[3]

We now have a conservatism with an instinct for the jugular.

THE DEPTH AND WIDTH OF NEW CONSERVATISM*

The individual is foolish; but the species is wise; and so the conservative appeals to what Chesterton calls "the democracy of the dead." Against the *hubris* of the innovator who scorns the past, the conservative invokes Cupid's curse:

> They that do change old love for new
> Pray gods they change for worse.

[2] *Ibid.*, p. 63.
[3] Kirk, *The Conservative Mind*, (1953), p. 212.
* The quotations at the head of sections are from Kirk's *The Conservative Mind* or *A Program for Conservatives*.

Kirk, we have said, both broadens and deepens American conservatism. He broadens it by including in it many things which most American conservatives, at least in the twentieth century, have left alone. He deepens it by going back to Burke and other British writers, by giving it a pantheon of thinkers whom most American conservatives have ignored, or simply glanced at in passing.

The aim of Kirk in broadening and deepening American conservatism is to shape an ideology.[4] He denies, of course, that he is treating conservatism as an ideology or even that it can be an ideology. What else is to be expected from one who distrusts thought as such? But not soon after denying that he is an ideologue he says:

Our time, sick nigh unto death of utilitarianism and literalness, cries out for myth and parable. Great myths are not merely susceptible of rational interpretation: they *are* truth, transcendent truth. . . . Conservatives always differ a good deal, among themselves, as to the better solution of any particular problem. What they have in common is a similar view of human nature, of the ends of society, and of the most nearly satisfactory methods for seeking the common good.[5]

Are not common myths, views of human nature, thoughts on the ends and means of society, the constituents of an ideology? And especially when these parts are bound together in a whole scheme which promises salvation to the believer?

What is the nature of conservatism as it comes to us from Kirk's hands? First and foremost it is Burke's battle against the

---

[4] See E. V. Walter, "Conservatism Recrudescent: A Critique," *Partisan Review*, September-October, 1954, for a description of the dangers of the "mythical tendencies of conservative thought" and the way they transform "observation into fantasy," as exemplified in Kirk's writings.

[5] Kirk, *Program for Conservatives*, p. 15; p. 7; (*sic*).

Revolution and John Adams' battle against perfectability and innovation. But Burke above all. It may be hard to believe, but a propaganda pamphlet written by a politician in terror of revolution's threat to his security is seriously recommended to present-day Americans as a guide to the reconstruction of American society in the mid-twentieth century. Conservatism for Kirk is what Burke wrote in his *Reflections on the Revolution in France*. Others may have embellished it, but unless they are in the line of Burke they are nowhere in his view. Indeed, Kirk goes even further and tells us that conscious conservatism did not manifest itself until 1790 with the publication of the *Reflections*. Seldom has so weighty a cause been based on so weak a foundation.

So lacking in substance is it in fact that Kirk himself is forced to give us a preliminary definition of conservatism in order to clarify the confused thought of Burke. Conservatism, he tells us, has six ideas: (1) a belief that "divine intent rules society;" (2) affection for the variety and mystery of traditional life as distinguished from uniformity and equalitarianism; (3) the conviction that civilized society requires orders and classes; (4) a belief that property and freedom are inseparable; (5) faith in prescription, distrust of calculators, and a belief that man is governed by emotion and not by reason and that therefore he must be controlled; (6) a conviction that change and reform are not the same, a "recognition . . . that innovation is a devouring conflagration more often than it is a torch of progress. . . . Providence is the proper instrument for change. . . ."[6]

In the incoherent rag bag that is the *Reflections on the Revolution in France* all of these principles can, of course, be found. There is Burke's defense of the English constitution against innovation and his view that society is a spiritual unity. It might

[6] Russell Kirk, *The Conservative Mind*, pp. 6-8.

be added that Kirk agrees with Burke that the eighteenth-century constitution was a very fine one indeed. Did it not protect Englishmen in all walks of life? (The answer is, no, it did not, but that is not at issue here.) As for the question of the peculiar voting practices of eighteenth-century Britain, why, "in good government, the object of voting is not to enable every man to express his ego, but to represent his interest, whether or not he casts his vote personally and directly." That is Kirk speaking, not Burke. It is certainly true as Kirk says, that "Burke would have dreaded the modern democratic state."[7] Further, the *Reflections* were strong on tradition. Burke saw the state operating through the prejudices and traditions that "millenniums" of human experience have made manifest. (How many traditions, by the way, go back for millenniums?) Religion, too, is approved by Burke not merely because it keeps the many in their place, but because he believed in the reality of the purpose of Providence.

"There is an order that keeps things fast in their place," said Burke himself, penetrating to the very root of conservative instinct; "it is made to us, and we are made to it."[8]

It is, of course, important to tie tradition and religion together because tradition is the way man knows the truths of religion. As Kirk says, "we may be sure that Providence, acting through the medium of human trial and error, has developed every hoary habit for some important purpose." One might inquire how these hoary habits could be developed through trial and error if the conservative will not permit innovating men to make trials and errors, but perhaps the question lacks veneration. Finally, it follows from such methods of "reasoning," a

[7] See Kirk's *The Conservative Mind*, ch. II for Kirk's use of Burke.
[8] *Ibid.*, p. 28.

word abhorrent to those bones of Burke still shaking, no doubt, in fear of the Jacobins, that to Burke government by majority rule is really not government by majority rule. Kirk has a rather neat way of putting the point: "Burke believed in a majority rule, properly understood."[9] And how is it to be properly understood?

Burke maintains that a proper majority can be drawn only from a body qualified by tradition, station, education, property, and moral nature to exercise the political function. In Britain, this body, "the people," included some four hundred thousand men, Burke said; and a competent majority should be a majority of these persons, not merely of the whole population taken indiscriminately. Sharing in political power is not an immutable right, but rather a privilege to be extended or contracted according to the intelligence and integrity of a population.[10]

One wonders whether there might not be a dispute on the question of the intelligence and integrity of the population.

John Adams shares second billing only with Burke; he is in a way the American Burke and we are lucky to have him and his whole family—"resembling in their stiff patriotism some ancient Roman house . . . ."[11] The main thing about Adams that delights Kirk is his keen sense that the many are not to be trusted, a profundity that enables Kirk to develop the conservative principles that exalt local rights and diversities and to state his belief in aristocracy of the natural variety. But what both Burke and Adams thought is so involved with Kirk's concepts of conservatism that we can leave those two gentlemen to their restless graves and turn directly to Kirk's concepts themselves as they are presented in *The Conservative Mind* and *A Program*

[9] *Ibid.*, p. 52.
[10] *Ibid.*, pp. 52-3.
[11] *Ibid.*, p. 65.

for Conservatives. Before we do, however, it is important to note whom Kirk does not mean to include as conservative.

He does not mean to include certain figures such as Sir Robert Peel. The reason Sir Robert is *out* is because he "obtained office by sacrificing principle," something, evidently, that cannot be said about, say, Disraeli or Salisbury. Besides, Sir Robert conceded everything to the Whigs in his Tamworth Manifesto. So Kirk tells us. But the real reason Kirk has such a dislike of what Peel did seems to lie well outside the realm of principle and to center on simple class expediency. When Peel yielded on the Corn Law it was not principle that was at stake but the security of the country gentlemen, "a class . . . most useful . . . in English society." Peel, it is clear, is among the damned, especially since Cardinal Newman has condemned him. There are other conservatives, too, who do not qualify for the elect; Lord Randolph Churchill together with the whole idea of Tory Democracy is out; and it is worth noting that in all the pages of Kirk's two books there is no mention of the reforming efforts of Shaftesbury and Oastler. To Kirk, Tory Democracy is merely the belief that any change is admissible as long as it is presided over by the Conservative Party. But fortunately Disraeli, Balfour, and Salisbury saved the Tory Party from this fate worse than death. As Kirk puts it primly, they "endeavored to provide old-style aristocratic leadership and precaution in a time of mass-action."

Who, then, are the conservatives, Kirk asks grandly? They include all types of persons. It is not wealth, or power, or class, or immediate interest or even timidity which makes a conservative but "rather a deep-seated prejudice in favor of prescriptive truth. . . . Conservatives are . . . a number of persons, of all classes and occupations, whose view of life is reverential, and who tend to be guided by the wisdom of their ancestors, instead of abstract speculation." Kirk grows quite eloquent on the subject; a true conservative may be a "resolute and strong-minded clergyman" [not a weak-minded clergyman? Or would he be a liberal clergyman?], a "worn farmer who holds fast to the wisdom of his ancestors," or a truck driver "retaining within himself a dignity of soul . . . doing infinite good to the human race by the example he sets in the station to which a 'divine tactic' has assigned him," or a landed proprietor of ancient name, or an old-fashioned manufacturer, or a physician, or a lawyer, etc.[12] The last two are of particular importance because they seem to be the only two major groups today who are alert to the threat of socialism in the United States.

Are the conservative types mentioned by Kirk of much importance? Or are they strictly marginal types, a truck driver or two who reads "good books"? Certainly conservatism has sustained some shattering defeats, and especially in the twentieth century, when society took on an ugly aspect and conservatism itself turned sour as the hard-faced men assumed power. The headings of two of Kirk's chapters tell the melancholy story: "Conservatism Frustrated: America, 1865-1918", and "English Conservatism Adrift: The Twentieth Century." Things certainly are in the saddle and the name of the things are industrialism, centralization, secularism, and leveling, all "unreasoning forces." One might well become just another despondent conservative as one looks around at the world which has used Rousseau as its guide.

However, the wheel of fortune is turning. Burke is proving to be correct.

But the course of events seems to have vindicated Burke's prophecies, after all, and our present time of troubles has seen the literal disintegration of those illimitable hopes of the Age of Revolution: the gods of the copybook headings with fire and sword return. Burke

---

[12] See Kirk, *A Program for Conservatives*, ch. II.

habitually thought in terms of long-run tendencies and consequences. All the vaticinations of Burke have come to pass: the dissolution of nations into mere aggregations of individuals, the reapportionment of property by political machinery, the era of merciless war, the appearance of men on horseback to forge tyranny out of anarchy, the ghastly sickness of morality and social decencies. Burke found the source of these terrors in the radical visions of the revolutionary thinkers.[13]

Burke is vindicated and conservatism once more has the possibility of true growth before it. And not a minute too soon, it should be pointed out, for America needs conservatism as never before "to redeem her from ungoverned will and appetite."

Kirk stands out among his fellow conservatives by virtue of his supreme self-confidence, but a degree of self-confidence generally distinguishes the New Conservatives from the Old— the latter having always a touch of nervousness about them. He is confident that conservatism is the only nostrum that civilization needs, and he is confident that the day of the conservatives is arriving with ponderous tread. Conservatism certainly has been routed in the past, he admits, but what of its adversaries, the liberals, the Jacobins, the sentimental socialists? They are in even worse shape. At least conservatism has been able to maintain continuity and as a result, "today . . . conservatism has such an opportunity for regaining grounds" as it has not had since 1789. For of the six conservative canons four still operate among the Anglo-Saxon people: religion, unaltered political institutions, private property, and respect for "established usage." There are difficulties, to be sure; the idea of class and order has suffered some nasty defeats, and the masses threaten to overturn established usage, but it is the very threat of such dangers that has, providentially one might say, led to a revival of conservatism. Collectivism especially has frightened everyone, even

[13] Kirk, *The Conservative Mind*, p. 22.

the "obdurate radicals." Hence the "recrudescence" of popular conservatism in the west.

The score is 4-2 and it is in favor of conservatism. It begins to look as if the nadir had been reached. Even many of the liberals who up to now had scorned conservatism are beginning to see themselves as true believers. But if they do they should not make the mistake of thinking they can make a deal with the reviving conservatism. The liberals will come to Kirk and his fellows on his terms, and on their knees, or not at all. Those conservative types mentioned by Kirk, those non-Sir Robert Peel characters, are about to inherit the earth. The possibilities for conservatism are widening, not shrinking, as the world goes spinning further and further away from liberal dreams. The way will be hard, of course, but one can assume from Kirk that the route is open. It is up to the liberals to follow the procession.

Before going on to describe the nature of the salvation that faces us it is worth saying that on the question of foreign policy Kirk has nothing to offer. Writing in 1953 and 1954, foreign policy in his view is merely a matter of expediency and, as we should know by now, conservatives do not fool around with expediency. All that Kirk has to say on the question is that if the conservative canons are realized, even in part, then "the problems of war and peace are likely to fall into some manner of settlement . . . ."[14] Such insouciance is truly breath-taking. And his ability to ignore the way international affairs might just possibly influence the domestic affairs Kirk is so concerned about is even more breath-taking. It is true that he does suggest getting back to the good old days of conservative diplomacy. But he concludes by saying that the best way of saving the states of Europe and Asia from revolution is by realizing our own conservative character.

[14] *Ibid.*, p. 416.

THE POLITICAL SYSTEM OF NEW CONSERVATISM

If the Constitution cannot be relied upon as a barrier against appetite and force, if the most capacious human intellects cannot apprehend the way to manage society, where may security against power be found? Why, said Randolph, in habitually restricting the scope of government to narrow limits, and in basing all government, and participation therein, upon practical considerations, rather than upon the fancies of the *philosophes* and of Jefferson.

The conservative attitude toward the state in America and the American political system has not always been crystal clear, and Kirk no less than other conservatives has to tread warily. The problem is derived from that old devil Hamilton and the unfortunate fact that The Founding Fathers erected a strong centralized state where there had been a weak decentralized confederation. Certainly The Founding Fathers cannot be repudiated. But does it follow therefore that the Federal government and its works must be accepted as supreme, in the last analysis at least, above the states? The Old South did not think so. The question must be answered therefore, which tradition of state action will the conservative follow, the Federalist or the Southern? Since both the views of the South and the facts of central power can be justified by an appeal to the past, it is difficult for even a conservative to bring both attitudes under the same rubric of tradition. Therefore a choice must be made. Kirk has no hesitation. He chooses the South.

In doing so he is forced to put Alexander Hamilton outside the pale of true conservatism and in the limbo where Sir Robert Peel and Lord Churchill also wander. True, Hamilton had certain excellent tendencies; he distrusted the people, for example. And he was a Christian who wrote of the errors of the French Revolution. But the man had fatal flaws. For one thing he ignored local distinctions, state's rights and all that, and thought that a strong government would be able to handle any difficulties that might arise in connection with them. Further, he was a mercantilist who, in his ardor for economic growth, rode roughshod over the prescriptions of others. Certainly Burke would not have been so brutal; he would "have delayed indefinitely any alteration if it menaced the lawful property and prerogative of a single tidewaiter . . . ." In fact it is hard to avoid the conclusion that Hamilton was definitely more interested in production and productivity than in tradition. Worse: he was interested in planned productivity. Hence it can be said that poor Hamilton did not understand what it was he was doing.

It seems hardly to have occurred to Hamilton's mind that a consolidated nation might also be a levelling and innovating nation, though he had the example of Jacobin France right before him. . . . He ignored the probability that the industrialized nation he projected might conjure up not only conservative industrialists, but also radical factory-hands. . . .[15]

One must record with regret, too, that "Hamilton never penetrated far beneath the surface of politics to the mysteries of veneration and presumption." The tests for conservatism are stringent, but failure will not be excused. Hamilton is out. And with him goes centralization.

The way is now clear to turn back to the South with its lovely old traditions of concurrent majorities and slavery. The latter, as Kirk says, is "bad ground for the conservatives to make a stand upon." Indeed it is. But he is solaced with the thought that there was "no satisfactory answer" possible to the question. Thus he is able to say with an obvious sigh of relief that he will "keep clear here of that partisan controversy over slavery." In passing, however, one cannot resist pointing out that there was

[15] Kirk, *The Conservative Mind*, p. 66.

a solution available that was both satisfactory and possible. It consisted of ending slavery. One is surprised that someone who is as religious as Kirk and who thinks that politics is about morals should be so obtuse on the moral problem of slavery.

The conservative's ideal political system comes down, therefore, to what Randolph and Calhoun believed it should be. Kirk points out that the Southern conservatives were disciples of Burke and that fact in itself is enough to make them O.K. with Kirk. They were conservative because they saw the world moving away from the decent life of agriculture and into the indecent life of industrialism. The affection for agriculture led, of course, to an affection for decentralization, and to a dislike of democracy. Randolph, having a firm conviction that men were weak, believed that man could be trusted with his own freedom, perhaps, but certainly with the freedom of no one else. Man is best when left alone. Prescriptive rights, common law, and custom must thus be used to prevent the democratic masses from riding over local rights. Calhoun, another great statesman, also exemplifies the defense of local interests and the good old conservative belief that there is no such thing as the People but only individuals and local groups.

But the southern point of view is too well known to require elaboration. It is what Kirk makes of it that is significant and what he makes of it is nothing short of *the* political position of conservatism. Randolph's spirit

was the conservatism of particularism, of localism. Without the spirit of particularism, the idea of local associations and local rights, perhaps no sort of conservatism is practicable.[16]

Randolph and Calhoun the mentors of American politics today? Why do Kirk and others like him seek in the dead Old South a model for politics? The answer is of course that the South gives

[16] *Ibid.*, p. 143.

them the authority of tradition for a stand they are anxious to make—a stand against democratic majorities. Calhoun's statement that there are two types of majorities delights the heart of every conservative, for it tells him what he had always hoped to hear—that counting heads is not a sufficient basis for politics, that the whole concept of "the People" is a myth.

But the espousal of the political ideas of the Old South goes deeper than even the normal conservative desire to arrest time (Randolph: "it [is] always unwise—yes—highly unwise, to disturb a thing that [is] at rest."), and deeper even than the desire to crawl back to a Garden of Eden. Kirk's contribution is to have spelled out some of the assumptions of the conservative philosophy of the state.

The conservatives have, Kirk informs us, a point of view on power. They have always looked upon power as a most dangerous thing. It is a most dangerous thing not just because men may misuse it in a sort of general way but because men are sinful and are bound to misuse it. For one of the major sins of man is his lust for power. Thus the conservative has always sought for means to restrain power, to keep it from any man or class by the use of prescriptive constitutions, by attention to local government, and by confining the activity of the state to a few well-defined objects. The totalitarian state is not, on the basis of this argument, a nonexistent threat in America. Granted that no one actually advocates the totalitarian state, it is still possible for it to come by stealth.

There *is* such a thing as "creeping socialism"; and the worst of it is that socialism never ceases to creep until it becomes totalitarianism, nor can it, in its nature.[17]

[17] Kirk, *A Program for Conservatives*, p. 262. (*Sic!*).

An example of such creeping socialism with all its threat of the totalitarian state is the federal school-lunch program. How much better, Kirk tells us nervously, it would have been if it had been left to local paternalism. Whether it would have been done at all in that case he does not discuss. He is not, it is only fair to add, against school lunches as such. In short, conservatives must "stand firm against centralization and specious legislation that offers to substitute a passing 'security' for a prescriptive liberty. . . ."[18]

Thus Kirk on power. As we shall see, the conservative attitude toward power is part of a linked series, or syndrome, of ideas all of which work together to establish a particular view of man and society. But it may be asked, to what extent does this view of power, by itself, differ from that of nineteenth-century liberalism? The answer is that it does not differ at all.

Kirk tells us that his view of power is identical with that of nineteenth-century liberalism. He tells us that in the early nineteenth century the liberal feared the power of the state and sought to hedge it about with constitutional restrictions. But then a fatal flaw appeared in liberalism; it became optimistic. It assumed that issues could be settled with reasoned discussion, that such discussions would replace the appeal to naked strength and—horror of horrors—that the people themselves could even be trusted with power. Hence the yielding to the sinful pleasures of the welfare state and school lunches. The bars were down. The liberals deserted the cause of constitutionalism and the twentieth century is the result. It is a century that vindicates Acton's old tag.

It is when he is face to face with the fact that man has nothing to depend upon but his free choice of limits that the conservative panics. Law itself suddenly looks like a very weak

[18] *Ibid.*, p. 266.

reed indeed. There is only one way out: prescription. When he takes his stand on prescription as the hedge on power we have the authentic conservative view of power.

THE BUSINESSMAN, PROPERTY, AND ECONOMICS

Only a few words need be said about Kirk's view of property and economic affairs, but more needs to be said about his view of the businessman, for the businessman is a headache for the high-flying New Conservative.

Having been told in all seriousness that "there *is* such a thing as creeping socialism" *[sic!]* we suspect that Kirk has little to contribute to questions of economic organization. When we also see that he is in despair because of the income tax we are more positive. The income tax, for those who may still be interested in the question, is described by Kirk as an "instrument for deliberate social alteration. . . ." So it is. As for the inheritance tax, it simply does not go down well with the conservative view of right reason. But these two economic injustices aside, Kirk's main concern with the question of economics is to show that it is not important; i.e., economics deals with material things, with physical wants, and it is the fact that we are a slave to creature comforts that is the problem, not how to solve the problem of their scarcity or their distribution. The conservative knows that material production is not the purpose of human existence. While Kirk wants it to be understood that he has no objection to anyone being decently clad, fed, housed, etc., he also wants to make it clear that he is not really taken in by the talk of planners and politicians about relieving poverty. They are not as concerned with relieving poverty as they are with satisfying dreams of avarice. Simplicity and modest contentment is better than unrestrained sensation, torpid satiety. How to obtain a decent frugality, it turns out, is Kirk's idea of the "problem of wants." A production and consumption society is neither universal nor traditional. Hence one need not bow down before its aim; humanity needs to restore those moral ends held by past and older societies; that is, the old motives of integrity and honesty.

Unfortunately it is not clear what honesty has to do with wants, nor is it clear either what was so honest about the past. Since its record of honesty is no better than that of the present and probably not as good, one may have some suspicion that Kirk is simply avoiding the issue of honesty in society as well as avoiding the issues of economics. Nonetheless, the conservative solution to problems of economics is not without its significance, for it is an easy attitude to take, requiring neither thought nor knowledge but just a blunt, old-fashioned emotion. The conservative view is, simply, that we should ignore economics; we have too much of it, so to speak. We should be moved to the following effect:

The American conservative will endeavor to exert some intelligent check upon material will and appetite.[19]

It sounds like a good idea.

Naturally, having the opinions he does have on politics, Kirk is not without some doubts about government economic planning. He seems to allow for some of it on the local level; but even there it should be kept to the minimum. He tells us that what we should do with the wealth we have is to make our communities beautiful; thus we should employ our industrial production for conservative ends rather than revolutionary ends. But he is anxious that he should not be misunderstood. Cen-

[19] Kirk, *A Program for Conservatives*, ch. VIII.

155

tralized planning for such purposes is not only not necessary, but positively a threat to society. Instead we should depend on private and local activities to beautify our communities. There is another point of view, however.

Only God can make a tree. But only the New Deal can make a park.[20]

The question of who is to create the beautiful communities of which he is so hopeful is nowhere faced up to by Kirk. One may assume that he, like this writer, is in favor of parks. But who is to build them? Bankrupt cities under the control of housing contractors? Or should the central government perhaps use its financial whip to push the cities out of the hands of the corrupt who desire to build new slums rather than new parks. Kirk avoids such questions because they were not discussed by Burke. They were not discussed by Burke, it is worth pointing out, because the wealthy, those of "unbought grace," already had their private parks.

Yet reality will keep breaking in and it breaks in especially with the swaggering, unseemly, and altogether upsetting presence of the American businessman. The problem he presents for the American conservative in general and the New Conservative in particular is a fascinating one. We have seen that Felix Morley has a rather aloof attitude to businessmen, considering their works to be considerably less than Godly. The even more intense Russell Kirk, dedicated as he is to a crusade, is still more perplexed about this buccaneer.

One of the problems that the businessman creates arises from the widespread belief that he is a natural-born conservative and perhaps the only real conservative. The unthinking American public, having a superficial view of what conservatism is about, and being somewhat materialistic and cynical, seems to have

[20] Anon.

the idea that business and conservatism are really the same thing. It is important for the conservatives to deny . . . to deny what? To deny that businessmen are conservative? Such a denial they would never make since it would not only lose them a valuable ally who possesses the riches of this kingdom if not the next, but would be untrue. Yet it is unfortunate for the public to think that a defense of business interests is all there is to conservatism. What the conservative must deny, therefore, is that conservatism is only a businessman's creed. But he must go further. The businessman must be told, and in loud enough tones so that everyone can hear it, that he must conform to conservatism, not conservatism to him. He must be told that there is an eternal conservatism that sprang full-blown from the ripe mind of Burke and that the businessman is in or out depending on whether or not he knows what Burke thought. But soundness on Burke is not all that the conservative requires of the by now somewhat baffled and even suspicious businessman. The latter must realize that his business activities almost destroyed conservatism in the nineteenth and twentieth centuries and produced the mass culture that is such a curse today, and that it is therefore his activities which have ruined the social order upon which conservatism must rest.

The poor businessman! He gets it no matter where he turns, from the left and from the right. We know what the left thinks of business. As for the right, Kirk tells us that conservatism struggles against both industrialism and democracy. And he leaves us in no doubt that both derive from the same source, that the two in fact are the same thing. Who would ever have expected the businessman to be told by conservatives that it was he who was responsible for democracy and that he should be condemned for it! No wonder American business has so little sense of ideological direction. No one loves it.

The main reason for the discontent that Kirk (and other conservative ideologists) feel with the businessman is the fact of his social revolutionary activities and his refusal to be a man of tradition. The shocking history of the businessman in the Gilded Age is an example of his careless revolutionary urge. We know already what Kirk thinks of Hamilton's businesslike view of the American states. And one must think of what the automobile did to America. It was a "mechanical Jacobin"; and "the productive process which made it so cheap was even more subversive of the old ways than was the gasoline engine itself." Mass production methods dissolved, Kirk tells us grimly, "station and family." Certainly it was an awful threat to tradition. For that reason it is all the more tragic and ironic to identify free enterprise and conservatism, although the identification has in fact been made, to the loss of conservatism, in the twentieth century.

It is for such reasons that Kirk will have nothing to do with the idea put forward by Arthur Schlesinger, Jr., that the real function of the New Conservatives is to "deal with American society in terms of the businessman." Kirk, believing as he does that a conservative is one "whose view of life is reverential," can hardly let that point of view go unanswered. Not only is the businessman a revolutionary. Even when he is trying to be a good conservative he is simply too busy to think conservative thoughts. Yet Kirk does admit that the conservative and the businessman agree on the defense of private enterprise because as Kirk naïvely tells us, it "is the only really practicable system, in the modern world, for satisfying our economic wants." That such unswerving devotion to the system of free enterprise might well cause the uninstructed layman and Arthur Schlesinger, Jr., to identify conservatism and business rule does not occur to Kirk.

But let us go a little further with Kirk before we accuse him of being an unconscious victim of self-interest or naïveté. While it is his claim that conservatism is confined to the single interests of no class, it is nevertheless true, as Kirk says, that conservatism finds it *essential*, not just convenient, to have a leading, upper class in society, a ruling class of some kind or other. Does the business class provide such leadership? Not necessarily, according to Kirk, because there is another upper class in American life that carries weight in political life and that forms an enlightened public opinion.

Old families are not without their influence, and gentlemen of substantial private means are not an extinct breed, and probably the number of persons endowed with leisure by the inheritance of wealth is actually larger than it used to be. An upper class, though amorphous, does still carry some weight in political life.[21]

They make a charming picture, these gentlemen of substantial private means. But does Kirk really think that they will save conservatism and modern society? If he does, the problems we face today cannot really be very serious. But evidently he does not have much faith in his well-heeled gentlemen, for he adds:

All the same, the businessman remains the great prop of American conservatism.[22]

It turns out, after all, that while there is sin in business it is, unlike the sin in the rest of us, not original sin, not inherent in and necessary to business. The businessman can, if he wishes, purge himself. But the trouble is that he is obtuse. How many businessmen, Kirk asks bitterly, take any interest in general ideas? In politics? Alas! he cries in great anguish, "how many,

---

[21] Kirk, *Conservative Mind*, p. 434.
[22] *Ibid.*

indeed are really conservatives?" The answer, it turns out, is, not as many as might be. Some give money to the Democratic party. Others let themselves be flattered by liberals and collectivists and almost all become Marxists without knowing it by accepting economic determinism and the primacy of economics. But these facts can be counterbalanced if the businessman is careful and nourishes the prejudices he was born with.

Such are [the businessman's] professions; but his actual prejudices are much more generous and sound, commonly, than the confused opinion he utters. In his heart, this businessman is really a conservative, substantially; but he understands neither himself nor his era.[23]

Businessmen need only be educated to constitute a ruling class. The reason they need education is that they "are inordinately vain." What have they to be vain about? Only material progress.

Kirk concludes by stating that the businessman must come to conservatism, not the other way around.

A conservative order is not the creation of the free entrepreneur; rather, the modern man of business exists only because a conservative order recognizes the importance of his function.[24]

But one must repeat, if free enterprise and conservatism are so nearly identical as Kirk seems to think they are (although, as usual, he is not clear about what he thinks in this connection) then perhaps a condition of unity has been reached in which conservatism is business and business is conservatism.

Whatever Kirk thinks on the question, it is a fact that business poses a serious problem for conservatism in America. Kirk

[23] *Ibid.*, p. 435.
[24] *Ibid.*, p. 436.

would not be so uneasy about the whole question if there was not in reality a dynamic, innovating, and revolutionary force in business. It is the existence of that revolutionary aspect of business which has always kept conservatism off balance. Hence in practice the potential identity between conservatism and business has in fact been broken time after time. And yet it has always reasserted itself. It has reasserted itself because, although business is revolutionary in the technological areas of life, it leads to the creation of a society of hierarchy in the economic and social areas. It is based on a system of free enterprise that creates and supports a class structure. In doing so it does nothing but good for conservatism. Although there is mutual antipathy and attraction between conservatism and business, on the whole attraction wins out. Kirk is correct, businessmen are conservative at heart.

From the point of view of the self-interest—if one may mention that word in connection with such a delicate and otherworldly philosophy—of conservatism, attraction had better win out. For despite all the grand talk about gentlemen of substantial private means it is a fact, and a fact known by Kirk, that without the businessman conservatism would have hard going. No doubt, it is time, as Kirk claims, for the forces of conservatism to spread far beyond the realm of the hardheaded businessman. Certainly conservatism is in the very fiber of American political and social life, and not only the gentlemen of substantial means but also many nongentlemen of unsubstantial means are conservative by instinct if not by conviction. One need not point out that the Democratic party is hardly a hotbed of radicalism. But nevertheless businessmen are the rock of conservatism in America. The relationship between the businessman and professional, ideological conservatism, is one of marriage— an uneasy marriage, but still a marriage.

NEW CONSERVATISM AND
NINETEENTH-CENTURY LIBERALISM

We are in danger of forgetting how strongly attached the old liberals were to *liberty*. Political liberalism before the middle of the nineteenth century (whatever may be said of economic liberalism) was conservatism of a sort: it intended to conserve liberty. The greater liberals were men imbued with the spirit of Burke. . . . In general the liberals feared the future.

We have seen that Old Conservatism is simply nineteenth-century liberalism in the twentieth century. Such attempts at total recall, at resurrecting a Garden of Eden, are the very essence of much conservatism in general and American conservatism in particular. How does Kirk finally regard the liberal nineteenth century? Does he too look back to it with longing? Or does his attempt to create a new conservatism, one based on a wide-ranging metaphysics, lead him to reject the whole dream and to plump instead for the eighteenth century and Burke?

It is a difficult problem for Kirk, partly because the act of throwing overboard one of the few traditions that conservatism possesses would be most unconservative behavior. More important, the nineteenth century did in fact possess many features dear to the heart of a conservative, New or Old. And most important of all, if the New Conservatives, like the Old, cannot find some roots in the nineteenth century, someone there to hold the flag for them, it would be a poor thing indeed.

Surely conservatism is not so sterile that it rests only on the rather overheated and not very lucid thoughts of one man and his political pamphlet? Yet, despite all these facts it is also a fact that there is little in the nineteenth century to which a modern Burkean conservative can look back and say, "that represents the continuity of the conservative tradition; that is Burkean-ism in action." There is the American South, of course, but other than the Old South . . . ? Kirk's attitude toward the whole problem of the past—and after all, what followed Burke but the nineteenth century?—is marked by ambiguity, doubt, and even some confusion. There are none of the clear-eyed certainties for him that come so easily to the Old Conservatives.

That Kirk is more aware than the Old Conservatives of the high cost of the nineteenth century is clear. Indeed, in describing the ravages of the century he sounds almost like a modern, twentieth-century liberal bemoaning the devastating effects of *laissez-faire*. Yet he cannot really be mistaken for a modern liberal; he sees the high cost of the century not only in its industrialism but also in its growing democracy, two features that will forever blacken that era of history. What further prevents him from being mistaken for a modern liberal is the fact that he judges the nineteenth century not in terms of its effects on those who had to live through that bloody time but only in terms of its effects on conservatism. He sees the nineteenth century as a time when economic change destroyed the old class structure—here he almost sounds like Marx himself—and broke the economic basis of a conservative society. The squires were replaced by the energetic men of Manchester, the commercial elite of eighteenth-century England and America was replaced by the trust makers and such impossible men as Joseph Chamberlin—definitely from the provinces. These new men were ignorant of tradition or if they were not they did not like tradition. They were clearly aggressive. As for the proletarians of the nineteenth century, why, they were brutes with brutish appetites. Naturally the old network of personal and paternalistic ties was broken down under these circumstances.

The wealthy man ceased to be magistrate and patron; he ceased
to be neighbor to the poor man; he became a mass-man, very often,
with no purpose in life but aggrandizement. He ceased to be conservative because he did not understand conservative values, which
cannot be instilled by mere logic—a man must be steeped in them.[25]

Mrs. Gaskell could not have put it better. But perhaps she
would have had a little more thought for the suffering which
the nineteenth century involved for those who lived in it.

But what gripes Kirk's soul is the blatant and quite candid
refusal of the nineteenth century to steep men in the juices of
the past. That sin is one not lightly to be forgiven by Kirk, and
he does not forgive it. The nineteenth century for him is a time
of desolation and defeat, a time of defeat in which the actual
military collapse of the American South was symptomatic of
what was happening elsewhere on a larger scale. For with the
defeat of the gentlemen of the Old South it was really quite
difficult to find someone to represent conservative beliefs.

But Kirk is constrained to try. It would be too devastating to
admit that no one in the nineteenth century outside of the South
spoke for conservatism, that conservatism had been defeated
everywhere. Therefore Kirk thumbs back through the intellectual history of the century trying either to find some genuine
New Conservatives (or should they be called old New Conservatives? The question of nomenclature becomes confused at
this point), or some liberals who can stand in for conservatives.
There is of course good old Sir Walter Scott and there is
Coleridge, not to mention Canning, but these are really men
of the eighteenth century. There is J. Q. Adams, but Kirk has
reservations about him; he fell for the possibilities of progress
once too often. There are Brownson and Hawthorne, Newman,
Disraeli, and J. F. Stephen—they will do in a pinch as con-

[25] Kirk, *Ibid.*, p. 199.

servatives, as will Henry and Brooks Adams. It is true that some of these men could hardly be called conservatives, although at various times they all had conservative thoughts. But above all there are the liberal conservatives: Macaulay, Cooper, Tocqueville, Maine, Lecky, James Russell Lowell, Godkin, and Bagehot. It is these men who are vital to Kirk, for if they cannot be made to be essentially conservative, the others will hardly do, since by themselves they are not the embodiment of a continuing conservative tradition but simply a group of eccentrics, of dissenters mainly significant because they did not embody anything but their own personal protest against the times in which they lived. In the final analysis Kirk is forced back to the nineteenth-century liberals to find the continuation of Burke.

He points out that after 1867 the conservatives in Britain were reinforced by recruits from the old liberal, Whig, and utilitarian branches of Victorian life. They came to conservatism because they were alarmed by the increasing powers of the state, and by Gladstone and the aggressive actions of labor. The middle classes began to sniff revolution in the air. (Kirk does not consider the effect of the Paris Commune on British opinion, but it will be gentlemanly to help out his argument and point out that the Commune certainly increased this swing of the British middle class against liberal beliefs.) Kirk can therefore point with pride to the remark of Bagehot that in his time there had ceased to be much difference between a liberal conservative and a conservative liberal. Both now had the duty of setting bounds to both collectivism and democracy. Herbert Spencer is a prime example of such conservative individualists as are J. F. Stephen, Maine, and Lecky. Panicking before the logic of democracy they all sought comfort in the arms of motherly old Burke.

Or did they? Kirk's notion of a conservative swing of opinion in Britain after 1867 certainly has a degree of historical truth. The middle classes, including their esteemed literary representatives, after 1867 clearly moved into the camp of the Conservative Party. But did they turn to the Conservative Party because they were fearful of democracy, as Kirk claims, or because they were suddenly aware of the virtues of Burke, as Kirk also claims? The two are not necessarily the same thing. That something drastic happened to nineteenth-century liberalism after 1867 is not to be denied. But that what happened was a return to Burke is definitely to be denied. It is to be denied because what happened to liberal thought in those years was an independent phenomenon unconnected with Burke and having its own life and logic. It was pessimism that enveloped the liberal ideas of the writers and thinkers of the years after 1867. And conservatism, as Kirk would be the first to acknowledge, is more than pessimism. As for the manufacturing middle class, it is true indeed that they moved into the Conservative Party, but, as we have seen, Kirk refuses to identify conservatism with the manufacturing middle class, and with the Conservative Party.

His failure to understand history, a failure common to most ideologists, causes him to make further mistakes when he deals with the liberals of the years before 1867. He tells us that the liberals of the mid-nineteenth century were conservative because they believed in liberty. Political liberalism before 1867 was, according to this theory, conservatism of a sort simply because it intended to conserve liberty. The men he considers— Macaulay, Cooper, Tocqueville—he describes as being aware of the leveling spirit of the age. They were therefore men in the spirit of Burke, Kirk tells us. Burke taught them that liberty was a legacy to be conserved; he taught them a "tenderness" for private property, and the virtues of limited government. Unfortunately for Kirk's argument the fact is that if Burke had never lived these men would have held essentially the same ideas since they are all liberal ideas, ideas which in fact lay dormant until liberalism took them up and made them a part of a creed. They are the ideas of Locke and Bentham, not Burke and Coleridge.

But such misreadings are not the main issue. What is important is the fact that Kirk has in fact perceived one of the most important traits of the nineteenth-century liberal. It was the tendency of the nineteenth century to get out of hand, to go beyond tolerable bounds, which did in fact make conservatives of many liberals. They did not necessarily turn to Burke as such; they did not necessarily worship old ruins. But they did begin to think as a conservative thinks; they did strive with increasing desperation to establish a fixed society that could enclose the freedom which now had suddenly passed beyond what they thought was its proper limit. Kirk has a bad sense of history, but he knows the panic men feel when they look freedom in the face.

The problem that split and broke nineteenth-century liberalism was this very question of whether freedom should be enclosed in certain categories or whether it should be a freedom restricted only by self-limitation. Those who believed the former became conservatives, finding their home in various conservative parties although not taking up the pure canon of Burke and all that. Those who believed the latter turned either to Progressivism or to labor parties and/or socialism. There was a conservatism at the heart of nineteenth-century liberalism. Morley and Burnham and Kirk all know it and love it. Others know it, too, but reject it, claiming that men are free and without any limits except those that they themselves establish.

5. New Conservatism and Democracy

So FAR WE have only circled around the periphery of Kirk's thought. Let us get to the center of his conservatism. How do the attitudes of his New Conservatism on democracy, aristocracy, religion, tradition, and change mix together to form a coherent ideology?

We have seen that the conservatives so far considered here are undemocratic both by instinct and conviction, that Felix Morley, for example, postulates the United States as a republic and not a democracy. Kirk would not deny such attitudes, but as a New Conservative he puts them in the wider context of European history since 1789 and the wider philosophical context of original sin. It is one thing to prove that America was never intended to be a democracy, although the point having been made one is not quite sure what one is to do with it. But it is something altogether more awe-inspiring and convincing if one can show that Great Thinkers Have Always Thought Democracy is Bad. And it is positively final and crushing if one can show that man is bad, for then, Q.E.D., democracy must be bad.

Kirk seldom attacks democracy directly; evidently the evil thing is too much with us to require or need open confrontation

—or would it be too open-faced? At any rate, his attack is revealed through identifying himself with his conservative heroes from the past. Should a conservative not cling to the tradition of antidemocratic thought rather than think his own original thoughts? There is however, one statement by Kirk that will show in brief his attitude toward democracy in its most important form of political democracy.

I believe, for instance, that we injured our political order by adopting universal suffrage, direct primaries, popular election of senators, and other measures calculated to substitute direct democracy for representative government. Yet I do not recommend that we try to reverse these measures; instead, we ought to adapt them to the concept of order. . . . Now the conservative, understanding this paradox, will endeavor to apply the principle of order to elections, encouraging in every community those coherent elements which make up a body of reasoned opinion by which the mass of men and women may be guided; and he will try to restore among the mass of men and women a respect for the idea of order, so that their votes are cast with some deference to the opinions of their natural leaders, not at random, or in obedience to this editorial or that radio-broadcast. In short, the conservative will seek to utilize and improve the orders which already exist in our nation, not to impose an exotic pattern of abstract hierarchy.[1]

This conclusion is the end-product of a long line of antidemocratic attitudes in which Kirk delights. Macaulay gives him the basis for thinking that the poor would plunder the rich if they got the vote—a well-known suspicion that has been confirmed by the welfare state. James Fenimore Cooper demonstrates that a democratic state must have the moral discipline of leadership by gentlemen who have the security of inherited possession of land. Tocqueville proves, of course, that democ-

[1] Kirk, *A Program for Conservatives*, pp. 247-8.

racy is or can easily become a despotism and that religion, custom, and aristocracy are required to prohibit such a development. Maine shows what happens to contract, the invention of aristocrats, when democracy is given its head; contract turns into collectivism, economic competition comes to an end, and so does progress. Lecky shows how to restrict democracy by dominating the many through the unearned income that comes from ownership of land. ("Unearned income from land," said Lecky, "is of all forms of wealth generally that most beneficial to society.") Godkin, Henry Adams, and Brooks Adams give the general impression that democracy and decadence are the same thing and that they are the same thing because democracy destroys tradition by making innovation possible. George Gissing describes the incompetence of the masses and their absolute inability to govern themselves, let alone anyone else. Balfour is the man who saved England from Tory Democracy and whose principle of action in the face of democracy was delay and amelioration, in order to preserve authority, prescription, and moral authority.

But while Kirk learns much from his grab-bag of antidemocratic opinions, his real mentors are J. F. Stephen, W. H. Mallock, Irving Babbitt, and Paul Elmer More. It is from these sages of the decadence which is democracy that he draws his main arguments. Kirk's choice of spiritual fathers is interesting, for he has chosen the most embittered, the most hopeless of the lot, those who see democracy as a poison only to be redeemed by religion. (It was the failure of Henry and Brooks Adams to be religious that keeps them off this select list.)

J. F. Stephen is a particular favorite of Kirk because he gets to the heart of the issue. Man is depraved, and therefore must be governed by force, not by discussion. Is law a method by which men rule themselves according to rational decision? By no means. Kirk approves of Stephen's belief that "law is the instrument of social vengeance, created to enforce morality."[2] The impelling power in "all" societies is not the power of discussion as J. S. Mill would have it but the fear of hell. And after all, one must not be surprised at that fact; "force, whether physical or moral, is ordained by Providence. . . . The survival of compulsion is the chief protection to our order and culture."[3] Kirk concludes grimly by comparing Mill's essay *On Liberty* with Stephen's book on *Liberty, Equality, Fraternity;* "whose book the twentieth century has vindicated in the debate over force versus discussion, there can hardly be much doubt. . . ."[4] The twentieth century just goes to prove the truth of what Stephen had always said: "the grand scheme of God is inscrutable; the object of life is virtue, not pleasure; and obedience, not liberty is the means of attainment."[5] The problem democracy raises for Kirk, therefore, is not so much one of whether democracy is bad or good, although, of course, there cannot be much doubt on that question either. It is rather that democracy negates obedience. The awful truth is that democracy may decide that it has had enough of God's inscrutable purpose and decide that it wants a few scrutable purposes of its own for a change. Hence its well-known weakness for discussion. And in fact one must agree with Kirk that democracy is not strong on obedience. Indeed, one might even demonstrate, although Kirk does not, that one of its functions is to bring a certain kind of obedience to an end, namely obedience to those who claim to know God's inscrutable purpose, by pointing out that if God's purpose is inscrutable how can anyone know what it is.

According to Kirk, W. H. Mallock starts off from the same

[2] Kirk, *The Conservative Mind,* p. 268.
[3] *Ibid.,* p. 272. Kirk's paraphrase of Stephen.
[4] *Ibid.,* p. 275.
[5] *Ibid.,* p. 273. Kirk's paraphrase of Stephen.

religious premises as J. F. Stephen but concerns himself with a slightly different problem of democracy, the question not of force, obedience, and discussion, but the question of equality and progress. Because of his brilliance in dealing with those problems Kirk claims that Mallock has had no equal among English conservative thinkers since his death. While such a statement may give a clue to what Kirk thinks is significant conservative dogma, one may doubt if Mallock is either profound or original. Mallock describes inequality as the key to progress and defends orthodox religion against the claims of positivism and science. Progress according to these theories, and they are too well known to need more than an indication of their existence in Kirk's mind, is a function of inequality; the main producer of wealth is not labor but ability. It is necessary therefore for the many to subject themselves to the influence and authority of the "super-capable few." If the barbarians should get a hold on civilization they will ruin it whereas those who venerate their ancestors will be able to carry on, and to prevent the vandals from doing their worst.

It is with Babbitt, More, and Santayana that Kirk finds the most satisfactory union of theology and antidemocratic thought. He announces that Babbitt brings American conservatism to maturity. It is Babbitt who tells us that men must take on the yoke of a definite doctrine, that the salvation of society depends on belief in original sin, and that therefore democracy must recognize those leaders who understand the truths of the inner life, of the higher will. On this basis democracy will be transformed into an aristocracy in which those who work with their hands will rank lower than those who work with their minds. Conservatives, it seems, never despair of simplistic solutions. More, therefore, confirms the ancient truth that men must look to things of the spirit, and that the great practical problem of this time is to persuade the many that they must resurrect an aristocracy in which the spiritually great can dominate. Thus it is that this type of conservative sees no hope for democracy in an improvement of the many but only in the rebirth of an aristocracy, an interesting paradox, to say the least. What kind of an aristocracy can save democracy? Not an aristocracy of money, or of inherited privilege, but an aristocracy of the "best." Finally, More also knows from his spiritual insights that, to a civilized man, the rights of property are more important than the right to life. To protect property one must get the fear of God back into society; religion will then be able to alleviate discontent and put a brake on innovation. We are back where we started, with More and Kirk communing with the higher powers.

Such are the opinions of a "conservative mind," according to Kirk. Some matters are not, one may think, treated with the fullness they deserve; for example, the question of who is to choose those lucky few to be included in More's community of the best, not to mention the question of what is meant by the phrase "community of the best." These questions are conveniently left up in the air. There is, in fact, a problem of leadership in a democracy but More and Kirk prefer not to face it. They might discover that democracy and leadership are not incompatible, and that would never do. They do not want to improve democracy; they want to destroy it. Democracy and conservatism are incompatible. They do not like it. They think it is anticonservative. They believe that man would be better without it. As Kirk himself says:

What men really are seeking, or ought to seek, is not the right to govern themselves, but the right to be governed well.[6]

[6] *Ibid.*, p. 113.

In the final analysis what is democracy, this attempt of man to govern himself, but discussion? And what is discussion but the possibility of calling tradition, prescription, and the past into question? It is the perpetual tendency of democracy to ask questions, to ask both the glory and the debris which has come from the past to justify itself. It is the nagging refusal of democracy to accept what has been given to it without question which sticks in the throats of the Stephens, the Mallocks, the Babbitts, the Mores, and the Kirks of this world. Questions, questions, questions. Is there to be nothing that cannot have its existence questioned? And when these conservatives find that in a democracy the answer is No, everything must be questioned, why then they feel that their existence too is in doubt.

But democracy not only puts the past—and therefore the present—into question. Of necessity it puts the nature of the future into doubt. Once men begin to ask questions they might discover any truth. They might discover any possible way of acting. The future, which had been carefully blocked, shaped, and—the conservative hopes—determined by the past, now suddenly looms as the unforeseeable—as an empty area of infinite possibilities. Tradition restricts the future. Discussion opens it up. Anything suddenly becomes possible.

ARISTOCRACY, CLASS AND ORDERS

The British aristocracy, as a body the most intelligent and conscientious upper class the Western world has known, never became decadent; they simply were inundated, so that after 1906 they were compelled to stand powerless while their property followed their political influence into the custody of the cities and the industrial masses.

It is for such reasons of anguish that aristocracy is taken seriously by the conservatives. The effort to revive an aristocracy

174

or to create a new and fixed elite is not a mere atavistic impulse but an earnest attempt to provide an alternative to democracy with its wild possibilities. Aristocracy, like tradition, will block the threat of innovation which freedom carries with it. Order, in the sense both of orderly living and living by a hierarchical order, will follow the restoration of aristocracy and class. If such a prescription sounds somewhat old fashioned, why, then, its old-fashioned quality is just the reason why the twentieth century needs it. Disorder is the very trait of this awful era. Quick! there is not a minute to lose! Man the barricades with the potent few.

The opposite of aristocracy is, of course, the masses, that phenomenon so characteristic of the twentieth century. It is the masses that the conservative fears as the source of anarchy and as death to unbought grace. The masses are the people who live in ugly urban conglomerations that this civilization has spewed forth so voluminously; they are the people who cannot control their own passions and yet who, because they lack control, aspire to the property of others. The masses are the threat contained in the glittering words of democracy, in Birmingham democracy as well as any other kind. But most of all and above all, the masses represent the equalitarian urge, the urge to level and to destroy those who are better than they are. Kirk does not go beyond such semihysterical descriptions of the meaning of the word "masses" but he is, from his own point of view, under no compulsion to do so. Although the word as he uses it is devoid of any scientific usefulness, it serves his aim of presenting a drama composed of the brutish many against the sensitive and lonely few. He swallows Ortega y Gassett's theory and thinks he has a basis for social analysis.

There are many persons who are not conservative but who nevertheless fear the masses (many of them being no more definite than Kirk as to what they mean by the word). They, too, see the masses as the barbarians against civilization. But their reactions differ from those of Kirk and his fellow conservatives in one important respect, and that is, what they propose to do with the masses. One possibility is to free the masses from their bondage to barbarism by raising them above their so-called brutish existence. That solution is, of course, a liberal solution, using the word liberal in its uncorrupted sense of having some faith in the rationality of mankind. The conservative solution differs in at least two respects. First, it would redeem the masses by destroying the urban life in which they fester and breed. Secondly, it would see to it that the masses are put into a proper hierarchy, in which whatever talents for work they have could be used but in which they would be so controlled and watched that they could do no damage with their passions. Man being what he is, in this view, it is too much to hope that the many can raise themselves to the possibility of self-rule; if the attempt was made, as in fact it has been made, the only result would be to destroy the possibility of rule by the happy and talented and wealthy few.

Hence the need for aristocracy. It is not just an idle romantic dream but an iron necessity. But of course one must ask, what kind of an aristocracy? One with ruffled sleeves or a button-down collar?

To answer that question we must, naturally, turn first to Burke. And from Burke we learn that in fact there is not really much choice as to whether we will have an aristocracy or not since hierarchy and aristocracy are the natural and original framework of life and society. As Kirk paraphrases Burke:

Just as it is a fact of nature that the mass of men are ill qualified for the exercise of political power, so it is written in the eternal constitution of things that a few men, from various causes, are mentally and physically and spiritually suited for social leadership. The state which rejects their services is doomed to stagnation or destruction. These aristocrats are in part "the wiser, the more expert, and the more opulent," and they are to conduct, enlighten, and protect "the weaker, the less knowing, and the less provided with the goods of fortune." Birth, too, Burke respects; but he mentions more particularly the clergy, the magistracy, the teachers, the merchants: not the accident of birth, but nature, has made these men aristocrats. It is wise and just and in accord with the real law of nature that such persons should exercise a social influence much superior to that of the average citizen.[7]

It sounds mild enough, but the teeth show when Burke-Kirk point out that one of the wants that men legitimately have is the need for a sufficient restraint on their passions, and when they then go on to point out that that object can be achieved only by a power distinct from and outside of the passionate masses. The masses, thus, have a right to be held down, says Burke. "In this sense the restraints on men, as well as their liberties, are to be reckoned among their rights."[8]

After this double-talk we are not surprised to find that Kirk draws on another great thinker, Disraeli, for a more detailed picture of what aristocratic leadership can and should mean. The idea that Dizzy has a solution for the problems of today is certainly a novel one—he would have been much intrigued by the thought—but so it turns out to be. He has the proper solution because he wanted a system of politics that would be based on social diversity, a hierarchy of those rights and duties that are so woefully lacking today. Dizzy went even further. He knew, unlike Marx, who was somewhat confused on the issue, that the interests of classes were not opposed but simply com-

---

[7] *Ibid.*, pp. 54-55.
[8] *Ibid.*, p. 53. Kirk's quote of Burke.

plementary. Hear Kirk on this question of "the vindication and restoration of class. . . ."

Class is order; without order, law crumbles. The intelligent Tory, invoking the old sense of order and obligation, must struggle to infuse into modern industrial life the aristocratic spirit, reviving that loyalty to persons and places which is the rudiment of every noble conservative impulse. British democracy depends upon the continued existence of a true sense of class.[9]

The sight of British democracy, bound and swaddled in its variety of classes, should be the example for all mankind. It is a system of recognized orders and classes each with its peculiar privileges and each balanced to give every large interest a voice in the affairs of the state, or realm, as Kirk calls it. Neatness is all. Certainly it is an enchanting picture, but is it democracy? Kirk obviously hopes not. But whatever it is, it is a society in which the workers would be Low People and the Crown, aristocracy, and Church the Top People. As Kirk concludes, "The Primrose League mattered more than Suez." It is, evidently, a regrettable fact that the Primrose League has not been able to establish a branch in the United States. However, we have the DAR.

The most significant aspect of Kirk's apologia for an aristocracy is the context in which he conceives its role of leadership. Kirk's desire to restore aristocracy comes not only from the hope of resurrecting "unbought grace," although that hope plays no small part in his scheme. It also comes from a haunting sense of social disorder. To bring the threat of disorder to an end, old canons of social ethics must be re-established. What is social justice? What is social order? His answer to those two vital questions is the clearest and most precise statement of the ideal

[9] *Ibid.*, pp. 234-5.

conservative society given by Kirk—or any other conservative for that matter.

His concept of the proper society is based on the fundamental assumption that

. . . justice has some source and sanction more than human and more than natural. Either justice is ordained by some Power above us, or it is mere expediency, the power of the strong over the weak.[10]

Since Kirk like all conservatives has an almost neurotic antipathy for expediency he finds it necessary to claim that justice on earth is an attempt to copy the perfect justice that exists beyond space and time. Such a task may sound more than usually difficult but it does not daunt Kirk. Indeed, he presents us with a general rule that is not as innocent as it seems. The general rule is, to each man his own. Each individual should be free to do the work for which he is best qualified, and each individual is to be rewarded according to his just deserts; which means, among other things, that no one has a right to the property of others. Kirk is able to go one step further. The Christian faith does not commend the sacrifice of the welfare of one class to another. With that sanction firmly in hand he is able to re-establish the good old idea of social station, of accepting the place which one has in the social order.

What really matters is that we should accept the station to which "a divine tactic" has appointed us with humility and a sense of consecration. Without inequality, there is no opportunity for charity, or for gratitude; without differences of mind and talent, the world would be one changeless expanse of uniformity: and precisely that is the most conspicuous feature of Hell.[11]

[10] Kirk, *A Program for Conservatives*, p. 166.
[11] *Ibid.*, p. 177.

This is Calvinism with a vengeance—and vengeance is the word. The poor we must have with us to enable the wealthy to be charitable. And it is worth noting how the argument changes in the latter part of the statement. Has anyone suggested that there should be no "differences of mind and talent?" Argument by untrue and malicious attribution is evidently one of the tricks of aristocratic leadership. But the times are desperate, and desperation can always be used as a reason for dishonesty.

In case anyone should misunderstand what he is driving at when he says that the general rule is to each man his own, Kirk tells us that we must not abolish the class system just because there has been some misspent wealth among the rich. Besides, the "old leading classes" are now beginning to act with courage and fortitude, and if they are effaced, why then we will be in the hands of the commissars. And think what happens when money is given to the "people": they waste it. Kirk proves his point by telling us how the lower classes of Britain let the free milk given them by the government stand out all day on their doorsteps. The necessity of resurrecting social stations to achieve order in society is manifest, especially because there is no injustice in inequality and because a mere grant of money will not bring real equality of opportunity anyway.

Order, in society, is the harmonious arrangement of classes and functions which guards justice and gives willing consent to law and ensures that we shall all be safe together. . . . It signifies those established usages which deserve veneration.[12]

When society lacks this particular form of order then only force rules. The great disorder of society today comes exactly from the decay of the

[12] Kirk, *Ibid.*, p. 228.

. . . idea of order in its traditional sense—that is, the spirit of class, duty, and honor, the sense of responsibility and common interest within long-established social groups, which is closely bound up with Burke's "unbought grace of life." The evidence of this disintegration of obedience to establish customs and of the prescriptive framework of the civil social existence are all about us.[13]

To understand Kirk's view of order in society the emphasis on "long-established social groups" as the basic element in this happy family should be noted. Indeed, he lets the cat out of the bag, although of course to Kirk it is nothing of which to be ashamed, when he tells us that the great problem of modern society is how to convince men that they are not sufficient unto themselves but require membership in an order, and that a number of orders with distinct functions and responsibilities are a benefit to free society rather than a violation of free institutions. Does Kirk discuss the question of a possible conflict between orders and free institutions? He does not, partly because he is not given to such discussions, and partly because he really is not interested in free institutions. What he is interested in is to get the many to accept the idea of orders in society. As he puts it, while the masses have always taken their morals from the natural leaders in every order in society, it is nevertheless true that they will be unlikely to do so today unless there is a restoration in the minds of the many of a general consciousness of order.

Thus Kirk comes to his appeal to the men of wealth in America today. One should not be ashamed of class; instead one should recognize how useful it is as a way of controlling direct democracy. There is no need to try to create a new elite, for that new elite will probably be composed of the commissars,

[13] *Ibid.*

the crude technicians, the men who only know how to do things and have no "unbought grace of life." Instead the men of wealth should simply recognize themselves as an order. We will have neither ruffled sleeves nor a button-down collar aristocracy but simply rule by those who always have ruled us.

I think we will do well simply to recognize and *preserve* our *present orders* rather than attempt to shape some New Order.[14]

Such is the utopia from the past offered to us today by the New Conservative.

THE NEW CONSERVATISM AND RURAL SOCIETY

Certainly the conservative elements in a nation are menaced when rural population commences to decline. . . . Our guardians of tradition have been recruited principally, although not wholly, from our farms and small towns; the incertitude of the cities disturbs the equanimity of the tradition-guided man.

Aristocracy obviously flourishes best in a certain climate and it is clear from Kirk that that climate is a rural one. His adoration of the rural, small-town life of America is not just a reversal of Sinclair Lewis for the sake of reversal but a part of the more general conservative conviction—which we have seen also at work in Felix Morley—that centralization robs man of his virtue. And what greater representation or symbol of centralization exists than the city? But Kirk has another reason for founding his hopes in small town life, and that is his search for community. To Kirk the small town is the antithesis of the individualism and resulting disorder of city life. His attack on the city, therefore, is part of an attack on individual freedom and part of a positing of orders, rural life, rule by one's betters,

---

[14] Kirk, *The Conservative Mind,* p. 246. Italics added.

and community as the best way to tie man down and enclose him in a network of fixed social duties and obedience.

The matter of community *vs.* the individual raises a nice problem for conservatism. On the one hand the individual is a particular care for conservatism in the mass age. Yet, as Kirk says, the conservative has been much too neglectful of community and much too anxious to espouse individualism. As we have seen, it is particularly the case with the Old Conservatives who have tended to think of man mainly as the nineteenth-century liberal thought of him, as an atom on its own. It is because of their exalted view of individualism that the Old Conservatives have detested centralized power and sought simply to free the individual from restraint. It is true that Felix Morley does put forward some communitarian sentiments in his talk about social democracy, but it is also true that his talk is vague and without content.

The New Conservative, however, is not prepared merely to accept the postulates of nineteenth-century liberalism on the subject of the individual. Having an overwhelming desire for Order and Orders he finds it necessary to put the individual in his place—a small town where he can be watched over by his betters and prevented from doing mischief. Kirk thus looks coldly at von Mises and his theory of free enterprise. He finds it good, of course, as a productive system and he gives no hint that he would do anything to harm the system one jot. But, as he says, and on this point we may agree with Kirk, the view of von Mises, and of Hayek too, leaves out love. Even worse, it leaves out traditionalism. And it postulates a rational man whom no right-thinking conservative can accept. "Once supernatural and traditional sanctions are dissolved, economic self-interest is ridicuolusly inadequate to hold an economic system together."[15]

The search for community, therefore, leads Kirk to put for-

---

[15] Kirk, *A Program for Conservatives,* p. 147.

ward the views of Wilhelm Röpke, an economist, contributor to
Modern Age, and advocate of a decentralized community
economy. Kirk puts forward his views as a middle ground between individualism and mass collectivism since they aim at
preserving a *laissez-faire* economy and community, too. The
method Röpke would use is simply to reduce the scale of economic life, to decentralize. In this way scope would be given to
peasants, artisans, small traders, small and medium-sized businessmen, and "trusty" leaders of the community. Having accomplished such a reduction of scale Kirk thinks that "we might
be as well balanced . . . as is Switzerland." Indeed, Switzerland
is not merely a dream for Kirk as it is for W. H. Chamberlin; it
is proof that such a program can be realized.

Would such a system be the *laissez-faire* system in new form?
Oddly, Kirk is quite reluctant to turn his back on the nineteenth-
century liberal and his individualistic *laissez-faire* ideas. He
claims that what he and Röpke envisage would be an "elevated
laissez-faire" which would create a society of autonomous
groups in which the basic unit would be church, family, guild
or union, local community, school, university—in fact all voluntary associations which "combine freedom with love. . . ." But
it is important to realize that this community existence would
indeed be an elevated one. It would be elevated by those
"trusty" leaders, those natural aristocrats who would keep the
whole community nicely under control. It would be nicely
under control because the object of the whole operation would
be

. . . not to reinstate a rule of force, but instead to venerate afresh
order, coherence, authority, and hierarchy, established by prescription and consent.[16]

[16] *Ibid.*, p. 151.

Gopher Prairie was a howling wilderness of freedom compared to this scheme.

Although Kirk's vision of a small-town paradise has richer overtones than Morley's dry concept of social democracy, its net effect on the national political system would be about the same. The object of such a vision is to defeat the French Revolution, Kirk tells us ("The work of the French Revolution must be undone. . . ."), to liquidate that old devil Rousseau and his totalitarian democracy. One example of totalitarian democracy which would be liquidated might be mentioned—the social security system. And it is interesting to note that in Kirk's mind the only group in America today that seems to have a sense of what the issue is all about is the medical profession in its ever-glorious fight against socialized medicine. The trade unions, who should be in the forefront of the Back-to-Main-Street movement, have missed the point altogether.

Thus we see that for all his fancy phrases, Kirk really does not differ significantly in respect to questions of community, individualism, political democracy, and centralization from Messrs. Chamberlin, Morley, and Burnham.

RELIGION AND TRADITION

Now belief in the dogma of original sin has been prominent in the system of every great conservative thinker. . . .

Yet there are significant differences in emphasis between Kirk, the New Conservative, and the Old Conservatives. In an attempt to create an ideology that is round, firm, and fully-packed, the New Conservatives like to deal with Man in all his various aspects. And what better approach to Man is there than religion? The ground of New Conservatism, the attempt to find a new basis for conservatism in America, is religion above and beyond all else because religion gives a "description" of the basic behavioral patterns of man. It provides the ultimate reasons for tying man down, for preventing him from indulging in freedom.

Since religion provides the assumptions on which Kirk creates his view of society, it permeates, as we have seen, all of his ideas on such matters as political systems, economics, democracy, aristocracy, and order. We have already, therefore, become acquainted with the ramifications of his religious thought, and the meaning it holds for those subjects. We know that his conservatism is one that leads to an undemocratic politics of Order. We are aware that this view is based on a distrust of man's potentialities—and we are grateful to Kirk for making explicit what other conservatives often refuse to admit either to themselves or to their readers.

Thus what Kirk finds so appealing in Disraeli, for example, is not only his attempt to restore a concept of a class society, but also his recognition of the divine character of the church as an immortal corporation independent of the state. As an immortal and independent corporation it can act as a guardian over both the state and the workers. What he finds appealing in J. F. Stephen is Stephen's belief that society needs religious sanctions in order to preserve itself and his belief that the state is, or should be, a religious establishment enforcing those sanctions. What he finds so appealing in his heroes, Babbitt and More, is their religious approach to the whole problem of man and society.

Babbitt believed that men must take on the yoke of a definite doctrine, that original sin must be revived and that democracy must recognize the leadership of those who have the inner light. As Babbitt put it, the proper question to ask in politics is: do men have souls? More thought along the same lines.

Things of the moment were of small consequence; indeed one of the awful aspects of pragmatism was that it yielded itself to the ceaseless flow. Instead one must get out of that ceaseless flow by belief in the supernatural. Hence his conclusion that one must get the fear of God back into politics, that religion is an alleviator of discontent and a brake on innovation.

Needless to say Kirk also sees John Henry Newman and Orestes Brownson in glowing colors as conservatives with a religious key to man and society. Newman's significant conservative achievement was his rejection of the idea that science is knowledge. Kirk is also pleased to be able to point out that Newman subjected his own reasoning to correction by authority, and that he fought against individual judgment. True education, in Kirk's interpretation of Newman, is "freedom to live within the compass of God's ordinances, not freedom to doubt or demolish." So much for the liberal critical intelligence. As for Brownson, he demonstrates to Kirk that free political institutions can be secure only when the people have a religious veneration. We shall not escape from the "deluge of change and perilous experiment until we recognize the principle of authority: God's authority. This cannot be apprehended without the Church." How such authoritarianism can be reconciled with free institutions is not, of course, a question that Kirk finds it necessary to ask.

Religion is of cardinal importance to the New Conservative not only because it shores up authority in the face of the disorderly many, but also because it provides a view of Man as a hopeless and perpetual sinner and the possessor of a fixed nature. It is those two attitudes that, more than any other, establish the absolute necessity of conservatism. Once they are accepted there is no place to rest short of conservatism.

Kirk is in no doubt as to the facts of the case.

The thinking conservative knows that the outward signs of disorder, personal or social, very often are no more than the symptoms of an inner ravaging sickness, not to be put down by ointments and cosmetics. He is inclined to look for the real causes of our troubles in the heart of man—in our ancient proclivity toward sin, in a loneliness of spirit that conjures up devils, in twisted historical roots beneath the parched ground of modern existence, in venerable impulses of human nature which, when frustrated, make our life one long lingering death. He knows, moreover, that the task for the prudent counsellor and the prudent statesman is to make life tolerable, not to make it perfect: there is something in the constitution of humanity that cannot be satisfied with the poor things of earth, and so what we ought to teach ourselves is honorable resignation, not frantic indignation. He knows, with Sir Henry Maine, that in the course of history nearly everything seems to have been tried, and that nothing has ever worked really well. He recognizes, with Burke, the wisdom of the Schoolmen of the fourteenth century: for they, detecting more in man than mind, distinguished from the intellect the *heart*, or will, that complex of impulses, held together by a mysterious power that is of ourselves and yet out of ourselves, able often to overrule our intellect, whether for good or evil.[17]

In the light of such an attitude, fooling around with such simple-minded gimmicks as social security is indeed a fatuous effort. If this view of man is accepted, to seek one's proper place in the social order, to sink into it with a sigh of relief, and let one's betters take on the worries of a fruitless endeavor (but if it is fruitless why do they do it? Is there something after all to be gained from pushing people around?) seems to be the only real form of existence. Indeed, passivity is then a positive emotional relief after the tension of hopelessly trying to better one's self and mankind. Passivity is a great good because Passive Man cannot be taken in by the Evil One, who has probably spread the idea of improvement and progress just to make victims of us

[17] Kirk, *Ibid.*, p. 81.

all. Kirk hints strongly at that possibility when he says that the idea of

... earthly perfection is a delusion, and in our time, quite possibly, a notion employed by the power of Evil to crush Good by the instrument of a pseudo-good.[18]

The implications of this conservative pessimism are obvious.

Conservative thinkers believe that man is corrupt, that his appetites need restraint, that the forces of custom, authority, and government, as well as moral discipline, are required to keep sin in check.[19]

Of all the justifications for conservatism this conviction of the sinful nature of man—because it is such an easy and thoughtless conviction—is the most important. It is an easy conviction because those men of ill-will, and they are many, who wish to convince themselves that The Other is bad can find much in the history of the twentieth century with which to convince themselves. It is a thoughtless conviction because sin is confused with what the observer happens personally to dislike about The Other. There is no sin like someone else's sin.

To a conservative, however, the problem of whether or not he is confusing other people's sin with his own does not arise because he is convinced that sin is an inherent part of the fixed nature of Man. The concept of man as fixed, for ever and ever, is fundamental to the thinking of the conservative because it enables him to find a stable point of reference in a world of ceaseless flux. He hates that ceaseless flux more than he hates anything else, and in fact conservatism is mainly an attempt to combat flux and to bring a stop to change. In that attempt he searches for the eternal, for eternal principles, for an eternal

[18] Kirk, *Ibid.*, p. 99.
[19] Kirk, *The Conservative Mind*, p. 212.

society, for an eternal Man who will always be and will cease becoming. This search for eternal being naturally finds most of its support in religion, which is also, it should be recalled, concerned with the eternal. If religion can show what Man is rather than what he might become but will not remain, as the disorderly liberal does, that achievement in itself will make religion a necessity to the good conservative.

As Kirk puts it:

Real harmony with the natural law is attained through adapting society to the model which eternal nature, physical and spiritual, sets before us—not by demanding radical alteration. . . . We are part of an eternal nature which holds all things in their places.[20]

"All things in their places"—if the conservative could only prove the truth of that statement for once and for all!

Kirk's search for the fixed nature of Man combines Burke and religion in a nice blend. Burke, he tells us, said that men do not make laws but instead simply ratify, or distort, the laws of God. There is such a thing as natural law; it is the law of God, not the law of nature that the perverse eighteenth century thought it had discovered. The true commandments are found in history, which, it seems, is not just a jumble of man's deeds and misdeeds but rather represents the "eternal enactments of Divine authority." Myth, fable and prejudice are also guides to this natural law, which will unveil the fixed nature of man. Kirk refers to "the *true* natural man . . ." *[sic!]*. What is the "true" natural man? Why, he is obviously Man not as he obeys his own mind but as he obeys the commands of God. Burke knew that fact when he said "Obey the Divine Design." Man may, of course, disobey the "Divine Design," but the Divine has also

[20] *Ibid.*, p. 56.

allowed for that contingency too, since disobedience is what sin is. Man may or not obey Divinity, but he is not free in the sense that he can make his own nature. That nature is made for him as a fixed part of a fixed natural law. There is a natural law and though we may or may not recognize its existence, we have no choice about being subject to it. What man is can be seen in what history, custom, and prescription say he is; what he *has been* is what he will *always* be.

Since Man is a scoundrel, and a perpetual scoundrel to boot, it is easy to see—or at least it is easy for Kirk to see—how important these religious insights are for America today. America, in Kirk's view, is (a) expansive, (b) complacent, (c) sensual, (d) bored, (e) lacking "that sturdy self-sufficiency its founders designed," (f) schooled but uneducated, (g) idle but not leisurely. It is obviously a nation in need of some kind of outside help, and it is quite clear that help will not come from liberals and/or sociologists. (Kirk considers them both to be the same thing since they are both radical in their views; i.e., lacking in veneration.) Help will come from religion since religion can restore the "real ends for which we have been joined in society. . . ." No people can live virtuously and industriously until a religious veneration permeates all their activities and lives, and until their society is permeated with religion. Kirk's prescription is "reverence for God and duty toward man and contentment in one's own calling. . . ." Certainly social planning will not provide any solutions to our many ills for all social planning does with its "fuss and pomp" is to thwart "the deep-seated human appetite for rest, permanence, assurance that things will be with a man as they were with his father."

When Kirk tries to bring religion back into the affairs of society it should be made clear that he does not mean that there should be a Christian political party of one kind or another. He means instead something much more dangerous, that we should "infuse Christian faith into politics." And what does the Christian faith in politics mean? Kirk tells us quite plainly.

Every man imbued with the spirit of veneration, acknowledging the presence of a Power superior to human will and reason, inclines in the hour of decision toward the cause of prescription.[21]

Religion and tradition are fused, for Kirk, into a whole which is the heart of conservative ideology. The two concepts act on each other so that religion is prescription, tradition, and tradition is veneration, religion. But they also permeate, as we have seen, all the other aspects of conservatism. Yet tradition is a separate conservative value in its own right, and as such demonstrates the deep-seated conservative appetite for rest, permanence, assurance that things will be with a man as they were with his father. Tradition is the means by which that stability is achieved, and is achieved for always. For tradition is a thing, a completed thing, which is real because it is not a becoming true but because it has been true and therefore is complete and fixed in itself. Tradition is full of itself and has no emptiness in it; it is a thing, therefore, to which unstable man can return as a sure guide just because it is complete. Tradition cannot contain the unexpected and surprising because all of it can be known; man can fasten himself to it; and, best of all, it will always be there, it will never disappear, because it is dead and therefore cannot change through a process of becoming. Tradition in the sphere of society is Sartre's In-itself, the condition to which all men aspire—but particularly conservatives.

Tradition, according to Kirk, means prejudice and prescription. That-which-has-been-long-established obtains a "just" presumption in its favor; a "tradition-directed man puts his trust,

[21] Kirk, *Program for Conservatives*, p. 100.

for the chief things of life, in Authority."[22] But perhaps the meaning of tradition can best be explained by the remarks of a conservative high in Kirk's list of Top Conservatives. John Randolph may not have been one of America's great philosophers but he knew perhaps better than anyone else what tradition really means when he said that it is "always unwise—yes—highly unwise, to disturb a thing that was at rest."[23] He should know, because the South of his time was, according to Kirk, the outstanding representative of conservatism in American history; since 1865 conservatism has never recovered the fine, free Southern air of success that it had before that year. We have seen how all conservatives have their own particular Golden Age; Kirk's Golden Age, the age during which he would prefer to have lived, is the American South as it existed in the time of Randolph.

But Kirk does not live then, and he must therefore face the difficult task of explaining to Americans today that tradition (and hence conservatism) is good for them, and that it will give them the solution to their problems. Kirk has told us that conservatives must be audacious and one can see what he means. One can especially see what he means when he admits that by 1914 "true conservatism" was nearly "extinct" in the United States and that "change was preferred to continuity." That fact might make some people feel that tradition is not really necessary in the United States, or at least that it is important to find out whether or not the American preference for change over continuity is not based on good reasons. But such doubts are a betrayal of ideology, and true to type Kirk does

[22] *Ibid.*, p. 110.
[23] Kirk, *The Conservative Mind*, p. 145.

not even consider such possibilities. What America needs now
is what all peoples have always needed, a tradition to fall back
upon, one to which the American people can attach themselves
so as to avoid the issues that change insists on raising.

Kirk attempts to tell us what tradition can do for modern
society by explaining that the problems that modern society—
and the United States especially—faces can best be met by a
belief in tradition as such. We have seen some of the specific
and particular traditions to which Kirk would have us return;
e.g., small-town life. But tradition as a way of life is of even
greater importance to conservatism.

What are the problems of modern society and how would
tradition solve them? They are the problems of social boredom,
of the heart, and of tradition itself, i.e., of change as a destroyer
of tradition.

Social boredom, social fatigue, comes, in Kirk's view, from a
pursuit of sensual and material pleasure to the exclusion of
other ends. The problem arises when the masses fall, as they
are bound to do, into a condition of lethargy through a surfeit
of goods. Then the longing for continuity disappears. Having
stated that general point of view, Kirk goes on to attack David
Riesman's *The Lonely Crowd* and to lay his claim for tradition
as the solvent of boredom. Riesman misses the point, we are
told, when he equates a high birth rate and a tradition-directed
society for he fails to ask why the two go together and why the
birth rate falls when the other-directed society comes upon
the scene. Since Kirk is not encumbered with the problems of
evidence or analysis, sociological or any other kind, he is able
to rise superior—in his estimation—to Riesman and give us the
answer. The answer is that the tradition-directed person thinks
life is worth living.

The tradition-directed person is not bored, for he feels himself to be a part of an immortal community and essence, and so put into this world for a purpose. . . .[24]

The answer is simple, and only Riesman's deplorable scientific instinct prevents him from seeing it. We must restore among men the "old objects of existence," namely religion, concepts of honor, self-reliance, knowledge of the "eternal contract of society." One other requirement besides religious veneration and all that is necessary if social boredom is to be defeated. There must be leisure not for the mases but for those who deserve it; i.e., "lofty minds" and those who inherit money. Further, he points out that it is impossible to be leisurely, "to find purpose in contemplation," unless one believes "that there is an order more than material. . . ."[25]—a statement that is, as usual, taken as one of those profound truths known only to those in touch with the eternal.

The attack on David Riesman is not the result of just an accidental peeve on the part of Kirk. He deplores Riesman not only because Riesman does not understand the ups and downs of the birth rate but also because he is all head and no heart; i.e., he sees the possibility of solving social problems on the basis of reason rather than tradition or religion—an accusation which will probably not surprise Riesman. Indeed, Riesman to Kirk's horror sees solutions coming from people who have severed themselves from all traditional values. But the heart, or at least Kirk's heart, says No. Mere planning and thought will not solve social problems; they can only be solved by an elite guided in part by the wisdom of their ancestors and in part by a Power outside of themselves. Social planning is the old fallacy of believing in the intellect, Kirk sighs, as he puts aside Riesman and all others foolish enough to believe in the human mind. A

[24] Kirk, *A Program for Conservatives*, p. 113.
[25] Cf. *Ibid.*, ch. V.

true and proper society should reject planning in the sense of innovating to meet new problems, and rely instead on Burke's concept of an eternal contract between those living, dead, and unborn and on "a conscious belief in the value of tradition." Resting on tradition will rid America of the uncertainty which comes from the individual taking thought on public policy.

Once most men should break the eternal contract, they would be thrown on the meagre resources of private judgment, having run recklessly through the bank and capital that is the wisdom of our ancestors.[26]

It is worth noting that included in the category of private judgment is scientific knowledge, for science is disrespectful—most disrespectful—of tradition, not to mention the eternal contract. Private judgment, then, is a snare of the devil, for it places the head above the heart; i.e., it may lead to a social planning that would violate America's obligations to its ancestors and future generations. America, indeed, must turn to ancestor worship.

Conservatism cannot exist anywhere without reverence for dead generations.[27]

The real meaning of the tradition and the past to Kirk is not that it is some pretty thing that represents the good old days. In postulating a severer and more metaphysical concept of tradition he goes well beyond the Old Conservatives. Kirk enables us to fathom the real meaning of tradition to conservatism. Tradition to a conservative such as Kirk is the way human essence can be grasped. Kirk, like so many of this day and age, is bothered by the failure of the human being to connect with essence, to become a thing. He refuses to face that failure and he therefore

---

[26] *Ibid.,* p. 298.
[27] Kirk, *The Conservative Mind,* p. 219.

seeks refuge from it in a search for essence as embodied in tradition.

The conservative knows that he is a part of a great continuity and essence. . . .[28]

He triumphantly announces that there is an eternal order into which we can fit.

There is an order which holds all *things* in their places, Burke says: it is made for us and we are made for it. The reflective conservative, far from denying the existence of this eternal order, endeavors to ascertain its nature, and to find his place in it.[29]

So says Burke. So says Kirk. And so say all the people who cannot bear the thought that they have to make their own life and therefore must be responsible for it. It is because the liberal insists on making up human life as he goes along, on recognizing its man-made, artificial quality, its need to innovate and create new things, and insists on acknowledging the unfinished, un-known quality of life—even worse, glorying in it—that Kirk hates (the word is not too strong) the liberal as much as he does. In the case of Burke this hate spilled over into the trembling fear that led him to give orders that he be buried secretly for fear the Jacobins would destroy his bones. But with Kirk it is only hate. He hates Emerson, who, "believing, like Rousseau, in the supremacy of benevolent instincts, . . . was hot for discarding all the old ways of society so that ground might be cleared for new edifices of emotion. . . ."

Emerson, it seems, never admitted the idea of sin into his philosophy. Kirk hates Bentham for being the great innovator, for his refusal to admit that Scott was right when he talked of

---

[28] Kirk, *A Program for Conservatives*, p. 47.
[29] *Ibid.*, p. 50. Italics added.

the contentment that might come from a happy union of cottage, castle, and piety, and who therefore insisted on legal reform according to rational principles. He hates John Stuart Mill, who was a secularist and therefore believed that man would have to solve his own problems by rational planning. And above all he hates John Dewey, the conservatives' own and very special devil. Dewey said, Kirk tells us, that the "past is trash" [Kirk's paraphrase]; his thought included every radicalism since 1789; his "destructive intellectual compound" appealed to the semieducated, was "intensely flattering to the presumptuousness of the modern mind," and was "a mirror of twentieth-century discontent" which gave a "philosophic mask" to the "imperialistic craving of America and the twentieth century." The crime of Dewey, for Kirk, was that he killed veneration; "veneration was dead in Dewey's universe."[30]

Indeed it was, a typical instance of liberal irresponsibility. Their sinfulness—and even if liberals have no place for sin in their system of thought they are nevertheless capable of it—is clearly revealed in the liberal liking for rational social plans. It is also revealed in the liberal liking for facts. The nineteenth-century liberal, Kirk tells us with an awful solemnity,

went in for facts, adorning the particular, however isolated, almost in defiance of the Decalogue.[31]

The liberal wants to do away with mystery and substitute for it—science! But the liberal will get his due, for "our time [is] sick nigh unto death of utilitarianism and literalness. . . ." One is not sure what the term literalness means, but the possibility that our time—or at least the past decade of our time—has had too much mystery and not enough utilitarianism is not one which would occur to Kirk.

[30] Kirk, *The Conservative Mind*, pp. 365-6.
[31] *Ibid.*, p. 229.

CHANGE AND INNOVATION

"People Can Be Virtuous Only In a Certain Routine."

Given Kirk's particular brand of conservatism and the peculiar cast of his thought, what possibility is there in his ideology for change and innovation? Is it as true with Kirk as it is with the Old Conservatives, stuck as they are with their Garden of Eden, that change is not a feasible phenomenon? In the smooth façade that conservatism presents to the strife of this world, is there a crack through which change can penetrate, through which the unknown can enter this enclosed world? The question is an important one, because one of the features of the New Conservatism that has attracted attention and should attract attention, is the possibility that it is a conservatism that can meet the problem of change and can encompass the unexpected. If such were the case, then there would truly be a *new* conservatism. There would be a progressive conservatism that could solve what is in fact a very real problem of social existence, the problem of uniting change and tradition so that both retain their vitality and contribute to each other and yet are not crushed out of existence by each other. Certainly no society can ignore that problem and conservatism should have something important to contribute to it because of its special concern for tradition. Old Conservatism fails completely on this question. What of Kirk's New Conservatism?

On the face of it New Conservatism is well equipped to deal with this problem. For one thing it is, ironically, less traditional, in America at least, than Old Conservatism and therefore can look at questions anew. Further, it came into being after World War II, when change as a fact of American life was so apparent that it would seem to have been almost impossible for an ideology not to have considered what role change must play in

society. But most important, the New Conservatives were not
so committed to a particular past as the Old; they were not so
determined to restore a particular Garden of Eden. In fact a
case could be made out that they were anti-Garden of Eden.
The New Conservatives, believing so strongly in the sinfulness
of man, could not have quite the same wistful hope as the Old
Conservatives that a restoration was feasible. They are, in other
words, blacker pessimists. Thus they might well try to face
this world, the one they live in now, and try to deal with its
problems rather than just pointing out how far it had fallen
from grace (although they would, of course, do that too). They
might well get to work in the world in which they exist because there is nothing else they can do. Pessimism is always
supposed to give a greater sense of realism. According to that
theory, the New Conservatives should be great realists indeed,
for it can be taken for granted that one attribute of realism is
the recognition of the existence of a real world in which change
is a fact.

There was good reason, then, to think that the New Conservatives might themselves be an innovation, if one may say so,
that they might be progressive conservatives. Unfortunately,
the conservative will be glad to know, such a thought was just
another example of the fatuous optimism of the liberal. Kirk's
brand of New Conservatism, and his is the most important
brand today, is incapable of coming to terms with change. It is
no better equipped to deal with change than is the old brand.
The threat of change is as awful and violent to Kirk's concept of
what life should be as it is to any previous form of conservatism.
Indeed, it is even more so, because the fears that Kirk has of
man are so great that he becomes even more rigid with hyste-
ria than the Old Conservatives, who have a certain relaxed,
the-worst-has-happened-so-let's-get-the-best-out-of-life air about

them. Kirk is a strenuous young man. The trouble with conservatives in his view is exactly that they have been too relaxed, too tolerant of sin. In the light of his general approach to man's troubles it would be difficult indeed for Kirk to admit that change could be a useful and good thing. For change means freedom and freedom only increases the possibility of sin and destruction of tradition. It was that devilish relaxation—is not relaxation the work of the devil?—that ruined John Quincy Adams as a conservative. He represents the sad degeneration that takes place if the conservative admits even the possibility of change, for John Quincy Adams believed in progress, in the possibility of human improvement. He was, in short, an innovator. He flirted with radicals. Such, in Kirk's view, is what happens when you relax.

Kirk's view of change is founded on his dislike and distrust of reason. There is no such thing, he feels sure, as a rational citizen. The nineteenth-century liberal was deluded when he thought that schooling would lead to the triumph of reason and decency. The public as a rational thinking machine will not save us in this day and age, or for that matter in any day and age. "Most men cannot possibly govern their lives according to the scanty stock of private reason which is theirs."[32] Hence it follows, just as Burke says, that reason is not the least bit useful in making change tolerable. That is, it is not possible to think out ahead what the consequences will be of a change, since man cannot think. It is all so clear. As Burke says, even if reason shows an innovation to be correct, the presumption is to the contrary. Anyway, Burke says—again—it may be better to continue with the errors of the past than to break radically with custom, because custom is good in and of itself. But can the rationality of science provide the means of orderly change?

[32] Kirk, *A Program for Conservatives*, p. 238.

Kirk cannot admit that possibility, since to admit the validity of science would be to destroy the need and function of tradition at one blow. Thus Kirk must see science not as a means of change but as bringing the threat of change. And thus science is to be brought to heel by being subordinated to religion.

Natural science, like the other high pursuits of life, has its traditional ends. . . . The end of science, says Paracelsus, is to teach the fear of God, through knowledge of God's handiwork. . . .[33]

Science today pursues power, Kirk complains. When he talks about science in these terms we know that he not only fears change but cannot tolerate it at all. Science is the main, indeed the only, hope of dealing with change, and a rejection of science is a deliberate effort to stop change. Kirk is honest at least to this extent, that he demonstrates to us that change is incompatible with conservatism as an ideology.

But whatever is true of conservatism as a system, it is also true that in practice some men are rational; Burke, for example, was an excellent reasoner. The problem of change is not solved simply by saying that the average man is a dolt unable to take care of himself since the elite few presumably could take change under their exclusive control and do well with it. Further, there is the undeniable fact that change does exist. What is one to do with this worm in the heart of tradition? Did not even Burke say that change was a law of society?

Change cannot be ignored. But it had better be approached with great and canny wariness. Tradition, we have seen, is one of the two cornerstones to Kirk's thought. Can change be allowed to disrupt it? The answer given by Burke-Kirk is that the "greatest of prudence" is required to accomodate tradition to

[33] *Ibid.*, p. 118.

the demands of new times. Change may be a law of society but it must be allowed to exist only as "a process of renewal." It must be only a means of preserving what already exists. Burke said that beneficial change is the Providential instrument for social preservation: change can be, must be, a conservative force. Hence it should not touch organic matters in society; those things which exist should continue to exist in their fundamentals. "Radical innovation," says Burke-Kirk, "would cut us off from our past, destroying the immemorial bonds that join generation to generation; they would leave us isolated from memory and from aspiration; and in that condition we would sink to the level of beasts." Further, let there be no dilly-dallying with the idea that even if the elite put their minds to it change should become a conscious thing.

> Our part is to patch and polish the old order of things. . . . By and large, change is a process independent of conscious human endeavor, *if it is beneficial change.* Human reason and speculation can assist in the adjustment of the old order to new things if they are employed in a spirit of reverence, awake to their own fallibility.[34]

One of the traits and functions of a conservative elite, in other words, is to admit that it cannot do anything.

What, then, is progress? It is certainly not progress as it exists in the mind of a liberal. Progress to Kirk is keeping change to a minimum. Progress is preventing change from disrupting tradition, what exists. It is, in other words, the admission that change exists only as a means of preserving what already exists; i.e., to prevent change!

Progress, beneficent change, is the work of men with a sense of continuity, who look forward to posterity out of love for the legacy

---

[34] Kirk, *The Conservative Mind,* p. 40; cf. pp. 33-42. (Emphasis added).

of their ancestors and the dictates of an authority more than human. The man who truly understands the past does not detest all change; on the contrary, he welcomes change, as the means of renewing society; but he knows how to keep change in a continuous train. . . .[35]

That one might think of posterity for its own sake and not for the sake of one's own ancestors is not an idea likely to occur to Kirk—or indeed, to Burke.

Is such an effort to make change no-change a serious attempt to meet the problem that society faces, a serious attempt to meet the problem that change poses for conservative values, for tradition? It is certainly the latter, for it is apparent that, despite the bow to the fact of change, Kirk would make change impotent, would prevent it from either disturbing tradition as a belief in itself or any of the other values of the conservative. By making change into no-change, Kirk's New Conservatism shows us that we can live and still be conservative, that we can eat our cake and have it too, and that change need not keep us awake at night. For tradition will not be destroyed; change can be tamed.

Kirk, however, does even better than show that tradition will win. He provides a rationale for the belief that it is impossible to reform, and shows that it is incorrect to include that particular change known as reform under the rubric of beneficial change. That possibility was one which opened up to conservatives as soon as they admitted that change existed as a fact. If change exists, then is not beneficient change indistinguishable from reform? Does "renewing society" mean the same thing as reform? The answers are No, not only because acceptance of reform also means acceptance of man's ability to use rationality to guide change, an idea, as we have seen, that Kirk rejects.

[35] Kirk, *A Program for Conservatives*, p. 301.

Beneficent change is fundamentally and qualitatively distinct from reform for another reason. It cannot be manufactured; it is something which grows. Hence society can cure its problems only by a natural and providential process.

Kirk thus grants that problems arise which may call for change, but he claims that that change is best left to Providence. However, even he has to break down and admit that occasionally men have to act. Still, they must not reform. The conservative instead will keep change in the pattern of traditional life, in "continuous train." Such was the great aim, in Kirk's eyes, of conservatism in the nineteenth century; although it fought against both democracy and industrialism yet it was able to take the changes that those two pernicious forces brought and contain them to a degree at least. The glory of conservatism is that it prevents change as such from having an impact on the basic qualities of society. Such an achievement is not only its glory; it is its function. The role of the conservative is to prevent innovation from overcoming prescriptive truth, to lead the waters of novelty into the canals of custom.

The conservatives have a charming construct for their use; they at least are well provided for by Kirk. But what of the rest of us? To what extent is this theory of change-as-not-change of any relevance to today's problems? Leaving aside the logical difficulties of the idea that change can be made no-change, none of which Kirk—or indeed Burke—even looks at, does such a theory help the suffering Many whom Kirk proposes to save? Such a question in its larger aspects is best left to the end of this book, but it is useful to consider whether Kirk thinks that the conservative theory of change bears on present-day problems in Britain and America.

True to his prediliction for generalities and his interest in other people's sin, the conservative spends little time on those problems. But he does drop a few hints. Thus Kirk tells us that in Britain the Conservative Party has been too enamoured of the idea of the inevitability of gradualness; now we know that even gradual change is not in the conservative canon. Yet he suggests that conservatives in Britain (and America) should propose a program of their own so that the radicals will not make all the running. What shall it be? (It is a difficult problem to draw up a proper program of conservatism for Britain since the fifth Marquess of Salisbury, "in some respects the most talented of Conservative leaders at present," is no longer influential in the Conservative Party.)

It is true that Kirk praises the "Industrial Charter" of the Conservative Party but he does not tell us why it should be praised. Thus the record of the British Conservative Party is not very good in his eyes. It has not, for example, restored university seats. Nor has it erected fundamental barriers against confiscation, or, in lieu of that policy, established a "system of attaching greater electoral weight to certain classes of property. . . ." Nor have British conservatives seen that mere efficiency in housing schemes is not important if most people continue to live in state-subsidized houses (Kirk calls them "state-subsidized tenements"). Such a program may be excellent as a work of charity, but "the reluctance of the present Conservative government to draw a clear distinction between assistance to the really poor and the collectivization of a whole people is one of their most striking failures of nerve or imagination."

We begin to see what Kirk means by the conservative idea of bringing change into the traditional structure of society. For he concludes by telling us that "nearly all the venerable institutions" of British society still stand and that the upper classes, the Church and Britain's "hearty working classes, most of them suspicious of organic change, most of them still as deferential as Bagehot found them," provide the means of preserving "Burke's English oak."

Since America is noticeably short on oak, at least of the Burkean-Kirkean variety, it presents the picture of a deplorable collapse. Kirk's conservative theory of change is put to a stiff test in these United States. But he has a point to make to those Americans not too busy to listen. It is that American energy is in dire danger of becoming a revolutionary influence, appealing directly to cupidity, class envy, and "the itch for change." Not all is lost, however, for there is still hope that change in America might be encompassed within the constrictions of tradition. Americans have a "predominantly conservative cast of . . . mind." We should pay attention to that conservative cast of mind.

We are not merely the pawns of impersonal historical influences; we have it in our power to preserve the best in our old institutions and in our old opinions, even in this era of vertiginous change; and we will do well, I think, if we endeavor to govern ourselves, in the age that is dawning, by the prescriptive values in American character which have become almost our second nature.[36]

So it seems after all that in America, too, change is to be no-change.

Kirk on change is not satisfactory. He misses a great chance to bring conservatism face to face with the problem that change presents. Surely conservatism is not incapable of meeting the problem? Perhaps it is. But whatever the case with conservatism in general—and we shall discuss that question below—it is clear that Kirk is incapable of facing the problem of change and for a very good reason.

The reason is that change is freedom. And freedom is not

[36] Kirk, *Ibid.*, p. 44.

only the new but also the unknown. Kirk, like almost all conservatives, flees freedom in search of fixity and the fixed society. His dislike of change and his inability to face up to its meaning or consequence is based in part on a very evident and real liking for tradition, for old houses, "ben-and-buts," and all that. He is against change, therefore, because it threatens—must threaten—his values. This love of what is old is one side of the coin. But every coin has two sides and one need not try to decide which is the more important side, a liking for tradition or a fear of change qua change. The two cannot be separated. Yet it is important to emphasize the fear of change qua change simply because it is the side that the Kirks and the Burkes of this world so seldom wish to look at themselves. They love to talk about their efforts to save traditional ways from the brutality of change. Yet they cling to the last shreds of tradition as their only hope in a confused world because they fear the very fact and existence of change. They would prefer change not to be. And they use tradition, and insist on obedience to tradition, as a way of stopping it from being. In that way they are able to disguise from themselves and others the depth of the repulsion they feel for that which is new, for innovation, and the slavishness of their search for the fixed.

It is not only tradition that is used as a disguise. The belief in an "eternal contract," in the fixed nature of man, and indeed the whole paraphernalia of religion, are mobilized to justify their refusal of change. If there is an eternal order—and conveniently the existence of such an order cannot be proved and therefore can be glibly assumed—then fixity is a fact. Whatever kind of a mess man may make here of his life, fixed and eternal principles nevertheless exist. Thus change can be seen as merely a ripple on a deep and unchanging ocean. And, thus, since it is only a ripple, and even if it is sometimes a large wave, it can be ignored as beside the point, the point being eternal things and ideas. In this mode of existence the conservative does not try to stop change. He simply ignores it as not being of importance.

If tradition/eternal principles are one side of the coin and if fear of change qua change is the other side, then what does the coin itself signify? It signifies the end of freedom. Without change there can be no freedom, for freedom is the right and ability to make something new exist, to innovate. No one is free if he has no alternatives and can only do the same things over and over again. Repetitive effort is exactly the nature of traditional society; it is exactly the nature of the society the conservatives would have us live in. Man is indeed condemned to be free, but he is condemned to be free, Sartre points out, because of the very nature of man—that he is not a fixed quality. It is the aim and object of the conservatives to make him precisely that, to make him a fixed quality by ensnaring him in eternity, in the past. It seeks—nothing less—to negate his freedom.

The threat conservatism holds for freedom is its most dangerous aspect. Conservatives like to talk about their belief in real freedom and how important freedom is to them. While one may argue that their particular form of "real" freedom is not as productive as some other type of freedom, this argument is still on the level of agreement on the ends to be pursued. As such it is an argument that masks the real nature of conservatism, even to conservatives themselves, who like to believe their own clichés and who in fact do believe their own clichés, and who are therefore quite sincere if not very profound in their professions of affection for freedom. It must also be said that conservatism like all political ideologies can often in practice avoid the logical results of its system of ideas and live on its clichés in happy ignorance of what they really mean. But logic is still important, and it even has a nasty way of forcing men to behave in ways they least expected to behave.

The logic of conservatism leads one to ask: can conservatism and freedom co-exist? The conservative is not, of course, a totalitarian brute. But can he be expected to care for freedom and want freedom, and to develop and broaden freedom? One may go further: can he be expected to preserve freedom? It would hardly seem so since he neither cares for, wants, nor develops freedom. And why should he preserve freedom? Has he not just shown that men must avoid change and that conservatism is designed to avoid change? Since he has demonstrated that change is a terrifying thing, and must be avoided at all costs, the conservative is of necessity against freedom. In his confusion he may seek to avoid that conclusion but it exists, nevertheless, at the very heart of his doctrine. Logic, too, has a certain eternal quality about it.

It would seem at first glance that there is a paradox in the thought of Russell Kirk which is revealed by the titles of his two books on conservatism, *The Conservative Mind* and *A Program for Conservatives*. Is it possible for a conservative to have a program? Is it possible—in the sense, one hastens to add, of advocating rationality as a way of dealing with social problems—for a conservative to have a mind? Is not the whole burden of Kirk's thought, not to mention Burke, that conservatives cannot have a program in the sense that a program is a plan for change, i.e., innovation, in the future? Surely one does not need a program if one is merely going to repeat what has already been done? A program implies planning for the unknown, not the known. Is not the burden of Kirk's two books the idea that conservatives do not believe in the mind as the means of

solving problems, since it is tradition and the higher powers
that must be relied upon and not the abstract mind working
unaided and without outside guides? Is there not an even
deeper paradox in the whole position taken by Kirk in that he
is adamant against change and yet proposes a society the attainment of which would mean a revolutionary act—even
though a backward one?

But such paradoxes exist only on the surface. We have already answered the claim made by so many opponents of conservatism that it is really a revolutionary dogma. The answer is
simply that such proposals may be revolutionary in the sense
of upsetting many established routines, values, and institutions
of present-day society but that it is not a revolution in the sense
that it involves the creation of new forms of social organization, in that it involves innovation. Since the word revolution
as it is applied to events in history and not to eternity includes
both aspects—although in abstract logic it could include just
one aspect—a proposal is not a revolutionary one if it confines
itself to just one of the aspects of revolution. But such distinctions are logic chopping, pieces of abstract reasoning themselves, and are of little consequence. If anyone wishes to consider conservatives as revolutionary they may do so: it matters
not.

It matters not because whatever the conservative may be in
abstract theory, in reality he is stuck on dead center. He is
stuck on dead center for two reasons. First, because of the sheer
difficulty in going back, in making even half-a-revolution. The
type of society suggested by the conservative would involve so
much upset that it is more impracticable than radicalism. It is
not likely that Kirk's program will really become a party plat-
form, not even for the Conservative Party of Great Britain. But
secondly, the conservatives are caught in a trap of their own
self-induced spasms of fear. The fact that they fear change so

much means that they themselves are incapable of taking the action necessary to jerk society out of the ways to which it is now accustomed, no matter how much they disapprove of those ways. In this sense the conservative prevents himself from being a revolutionary, from taking action to realize his heart's desire. Hence the peculiar note of frustration and bitterness which one hears.

Conservatism is a peculiarly self-stultifying doctrine, a fact that can be seen in an Eisenhower administration which detested the large welfare state it had to administer but could not find the courage to dismantle it simply because such an action would open the floodgates to all sorts of possibilities. The conservative is not a revolutionist. But there can be no doubt that his proposals suggest change on a large scale, a fact that renders him impotent. He cannot for the life of him figure out how to change by going backwards and yet not change. It is, one must admit, a difficult problem.

Yet conservatism is more than an exercise in frustration. It may not be able to do anything but stand still with a giddy feeling on dead center, but that particular form of stasis, although far different from the form of stasis of which Conservatives dream, has its own peculiar significance.

Conservatism may not be able to realize its ideal in the here and now, or even, for all one knows, in the eternal there and then, but it can postulate social values that in themselves can have effects in the here and now. And it does. Granted that the conservative struggle against the French Revolution is somewhat out of date and excites little interest in the average newspaper-reading public today; granted that there is something odd and even pitiful about the conservative effort to fabricate a tradition; granted that a belief in the fixed nature of man and society is not susceptible to scientific verification—not that that detail would bother the conservative; granted all those points and many more, it is nevertheless true that conservative values, whether taken singly or as a group, can and do have relevance to the society of today. Relevance, that is, in the sense that they can be believed by the citizen of today.

Is the idea of tradition as Kirk states it too extreme for anyone to take seriously? Perhaps it is as Kirk states it, but is it possible to deny that today there is a deep longing on the part of otherwise normal citizens for a tradition in which they can believe? Is that desire on the level of *kitsch*? Undoubtedly, but as a social and political fact *kitsch* can be potent beyond the weirdest dreams of the *kitsch*-makers of Madison Avenue. The search for an American tradition may or may not be vain but it can become a powerful force in American life. Whether it will overwhelm and obliterate the need, and the sense of need, for innovation cannot be answered. But who can deny today that this particular conservative value has invaded the body politic in America? And so it goes with most of the values we have discussed here. In fact, one might even agree with Kirk on one point, that as alienation grows in this society there will be an increased and even frenzied search for the security, the assurance, the *fixity*, that conservatism promises.

Conservatism has another source of influence and power to its credit. It may not be able to reach the land of its dreams. It may not be able to have every American weep for Marie Antoinette as Burke did and gird himself to fight the French Revolution as Kirk does. But it can prevent thought about the future by spreading the doctrine that the best way to face the future is to turn one's back on it. The belief that man should do nothing about the future because there is nothing he can do about it is the most vicious aspect of conservatism. The idea that one cannot take purposeful and correct and rational action for the future—even if there is no immediate crisis at hand —is one that is quite capable of passing from the somewhat feverish minds of the conservative ideologues to a whole nation. We know that the threat of that form of social paralysis is a real one because in fact it has at times come close to gripping America and Britain. Some may say it has done so. Is that threat the result of the books written by Kirk and other conservatives? It hardly seems likely. Does it represent the same conservative frame of mind as that represented and presented by Kirk? Yes, it does. Whatever the source, and it certainly is doubtful that Kirk is its source, social passivity is a perfect representation of what the conservative thinks about society. If society could only be quiet!

For these reasons the conservative syndrome, if James Burnham will allow the loan of his phrase, presented by the New Conservatives—and Kirk is the first, the greatest, and the most original of the New Conservatives—is of no small importance, for it is a collection of symptoms that can be found in the minds of many Americans today. The syndrome operates in a circle no one point of which is more important than any other. Sin: Lust for Power: Decentralization: Tradition: Aristocracy: Fixed Man: Eternal Law: Religion. These terms are the concepts with which the New Conservativism operates. Each one refers to the others and can be understood only in conjunction with the others. Taken as a whole the syndrome succeeds in doing what the Old Conservatism never did. It bases conservatism on a solid view of the nature of man in society, on the nature of man outside of society, and on the relation of both these concepts to the religious principle of eternal law.

And yet, is New Conservatism so different from the Old? The depth and scope, the stresses and strains, are different, but do we end in a different place after plowing our way through original sin and all that?

6. The New Conservatism of Clinton Rossiter

THE NEW CONSERVATISM of Russell Kirk and that of Professor Clinton Rossiter and Walter Lippmann are alike in fundamentals while differing in emphasis and temper. They agree in their attitudes toward man and his incorrigible propensity to sin, and they agree on the consequences of that desire, the need for a stiff social hierarchy, and the need to be sceptical of democracy and freedom. But Rossiter and Lippmann do not have the same torrid rock-and-roll desperation about them that Kirk has. They are both cool, detached, and aware of the historical realities and complexities of the world they live in. Therefore they struggle energetically to make their New Conservatism useful as well as logical.

Professor Rossiter is especially important for his strenuous attempt to bring his conservatism into line with the everyday realities of the United States in the 1950's, with the changes that the New Deal and modern statism have brought about. One of the oddest things about Russell Kirk, as we have seen, is that his New Conservatism is at least as far away from the normal experiences of mankind in the middle years of the twentieth century as Old Conservatism is. Kirk's ideas may be rousing stuff for his followers, but once having been roused they have a tendency to look bewildered about the next step. Kirk refuses to contemplate the fact that he cannot start all over with a clean slate. Rossiter, on the other hand, is thoroughly modern, thoroughly willing to come to grips with the facts of modern society. He is, it should be said now, a brilliant scholar in the field of American history and political science. Being aware of what society is really like, being aware, for example, that the presidency of the United States can hardly return to the position it held at the time of Hayes or Garfield without grievous danger to this nation, he desires above all else to bring conservatism into accord with the life of today. Indeed, it is precisely the attempt to accomplish that aim that *is* New Conservatism in the eyes of Rossiter. And one must agree to some considerable extent; if New Conservatism cannot develop ideas that comprehend the facts of society as it exists today, then it will not really be new. But if Rossiter poses the proper question, it still remains to be seen whether or not he answers it. Certainly, he goes as far as possible in making conservatism a modern up-to-date creed, one that might be *useful* to an American in the middle years of the twentieth century, and to the American nation in the middle of a foreign-policy crisis. If anyone can transform conservatism and present a modern new variety, Rossiter is the man to do it. But does he do it?

Walter Lippmann has one trait in common with Rossiter— a deep sense of historical reality—and another trait in common with Russell Kirk—a profound and even bitter pessimism. Before one can make such statements, it is, of course, necessary to say which Walter Lippmann one is talking about. His newspaper column is not named "Today and Tomorrow" for nothing; what Lippmann thinks today he may not necessarily think tomorrow. In his long career as a writer Lippmann has been all

over the lot. But whatever the vagaries of his personal development, in the 1950's he published a book that was thoroughly
New Conservative in character. *Essays in the Public Philosophy*
has much of Lippmann's drooping *fin de siècle* fatigue about it,
much of his pseudodetachment, but it reveals that the New
Conservative would solve the problem of disorder in our civilization, not by giving men more freedom, but by taking freedom
away from them. Lippmann sees modern Western society in
decline because it is a place of disorder. He would therefore
establish a public order that does not depend on the free decisions of men, but on a higher law, which is above men, which
is eternal and natural, and to which men must bow down. In
one sense Lippmann is the most significant of the New Conservatives of the 1950's, for his profoundly deep fears for our
society show how fear leads men to clutch at the idea of a fixed
law, a fixed society, and a fixed order to save themselves from
the consequence of freedom. Let us devote the present chapter
to a consideration of Rossiter's case for conservatism, and the
succeeding chapter to a discussion of Lippmann's "public
philosophy."

Professor Rossiter is a Cornell University political scientist
with a well-deserved reputation as a scholar and as a student
of American government and politics. We shall discuss some
of his political studies, especially the *American Presidency*
(1956) and *Parties and Politics in America* (1960) for the light
they throw on his conservative convictions. But before we do,
it is necessary to look at the way he sees American conservatism
and to understand what he is advocating. For Rossiter has not
only published works of scholarship but a book that is the attempt of an intellectual—and that Rossiter is an intellectual in

the best sense of the word cannot be doubted—to formulate a conservative belief that could be a significant ideology for the United States. His *Conservatism in America* (1955) is by all odds the best book on the subject in terms of quality. It attempts more than any other to come to grips with the reality not only of modern America but with the possible role of conservatism in modern America. It is a mighty effort by Rossiter to save conservatism for this life.

The task he sets for himself is not an easy one for many reasons, one of which is that his ambitions for conservatism are high, so much so that it is quite possible that in the end it has been left high-and-dry in a realm of purity but irrelevance. He tells us, for example, that "the new conservatism . . . will be conservative without being Conservative." He tells us, too, that the most difficult task of the new conservatives is to steer a middle course between ultraconservatism and the liberals, a task in which they will have to identify themselves with the moderate liberals in the "vital center." Yet he also tells us that conservatism must not be identified with the middle of the road.[1] One wonders exactly where one will find it after these subtle qualifications have been made. One wonders even more when he quite explicitly condemns American conservatism in the past for being so American, for having been individualistic and for having underrated the ability of government to do good, and then stresses that American conservatism must detach itself from a European ancestry in order to fit the unique qualities of American life.

It must be stated now that Rossiter is no word spinner and that he is in search of a new position for conservatism because

[1] Clinton Rossiter, *Conservatism in America* (1955), p. 300.

he believes that it is of great importance to America. Why is it of importance to America today? What hope is there that conservatism is *capable* of being important to America? Certainly Rossiter is in no doubt of the need for it.

I hope to make plain my conviction that a new conservatism is America's most urgent need for the years ahead.[2]

The reason Rossiter thinks conservatism is important to America today is two-fold. One is the quality and nature of conservatism itself, a matter that we will discuss as we study Rossiter's concepts. The other reason is that America today is in a conservative mood, a frame of mind that makes conditions favorable for conservatism. The reasons he gives for believing this do not seem to be complimentary to conservatism:

. . . our triumphs are soured with frustration, our prosperity with apprehension, our taste for peace with preparations for war. We are all more conservative than we were ten years ago. Even the liberal, the man with his heart in the future, speaks the language of tradition, loyalty, and preservation.[3]

Perhaps it is meant to be a compliment after all; we turn conservative when we are frightened. At any rate, Rossiter assumes a deep and significant conservative revival which is based not only on the fact that we have something to be conservative about—our well-being—but also on our need of a rest after all the frustrations and apprehensions of the past years. Further, the whole nature of American life is turning gradually, like some great prehistoric monster stirring in its sleep, to conservative ways. Our social structure is no longer as "plastic" as it was; there is an increased emphasis on status; the economy is matur-

[2] *Ibid.*, p. 246.
[3] *Ibid.*, p. 172.

ing and stabilizing; there is a decline in individualism and more interest in security; there is a diffusion of property and an air of nostalgia and satisfaction with our institutions; and finally the left wing in America has been discredited. Rossiter is happy to report:

For the first time in more than a hundred years, conditions are favorable for the flowering of conscious conservatism as a major force in American culture and politics.[4]

It is interesting to note the type of society which Rossiter considers to be conservative. It is one marked by smugness, torpidity, status, security, nostalgia.

What is the nature of the conservatism into which we will so soon be snugly fitted? Rossiter does not fudge the question. What he has to offer us he does not call an ideology because like all conservatives he brags about his love of mystery, of "things unseen," of the undefined. The conservative's desire to be fascinated by hocus-pocus is one of his most endearing features. But if Rossiter prefers not to use the word *ideology* it is of small matter, since the principles that he gives us amount to the same thing. Like any good ideology they encompass both man and society.

Let us turn to society first, for Rossiter's most original contribution is his treatment of the role which society should have in conservative thought. We have seen the Old Conservatives discuss this problem in a very tentative and most incompetent way; they had a glimmer of the idea that a problem existed but knew of no way to synthesize their ideas of nineteenth-century liberalism with their dim sense that society as well as man has

[4] *Ibid.*, p. 245.

rights and powers and existence. Kirk too has a glimmer of the problem, but he is so fascinated by his hell-fire metaphysics that he never gives time to the question. Rossiter, on the other hand, starts from the position that conservative ideology is unique because it has something special to say on the subject. He takes society and community seriously; one of the few conservatives to do so, he attempts nothing less than a basic reorientation and comes closer to it than anyone else.

Rossiter sees society as

. . . cellular. It is not an agglomeration of lonely individuals, but a grand, complex union of functional groups.[5]

He attempts to look upon society as having an existence in its own right, so to speak, an existence that does not dominate the concerns of the individual but is inseparable from the individual. His view of society is a pluralistic functional view, but also a view in which a balance of institutions must be welded into an ultimate unity. In such a society power of all kinds would be diffused within a system of operating equilibrium established by law, custom, and constitution. If his *desiderata* sound like one of Coleridge's pipe dreams they are nevertheless meant to be taken seriously because Rossiter believes that conservatism alone can give an answer to the pressing problems that face society today, and especially to the problem of lack of community. He postulates that conservatism, through its affection for groups and institutions, will transform a mass of men who have no ties to one another into a living community; in his view it is the role of the conservative to point out the importance and necessity of community as against the brutal individualism of the liberal. Hence the conservative must concern himself with such questions as the nature of the good society; the search for

[5] *Ibid.*, p. 27.

a balanced society as the only alternative to serfdom; the nature
and extent of class division in our society; the role of an aristocracy; the function and place of groups; and the methods of
diffusing power throughout state and society. All of these problems should be fused into one whole by the conservative's
unique concern for placing man in a community. For only he,
with his particular sense of the need to tie man down by giving
him a fixed place, can come to grips with the problem of community in modern society.

The answers Rossiter gives to these questions, and even the
questions themselves, will show us that while he has a very real
sense of society, lacking in other conservatives, the effect of
being a conservative is to drag him back to fundamentally the
same beliefs about society as those held by Kirk, and even to
some extent by the Old Conservatives.

What is the good society for Rossiter? It is the balanced
society. But what is a balanced society? We are never given a
definition except the statement that it does not consist of the
liberal harmony of interests. Perhaps the answers to his other
questions will clarify the problem. What kind of a class structure do we need? In brief, he thinks we need a class structure in
America of the type we already have, for the American system
could not operate as it does if it did not possess the status system " 'which it has been [its] good fortune to develop.' " [Rossi-
ter quoting W. Lloyd Warner] Should Americans have an
aristocracy? Yes, in some way we should, but it will have to be
squared with our ideals of democracy and the interests of the
middle class; we must also recognize that any aristocracy in
America will have to be composed of the business class. Hence
the conservative must take on the heavy task of showing how a
plutocracy can become an aristocracy. Rossiter does not tell us
how an aristocracy of business or any other kind can be squared

with democracy. What is the place of groups in his society? American conservatism has up to now mainly ignored man's need for community; therefore it should recognize the necessity of the organic and voluntary group. We are not told, however, how such groups can function in the face of modern mass society. Finally, how can power be diffused? Through regional and cultural pluralism, through new pluralism which would accept a mixed economy and countervailing power.

Such is Rossiter's general view of society. He does not detail his points, which is unfortunate, but as we have seen conservatives have a congenital liking for leaving everything up in the air. One cannot help but feel that if Rossiter, or someone on his side, would write a book on the conservative view of the realities of society and stop writing books on conservatism as a theory of society we should all be better off.[6] But they do not write such books for a very good reason; they have a positive antipathy to analysis, an antipathy based not just on a sort of dithering old-maidishness, but on the profound distrust—or fear —of analysis.

We will examine below the question of how and to what extent Rossiter differs in his view of society from other conservatives. Before we do this, however, it will be useful to consider the way he looks at the individual, and at his metaphysical view of man.

The conservative, Rossiter tells us, tries to make a workable

[6] For an attempt to analyze American history in terms of conservative order, see Rowland Berthoff, "The American Social Order: A Conservative Hypothesis," *The American Historical Review*, April, 1960. Professor Berthoff, in looking at American social history, rather than the history of ideas, finds a revived and conservative social order emerging in the twentieth century which is similar to that of the eighteenth century. He does not, however, come to grips with the question of whether or not the order of the twentieth century is conservative or liberal since he equates social order with conservatism only. There may be, however, a liberal form of social order; liberalism is not anarchy.

compromise between the needs of society and the rights of
the individual, but where there is a conflict the interests of the
community must come first; "conservative doctrine speaks of
the primacy of society."[7] Rossiter, in other words, goes further
than any other conservative in seeing what the modern liberal
has seen, that while the individual must be succored and be
allowed to roam his green pastures he cannot be allowed to
have everything his own way, he cannot become an anarchist/
gangster. Thus the New Conservative of Rossiter is not an
extreme individualist, and in particular he refuses to go all the
way with economic individualism. Unfortunately, his defense
of the community against the predatory individual is muddied
by his defense of the rights of property, which, he tells us, are
"to be honored without quibble and championed without re-
serve." What should be done when the rights of the many conflict with the unquibbable right to property? The solution seems
to lie in a briefly expressed statement that man has duties as
well as rights, and that there is no real or fundamental conflict
between the state and man since the state is essential to man.
Perhaps there is no "fundamental" conflict, but there have been
some pretty vivid conflicts. Thus, Rossiter's conclusion tends to
bathos:

... the undoctrinaire Conservative refuses to pursue the issue, except
to preach again from his favorite text: In regulating the economy
in the public interest, government cannot by right treat men un-
justly and cannot by nature solve all or even a majority of their
problems.[8]

He tries hard to be kind to the individual and at the same
time to stress the sense of community; his effort is not only

[7] Rossiter, *Conservatism in America*, p. 36.
[8] *Ibid.*, p. 42 [sic].

needed but highly original for a conservative. And one must say that one can believe that Rossiter has a sense of community. But he has in no way solved the problem of the individual in his relation to community, property, and the state by simply stating what the conservative would like to think. Even worse, one has the uneasy feeling that whereas the modern liberal would restrict some men in order to increase the liberty of more men, Rossiter's New Conservatism would simply restrict all men in a tight and firm community existence. Certainly he gives no indication that his affection for community is based on a concern for the ultimate freedom of man, on a conviction that community would increase the freedom possessed by men.

But assuming that Rossiter himself is both kind to the individual and solicitous of the community, what does his kindness to the individual mean in view of his willing acceptance of another conservative assumption about society, the concept of hierarchy and aristocracy? His acceptance of that principle means that the community he conceives is based on hierarchy, on inequality. Rossiter, to be sure, would cease the fight against universal suffrage and even admit that the vote is everyman's right. But "beyond this the Conservative is unwilling to go." Variety, it seems, extends vertically as well as horizontally, as neat an expression of the conservative addiction to placing one man over another as exists. Since vertical variety is a fact of life one must be grateful for class structure. In the class structure of a "good" society,

most men find their level *early* and stay in it without rancor. . . .[9]

True, equality of opportunity keeps the way at least "partially" open to ascent and decline; and a good social order tempers

[9] *Ibid.*, p. 23. Emphasis added.

those distinctions that are not "natural." What does "natural" mean? We are not told. But we are told that not only does conservatism recognize the inevitability and necessity of class; it also deeply believes in a "ruling and serving" aristocracy. Indeed, Rossiter insists that the belief in aristocracy is the one belief that really distinguishes conservatism from liberalism. (Now and then the cloven hoof peeps out.) What does Rossiter mean by aristocracy? Just the bright boys of Harvard, Yale, Princeton, and, of course, Cornell? Evidently not, for he speaks not only of an aristocracy of talent that is trained for special service and receives special consideration—how early, by the way does one begin to train this Samurai class?—but he also tells us that a conservative "continues to believe that it takes more than one generation to make a genuine aristocrat." Indeed it does.

Although Rossiter does not pursue the subject of hierarchy and aristocracy to any great depth, he enables us to acquire a distinct idea of what he means by a conservative society. It means, to borrow a term from another field, a feather-bed society, a society in which the individual will be snug and secure in his place, in his little community run for him by little tyrants and in which he will have the great honor of taking "pride in doing a good job in the station to which he has been called." Who called him to that station is never made clear, but we can make a good guess. His Master's Voice called him, the two-generation aristocrat who enjoys the beauties and expensive privileges of vertical variety. The possibility that some people do not like being called to a particular station and might even like to do a little calling themselves, indeed, might even like to change the call once in a while, does not occur to Rossiter any more than it does to any other conservative.

Rossiter on Man and the metaphysics of Man may be quickly

summarized. While not having quite the same gloom-and-doom approach that Kirk and Burke have, Rossiter shares their basic attitudes. First, conservatism is based on religion, and the idea of original sin. He accepts without hesitation the meaningless statement that society, government, family, church, "all are divine or divinely willed."[10] As for original sin, it is derived from the nature of man, which "is essentially immutable. . . . The immutable strain is one of deep-seated wickedness."[11] Hence we come to the comforting conclusion that "we must search for the source of our discontents in defective human nature rather than in a defective social order." After that statement Rossiter can say that this religious view of man is saved from cynicism because of two "splendid" beliefs, the belief that man is intricate and that man is "touched" with eternity. What price eternity!

Although the conservative is happiest when he is contemplating the eternal, he also has a deep affection for history, an affection that Rossiter shares. Values come from history, which is, of course, guided by divine intent. What does the conservative find in history? Rossiter is not as dogmatic as Kirk is on the question, but he too finds it mainly a record of tragedy and not a source of hope. Finally, out of history and religion comes the third element in the conservative trinity, the higher law, a system of abstract justice to which mundane law "must" conform and which provides a line of demarcation for the role of government, and a set of human rights. If anyone should think that the vagueness of higher law is a way of avoiding issues he would be correct, but it must be stated that Rossiter is aware of the need to tie higher law down to something a little more helpful than divine intent, for he recognizes the necessity for

[10] *Ibid.*, p. 43.
[11] *Ibid.*, p. 21.

conservatism to "carry on the progressive discovery of the commands of the higher law." One wonders, however, if the higher law can be progressively unfolded, how much higher it is than anyone's opinion. Is not the essence of the higher law that it is fixed law? The conservative will reply that it is a fixed law that is not yet all naked to our eyes. However, one may still wonder at such a law; how many centuries does dense and fallible man have to wait for this great unfolding? Is it not about time that the thing be revealed in all its majesty? But such thoughts are perhaps irreverent. As Rossiter says, "the Conservative engages reluctantly in political speculation." Quite so.

He engages so reluctantly in political speculation partly because of his distrust of reason, which, as Rossiter makes clear, is fundamental to conservatism. Rossiter, being more sensible than most conservatives, is careful not to carry this distrust too far; he talks about the distrust of "pure reason," of "abstract speculation." But he too must give the show away. He says that the conservative distrusts especially that speculation "aimed at ancient ways and natural urges." That is, he dislikes logic that proves him and his beliefs and desires to be wrong. Thus reason must be limited to instrumentality, to operating "within the limits of history, facts, and human nature *as we know all these to be.*" [Emphasis added][12] One may ask, how can we know all those things if man has no use for reason?

Rossiter's conclusion concerning the metaphysical thoughts of conservatism is that they give the faithful a mission to perform. The conservative must support the established order; identify and protect the "real" values of the community and thus work against moral relativism; must pass on the heritage of the community and recognize that he is not a creator but a trustee; must remind men of their sins; must champion organ-

[12] *Ibid.*, p. 52.

ized religion and private property; must foster social stability and social unity. This statement of mission is the clearest summary we will find of what it means to be conservative. The conservative mission is to create a society of feather beds. Doltish man is to be gently eased into his station and kept there so that he may do no damage. Remember the French Revolution!

How do Rossiter's concepts differ from those of the Old Conservatives and from those of Kirk himself? Rossiter must differ appreciably if he is to achieve his goal of establishing a *New* Conservatism. He must establish reasons for thinking that there exists a sharp break between those who are conservatives because they cling to nineteenth-century liberal attitudes and those who are conservatives in the new mode. The task of repudiating the Old Conservatives, as we have seen, was a most difficult one for Kirk, a task so difficult in fact that he was unable to carry it through. Can Rossiter do any better? He works hard at the subject, but in the end he, too, must settle for a tolerable existence with his ancestors.

His problem arises from the need to have a unique view of the American past. Has there ever ben a conservative past in America if one excludes the Old Conservatives? If not, if the American past is nothing but liberalism, then presumably Rossiter would be in a fine position to start his *New* Conservatism. But in that case what would conservatism be but a creed postulating a nonexistent tradition? It is small wonder that Rossiter veers back and forth trying to find his way across this treacherous ground. First he tells us that the great ideal of the American past is liberty, and that therefore the American mind has been a liberal mind. Does it follow, therefore, that "the American political mind has been a liberal mind [because] change and progress have been the American way of life?" It would seem to. But then, on the other hand, it would not seem to. For while the American mind has been "liberal about techniques and prospects, it has been conservative about institutions and values." But one is still not sure, for America has had no feudal past, and hence it has been more liberal than anything known by Europe. Yet, since America began in liberty the American mind has been conservative because it had a heritage of freedom for which to fight. The nice balancing act which Rossiter performs, and certainly the performance is as well done as it could be, ends with the climactic statement:

Having said that the most sacred articles of the American faith are Liberal in essence and purpose, I add this qualifying remark: if this faith is truly liberal, then somewhere in it lies a deep strain of philosophical conservatism.[13]

One is tempted to applaud.

Rossiter himself seems to be worried by his dizzy performance, for he insists on finding in the American past the conservative qualities of traditionalism, unity, loyalty, and constitutionalism. But none of these except traditionalism are really outside the domain of liberalism, as he has to admit. Is there an American affection for higher law, religion, and private property which can provide a groundwork for conservatism in the American past? Rossiter thinks there is, but curiously he has little to say about the role those things have played in that past. Even more curious he concludes:

Our tradition remains Liberal, but we are ever more insistent that it is just that: a tradition.[14]

[13] *Ibid.*, p. 71.
[14] *Ibid.*, p. 75. The section of *Conservatism in America* in which Rossiter describes the trend of conservative thought in American history is probably the best single survey of American conservative thought available; it is well-informed and dispassionate.

Thus Rossiter spends most of his effort explaining why American liberalism has not been radical; he finds it necessary to conclude that the American "mind is a prominent Liberal structure resting on a solid conservative foundation."[15] In other words, the American is both liberal and conservative. Or, as he puts it, "the American, like his tradition, is deeply liberal, deeply conservative. If this is a paradox, so, too, is America."[16]

But paradox aside, the search of this New Conservative for the essence of the American political tradition has not had results much different from that of the Old Conservative. Both find in one way or another the roots of their ideas in the past, in nineteenth-century liberalism. It is nineteenth-century liberalism that Rossiter is talking about when he tells us that the American is both liberal and conservative, that the American mind has a liberal structure and a conservative base. There is, however, an important difference between the way Rossiter looks at the past and the way the Old Conservatives do. The Old Conservative is not worried by his adherence to the nineteenth century, while Rossiter is most unhappy about the nineteenth century. The result is the delicate balancing act we have seen, the ambiguous and ambivalent attitude that Rossiter assumes toward American political ideas.

What is it that Rossiter finds so discouraging about the nineteenth century, the Old Conservatives, and the conservative past in general? Briefly, it is that American conservatism has generally been taken in by *laissez-faire* and economic individualism. The American conservative in the past has ignored the need of man for the "sheltering community." Thus he has rejected the very foundations of conservatism.

[15] *Ibid.*, p. 76.
[16] *Ibid.*, p. 98.

In rejecting the primacy of society, in underrating the capacity of government to do good, in passing lightly over groups and institutions that serve as buffers between man and political authority, it has pushed the precious concept of the free individual to an extreme position that no Conservative can occupy with peace of mind.[17]

Evidently nineteenth-century liberalism was really liberalism after all.

To turn now to the familiar conservative problem, the American businessman. What to do with him? It is apparent that Rossiter hardly finds him, anymore than does Kirk, an upstanding exponent of conservatism. Indeed, he says that "many men we like to think of as models of conservative thought and purpose —Morgan, Rockefeller, Ford—were in an important sense radicals. . . ."[18] And what was true of the nineteenth century, Rossiter glumly concludes, is true even today of our industrial leaders. Yet, like Kirk, he is forced to the conclusion that without the businessman there is no hope for conservatism.

The new conservatism will not flourish unless it appeals to the leaders of business. The claims of these leaders to respect and power will not be honored unless they serve the public in the spirit of the new conservatism. Only through a great tradition of public service in government, community, and vocation will America's valuable plutocracy become at last an invaluable aristocracy—an aristocracy, I hasten to add, of an American cut and therefore called by some other name.[19]

Rossiter has no doubts that the new elite aristocracy he requires must come from the business class in America. He therefore says that the conservative thinker must show how a plutocracy can become an aristocracy. He describes the con-

[17] *Ibid.*, p. 218.
[18] *Ibid.*, p. 220.
[19] *Ibid.*, p. 278.

servative thinker who will perform the task as "bold." Indeed he will be bold. He will have to be positively unique, and so far he has not appeared. Certainly Rossiter is not that thinker, for he gives no indication at all about how the plutocrat, as he so unkindly calls the businessman, will become the aristocrat. He hopes that the transformation will take place. He believes that it *must* take place if conservatism is to live well in America. But he does not even attempt to show us how it *might* take place. On such a vital topic both he and Kirk are mightily mysterious. But that is conservatism; mystery, mystery everywhere. Still, one wonders how they can let their best bet go so easily.

The businessman is as intractable as ever. But one must not get the impression that all is gloomy. Given the lack of decent conservative political tradition, there are still some sources of comfort. One is the existence of John Adams as a part of the American past. Now, *there* is a conservative. Adams had a realistic appraisal of the inequalities of man, a distrust of unchecked democracy, of all concentrated power, of rule by simple majority, and a devotion to private property. He was "grimly hopeful that the best of the old ways would somehow survive the surge to democracy and equality." It is interesting to note that Rossiter, like Kirk, has nothing but contempt for Hamilton, who embodied a regrettable plutocratic and mercantilist type of Federalism. Then there is the conservative minority of today—Southern agrarians, Catholic political theorists, conservative intellectuals. These men refuse to accept industrialism and have a deep affection for Burke and Adams. There is also the fact that modern conservative practice has become more so; i.e., less individualist, more middle-of-the-road, less optimistic, more traditionalist and nostalgic, more religious. Yet they are not much, these straws. Rossiter comes back to the liberal nature of American society as the cause of conservative weakness.

> When the one glorious thing to be conservative about was the Liberal tradition of the world's most liberal society, how could a conservative be expected to be Conservative?[20]

But is America such a liberal society? Has Rossiter been taken in a little too easily by his colleagues, the liberal professors? On his own showing it would seem that he has, for the most brilliant pages of *Conservatism in America* are those in which he describes "Conservatism in American Political Practice." He tells us that in American political thought liberalism almost always wins, but in the workings of American politics conservatism almost always wins over liberalism. His point is valid and important. Americans, he says, are conservative in their constitutionalism, in their two-party system, in their individualistic collectivism (i.e., collectivism on a local level to protect the community without harming the individualist tradition), in their community ties and voluntary co-operation, in their class structure, in the traditionalism of their patriotism. We have, according to Rossiter, long been a "citadel of conservatism," and have been radical only in economics and technology. And the "political American is the most conservative of all." Only under the stress of necessity in the early years of the Republic have the Americans innovated in the political realm. There is, it seems, something to hope for, some basis for believing that conservatism has an important hold in America. Americans may talk big, but they act conservative. Given that conclusion—and who can disagree with it?—the conservative may indeed feel that things work for him, whatever the words of liberals may say.

We have seen that Rossiter seeks to make a profound division

[20] *Ibid.*, p. 224.

self and the Old Conservatives, and to some extent although at the peril of his whole enterprise. Certainly he differs from the ninenteeth-century capitalist. Insofar as the Old Conservatives, e.g., such writers as Morley and Burnham, are devotees of *laissez-faire* capitalism, Rossiter is at variance with them. But as we have seen, the significant aspect of Old Conservatism as it exists today is not its adherence to *laissez-faire* economics, but its insistence on creating a tradition of nineteenth-century liberalism. Rossiter clearly cannot be accused of doing this. His whole effort is directed to distinguishing conservatism from the liberalism of the nineteenth century. That effort is what makes him a New Conservative.

But while he will have no truck with nineteenth-century liberalism it has yet to be proved that he differs in any significant way from the attempt of the Old Conservative to hold to it. The Old Conservative, it will be recalled, attempted to create a society in which change will have come to a stop, in which the future will have ceased to exist, in which a fixed society will run along its endless rounds of repetition. Rossiter attempts to achieve the same ends, the same fixed society. The means may differ; he would not consider freezing society in its nineteenth-century mold as a proper enterprise, and to that extent there is a real difference between the New Conservatism of Rossiter and the Old Conservatism of today. But if the means differ the ends are the same: a fixed society. And the ends being the same, one wonders if in practice the means would differ so much.

How does Rossiter attempt to modernize conservatism, to bring it up to date, to avoid the stigma of being an Old Conservative? Does he come out at any place significantly different from that occupied by Russell Kirk? Does he succeed in the

gigantic task of creating a progressive conservatism? His most
valiant effort to bring conservatism into line with twentieth-
century America is not to be found in his statement of principles—these, as we have seen, hardly differ at all from those
of Kirk. It is to be found in the important last chapter of his
Conservatism in America, "A Conservative Program for American Democracy." What is this program, and how does it square
with his principles? Does it show a deviation from Kirk on
matters of fundamental importance? Or is Rossiter's attempt at
a modernized, progressive conservatism simply a reflection of
Kirk's basic principles, a way of giving life to them? If it is,
then one must say that Rossiter's conservatism would only
seem to be progressive; it would be only a realization of principles which have nothing to do with modern problems.

Rossiter calls upon the conservative to create and honor a
tradition of public service, an attitude which, he points out,
calls for an end of antistatism. Presumably what he is suggest-
ing is an elite civil service corps similar to that of Britain. In
addition he suggests that the conservative be active in another
type of public service, voluntary action. The conservative
should carry on voluntary action on a tolerant basis; i.e., he
should not be unhappy if liberals do the same thing. Further,
he should see to it that an elite group of businessmen comes into
being and is transformed from a plutocracy into an aristocracy.
What do these proposals mean? Do they mean that the conservative has changed his stripes and become a liberal, a progressive who can accept the fact that modern society requires
a state and that co-operation in equality is a necessity of modern existence? Not on the evidence presented here. What these
proposals mean is that conservatism is simply going to be more
sophisticated, if it follows Rossiter's prescriptions, in creating
a fixed elite. The most noteworthy characteristic of the British

civil service, for example, is its quality of fixedness. A Socialist political party has come to and gone from power—and perhaps gone for good—and still the civil service elite reigns; it continues to hold British society in a viselike grip. Such is the elite that Rossiter would want us to adopt, except that he goes one step further and suggests a stiffening and increased fixity for the elites in business as well as government service. Plutocracy, like the spoils system, at least has the virtue of a certain democratic fluidity and freedom about it, rough and ready though it may be. But Rossiter, following sound conservative principles, wants an aristocracy. We are to be run by a combination of The Great God Luce and Massive Dulles.

It seems, therefore, rather odd for Rossiter to tell us that his next suggestion for conservatism is that it pledge itself to the defense of liberty. However, the suggestion seems less startling when we see that the conservative is to confine himself strictly to the *defense* of liberty. "If it is for the liberal to expand liberty, it is for the conservative to defend it, especially against experiments that appear to sacrifice real liberty for specious equality."[21] He does not discuss whether or not (a) it is possible to defend liberty in this day and age without expanding it, and (b) whether or not some of those "experiments" might not be necessary to an expansion of liberty. When it comes to problems of liberty today what would Rossiter have the liberal do? Ask permission of the conservative if he can try a few experiments or not? Rossiter's belief in an elite would indicate that such is the case. But what if the conservative happens to be in a bad mood that morning? What if he says, "No! No experiments today. Back to your place!" We will discuss the problem of liberty and change in Rossiter's thought below, but it is worth

[21] *Ibid.*, p. 281.

saying here that his suggestions as to how the conservative is to defend liberty do not advance his position one iota.

But his position does have certain interesting consequences, which he displays for us. To defend liberty, the New Conservative should, first, support organized religion. Indeed, in this particular case the New Conservative is evidently to go beyond defense and become an aggressive type, for Rossiter tells him to strengthen as well as defend religion—*organized* religion, that is. Second, he must take a close interest in education. He must protect it from both such Rightists as William F. Buckley, Jr., and from Leftists (unspecified). The conservative leaders of school boards should represent the whole community—a nice trick if it can be done. And the gap between the business and the academic worlds must be narrowed. Elite, it seems, must call to elite. (Why the gap should be narrowed we are not told.) In other words, according to Rossiter, "in the field of education, the new conservatism can steer a steady course down the middle. . . ." There is not much to say about such an idea except that it sounds good but uninteresting. However, when one thinks about it the whole idea really vanishes into thin air.

But what Rossiter has to say on the conservative program for economics and business does not vanish into thin air. It has a good solid tone about it. As he says with a wink, "the New Conservative will need no persuasion to take an active interest in the American economy."[22] Indeed he will not. But under Rossiter's urging what will he do? First, he will defend private enterprise and property against "careless tinkers." That being done, he will, second, make American capitalism the servant of American democracy. How?

[This goal] calls for . . . [the] construction of a "welfare community" that will prove less dangerous in power and more benevolent in

[22] *Ibid.,* p. 284.

operation than the "welfare state" proposed by enthusiastic re-formers.[23]

What is a welfare community as distinct from a welfare state? It is based, first of all, on an acceptance of capitalism. But so is the welfare state, for that matter. Second—and this quality is its unique quality, the thing that distinguishes it from the welfare state—the welfare community is based on business itself. Rossiter, in fact, is not very clear exactly what it is he is talking about, but it is clear enough that business, not the state, is to provide welfare. The New Conservative

. . . must carry forward a number of trends that are already under way in business and industry: acceptance and integration of unions, application of "the new *science of human relations*," and extension of the pattern of pensions and benefits. . . .[24]

Another word for the welfare community of Rossiter is the old-fashioned word *paternalism*. The new conservative elite is going to be put to work. Its slogan will be "you've never had it so good." Its methods will be manipulation of the workers through their unions and the "new science of human relations." Marx said that religion is the opium of the people; today, along with religion, there is a new opium. The important point, however, is that Rossiter wants to get welfare away from the state —which is, after all, responsible to the people, no matter how remotely—and into the hands of the business-elite-cum-plutoc-racy-cum-aristocracy—which is not responsible to anyone no matter how remotely. The point becomes clear when he discusses government intervention in the economy. The New Conservative should counter "a proposal for stiffer regulation of industry with one that would encourage self-regulation . . . a

[23] *Ibid.*, p. 285.
[24] *Ibid.* Emphasis added.

master plan for 'socialized medicine' with one that is voluntary, decentralized, and self-supporting."[25] Rossiter also says that the New Conservatives should allow private enterprise to be regulated in the public interest. But what does he mean by regulation in the public interest? He never tells us. What if the public interest requires a little chipping away at private enterprise—a not remote possibility? That problem is not discussed either. But he does tell us that

. . . the historic mandate of the new conservative in business [might well be] to prove that non-governmental institutions can satisfy the tremendous human needs that have spurred the rise of the positive state.[26]

In the light of such a remark, one does not think that the efforts of Rossiter and the New Conservatives to regulate private enterprise will be very strenuous. It is doubtful that they would be perceptible. And we are still waiting for a conservative, New or Old, to prove to us that nongovernmental institutions can satisfy the needs that have spurred the rise of the positive state.

It is only fair to conclude this discussion of Rossiter's views on conservatism, economics, and liberty by pointing out that he believes the conservatives in America to have been at fault in not defending civil liberty more than they have. The leaders of business and industry, he says in a somewhat peeved tone, should show sympathy for the rights of men with different opinions from theirs.

Finally, in his conservative program, Rossiter turns to "the unfinished business of American democracy." Unfortunately for his attempt to convince us, he has little to say on this subject. He suggests that we develop a foreign policy based on hard

[25] *Ibid.*, p. 286.
[26] *Ibid.*, pp. 287-88.

facts and good will and that conservatives should aid the Negro to have his full rights. On the latter point Rossiter does strike a new note, for all the other conservatives we have discussed have shown either no interest in the subject or have shown a positive antipathy towards equality for the Negro. But in true conservative fashion Rossiter warns that one should not move too fast in this respect; one must steer the "natural conservative course between standpatism and liberalism. . . ." One would agree that that course is the natural conservative course. Whether it would achieve anything—whether it achieved anything in the hands of the Eisenhower administration—is another question, and not, of course, a question discussed by Rossiter. Finally, the conservative should stand up for intellectual endeavors and stop attacks on the mind. We are never told, however, how this attitude squares with that part of the creed that states a basic lack of trust in abstract reason. If the intellectual does not indulge in abstract reason, it is hard to know what it is that he does do. In this case it would seem that the more conservative conservative has the advantage of logic over the tolerant and humane Rossiter.

It must be understood that Rossiter is tolerant and humane. The personality that comes through his pages is a kindly one, an intelligent one. The reader feels, as he does not in the case of Kirk, that here is a man he would trust; even if one disagrees with his opinions, here is a man who really seeks the truth and values human welfare. Alas! It is all the more depressing to have to ask and to answer the question: does Rossiter at the end of his attempt to bring conservatism into the mainstream of human affairs differ from the principles of Russell Kirk? True, there is a change in Rossiter's book from the dark and lurid thunder of the conservative canon in the first part to a sort of light and cheerful pink glow of American optimism in the last part. But the more humane tone, it would seem, is simply a reflection of Rossiter's own personality. For, whatever the reason for the change in tone, the brutal fact remains that on the intellectual plane of ideas, concepts, assumptions, and logic there is no break in his material. Rossiter ends as he began, a true-blue conservative whose ideas do not differ significantly from those of Russell Kirk.

Yet having said that intellectually Rossiter's conservatism leads to the same place as Kirk's, there still remains the difference in tone. And there is also the fact that Rossiter is not merely aware of the dangers from what he calls the Right in America, but wrote his *Conservatism in America* to try to pull conservatism away from its grosser manifestations.

The attempt made by Rossiter to pull conservatism away from the concepts that have motivated the Old Conservatives and away from some of the more turgid ideas of Kirk is shown by his views on two important topics, the role of government today and the question of democracy. We have seen what the Old Conservatives and Kirk think on those questions. Does Rossiter have a new and different point of view? To answer the question we must look not only at his *Conservatism in America* but also at his *American Presidency, Parties and Politics in America,* and *Seedtime of the Republic,* the books of a scholar written with a scholar's respect for facts and logic.

Despite his remarks about private enterprise doing what the state is nowadays expected to do, Rossiter is aware of the complexities of the problem. He is not, he says, an antistatist as such. Thus he is willing to accept the general responsibility of the government to secure social equilibrium, to promote public and private morality, to increase equality of opportunity, and to act as an agency of humanitarianism. And thus he is able to claim that his conservatism rejects the negative theory of government set out by the old Right (i.e., the Old Conservatives). We may accept that statement in good faith, not only because we do not suspect Rossiter of chicanery, but also because in his *American Presidency* he accepts wholeheartedly and without reservation the strong presidency as created or revived by Roosevelt. The strong presidency has always been identified with the political position of the modern liberal and rightly so, for it has been a means by which the federal government has acted in the interest of the nation as a whole; and that, of course, is the very reason it has been a grievance to the conservatives. But Rossiter accepts the results of Roosevelt's use of the presidency with such enthusiasm that even a modern liberal would hesitate to go as far as he goes in adulation of the strong president. He tosses off the criticisms of a strong presidency made by the conservatives with the curt observation that they do not matter. Well! One is even more surprised to see that in the second edition of *The American Presidency* Rossiter has only the harshest of words—insofar as this polite and courteous man can be harsh—for the weak presidency of President Eisenhower, whom he describes as a moderate conservative. Since Rossiter would describe himself as a moderate conservative, what, as they say, goes on here? The problem becomes even more complex when we consider that he also has advocated the concurrent majority of Calhoun as a "prime weapon" of the conservative, and that he has praised the two-party system as

the most conservative political arrangement in the Western world, designed to delay, check and frustrate . . .[27]

[27] *Ibid.*, p. 78.

Is Rossiter simply being inconsistent? It is not likely with someone of his stature. Is he a split personality? Nor is that likely. The answer is that he is a man with a terribly difficult task, the task of modernizing conservatism. But before we try to show what is going on, let us look further into some of Rossiter's subtleties.

The crucial question which he must face in his attempt to create a really new conservatism is the question of democracy. If he can settle that problem, then the other problems such as strong presidents and political parties fall into place. What are his views on democracy?

Rossiter, first of all, varies from the usual conservative position by accepting both constitutional government and democracy and by refusing to see any conflict between them. He does more, for he encompasses both the American Constitution and the American Revolution within the conservative framework by claiming that they complement rather than conflict with each other. Thus, in his *Seedtime of the Republic,* he demonstrates how the thought of the colonies developed toward democracy *and* liberty, he praises the rationalism of democracy, and sees the significance of the colonial period as a seedtime for the democracy that came to full bloom later. However, in the final two pages of the book he summarizes the political theory of the period as possessing a "deep-seated conservatism" because, in his view, the colonies had achieved freedom and did not have to hope for it. The goal, thus, "was simply to consolidate, then expand by cautious states, the large measure of liberty and prosperity that was part of their established way of life." He goes further and tells us that the mood and idiom of the American Revolution is still used by modern American political thought today. And he finds that use good and wise; he believes that the assumptions and language of the political theory of the American Revolution are still adequate.

We will discuss the significance of those ideas later. Let us now push a little further with this subtle and excellent scholar, for he has other salutations to make to democracy. He sees both the presidency and American political parties as working for democracy. As he says in his *American Presidency*, "if there is any one point I have hammered on in this book, it is that the Presidency is essentially a democratic office."[28] As we have seen, that statement is nothing new in conservative literature; Burnham, for example, would agree wholeheartedly. But it is clear that Rossiter does not make his remark in reproach. To Rossiter constitutional democracy is "the way of life that speaks of liberty and the rule of law." Again he refuses to divorce constitutionalism and democracy, finding them both good.

We receive even more surprising news when we are told that

"The new conservative will stand fast in the democratic faith. He must doubt the full promise of democracy; . . . Yet he must neither hold nor express any final doubts of the practical and spiritual superiority of constitutional democracy over all other forms of government. . . ."[29]

Franklin D. Roosevelt taught the American people the "proper relations of private enterprise and public authority." Further, in his *Parties and Politics in America,* he makes a clear identification between democracy and political parties, and he makes it equally clear that he thinks our system of political parties and the democracy that gave it birth are both excellent arrangements. Finally, he tells us that the political parties in America of which he approves so highly can check but not suppress majority rule. What price Calhoun now!

We return to our earlier question, how does all this praise of

[28] Clinton Rossiter, *The American Presidency* (rev. ed., 1960), p. 122.
[29] Rossiter, *Conservatism in America,* pp. 252-3.

democracy and strong presidents and the American Revolution square with Rossiter's principles of conservatism?

There are four possible explanations:

1. He is confused, or he has changed his mind since the publication of *Conservatism in America* in 1956. As we have said, such a possibility is not feasible with Rossiter and may be ignored. There are a few contradictions in his works; e.g., between his statement in *Parties and Politics in America* that Roosevelt gave a proper definition to the role of private and public power and his statements in *Conservatism in America* about the role of government. But these need not concern us.

2. His opinions show that there is no real difference between conservatism and liberalism today, a popular position but one which this writer, or Rossiter, so far as one can tell, would reject. The whole point of Rossiter's work (and this book) is to mark out a difference; if he does not do so he has failed. Further, one must not forget that he has in fact stated the conservative principles in which he believes and they have little to do with liberalism. No, the let's-smooth-it-over boys will not be allowed to get away with it.

3. When a conservative faces the facts of life a fissure opens in his conservatism, and he enunciates conservative principles that are contradicted by the facts of life which he describes as an accurate observer. For example, one may want a weak president but the fact is that America must have a strong president. To some degree this explanation fits the situation. Rossiter, being a scholar, cannot burk the issues as neatly as Kirk, whose responsibility is only to his own emotions. He cannot carelessly ignore the reality of American life; democracy, strong presidents, and the democratic surge of opinion in the colonies are not to be, cannot be, rejected. If a fissure thereby opens in his ideology, the scholar may be unhappy but he may not neglect

his scholarship because of his personal interest in an ideology. Rossiter, true to the creed of scholarship, does not do so. Nevertheless, while there is such a fissure in his thought, it is not the only explanation for his views. He is aware of the problem that his views as a scholar and as a conservative present; he grapples with it and grapples willingly. As we have said, he is a man with a great problem.

4. The fourth explanation comes closest to the mark and to meeting the facts, to explaining the ideas he expresses here and the ideas he expresses there. Rossiter is striving mightily to get conservatism out of the hands of what he calls the traditional Right. Hear what he tells the conservatives in the last pages of *Conservatism in America,* and note the despairing tone.

If [the enlightened minority of conservatives] will not lead bravely in the spirit of the new conservatism . . . the Republic will have seen its greatest glory . . . American democracy needs thousands of large-minded conservative leaders. . . . Their practices . . . should be relevant to America. American conservatism cannot and must not be as suspicious, gloomy, passive, and elitist as Conservatism in other countries; it can and must be more daring, hopeful, individualistic, and democratic. . . . For the present at least, while the Right rides high, conservatives should seek to steer a middle course between ultra-conservatism and liberalism. This may well prove their most difficult task. The commands of common sense call upon conservatives to associate with moderate liberals in "the vital center." . . . Over the long run, however, they should take care not to identify conservatism with the "middle of the road" or the conservative mission with the arts of compromise.[30]

In the light of his project Rossiter's seemingly conflicting ideas take on coherence. He is trying desperately to bring conservatism into the mainstream of American life, and in the light of

[30] *Ibid.,* pp. 299-301.

that effort his willingness to accept the strong presidents of the New Deal and democracy becomes a significant enterprise.

In discussing the presidency Rossiter tells us that pluralism, one of conservatism's favorite thoughts, is anarchy if it lacks a common point of reference, i.e., the president. In this instance he goes on to suggest that the president's power as a legislative leader be actually increased, an idea that really lights the fuse in the minds of most conservatives. But he is also able to put the presidential growth of power in the stream of American history and see it as a tradition, so to speak; as he says, those against a strong president "cannot win a war against American history." Because he does not dislike the America that exists in the here and now he is willing to accept the presidency as it is. It is noteworthy, too, that he tells us that a strong executive was favored by The Founding Fathers. But whether they would favor it today or not is not the main issue for Rossiter. Does the conservative love the lessons of history? So Messrs. Burke and Kirk tell us. If they do, Rossiter thinks the conservative should absorb a few, and one of them is the growth of presidential powers. A strong president to Rossiter is in the constitutional tradition of America. We have already raised the question in discussing Burnham of how far back the conservative went to discover a tradition to which he could cling. Rossiter does not go back very far, and he certainly includes the New Deal—or at least part of it. Further, he describes the presidency in good conservative fashion as a "breeding ground of indestructible myth." Finally, the presidency as it operates today fits into a broad "constitutional morality," and thus is prevented from being dangerous. There are many restraints on the president, but the point which Rossiter stresses is that no one of them alone works to restrain the president. Instead they form a network, the strength of which comes from the interlockings of its parts.

Thus, and this conclusion is a triumph, what we have working in America today is Calhoun's concurrent majority.

Having got the strong presidency safely within the conservative creed, democracy too can be made part of the creed. For, once it is seen that there is a pluralistic system actually at work in America *now*, it can be seen that democracy is no longer a threat. His point is made most clearly in his *Parties and Politics in America* in which he poses parties as the embodiment of democracy. For the party system of America is not only a democratic arrangement; it is a conservative arrangement. It makes the checks and balances system work more effectively. American parties do not exist to use political power purposely to remake society but rather to make the mechanics of government more effective. And in addition the parties succeed in working the checks and balances system while they also succeed in making a national unity, a consensus, from the variety of a pluralistic society.

Anyone, conservative or not, must admit that Rossiter has made a gigantic effort to bring conservatism face to face with realities. He has tried to do it by the virtuoso technique of showing the conservatives that those things they hold dear exist *today, right now,* in America, and they should therefore come to the aid and comfort of those values instead of sulking in their tents. Now is the time for all good men to come to the aid of the party. It is simple but breathtaking. What conservative before Rossiter had ever thought that he had it so good! Yet with all his achievement Rossiter does not give up any of the values held dear by the Kirkean-Burkean brand of New Conservative, nor, in fact, many of the values held dear by the Chamberlin-Morley-Burnham axis of Old Conservatism. True, the Rabid Right will be aroused, but he intends to arouse them.

As for the other conservatives, he intends to show not that they are wrong but simply that they are misguided.

Rossiter's theory is magnificent, but does it solve the problem it starts out to solve? Does he succeed in creating a progressive conservatism? That is, does he create a conservatism that can work with *change* and can contemplate change without feeling ruptured? Can his New Conservatism encompass change, progress, within its system and still be conservative? Certainly there is no one else as tolerant and openminded among the conservatives of the 1950's as Rossiter. But nevertheless the question must be asked: does he succeed in modernizing conservatism? Or does it leave his hands unchanged from what we saw it to be before we considered Rossiter?

The question must not be treated cavalierly, for we know how hard Rossiter has worked to bring conservatism into a progressive framework, and how important he considers the task to be. Nevertheless there are several disquieting reasons for suspecting that he has not done so and several solid reasons for being quite sure that he has not done so.

The disquieting reasons are: (a) the program for the unfinished business of American democracy, which we have already discussed. The program he presents presumably represents his idea of what kind of a society he would like to see. If so, there is no reason to believe that the society for which Rossiter hopes is any different from the society for which other conservatives hope, including Kirk. It may be more streamlined, and full of General Motors executives telling us our duties instead of lords of the heath, but it is essentially the same. (b) Rossiter's statement of principles, as we have also seen, is in no wise different from that of Kirk. So far, in other words, New Conservatives of a feather do, in fact, flock together.

But such considerations are minor beside the effort Rossiter has made to jerk conservatism around to face the present. And that effort raises the real problem. Can he get the conservatives not only to turn their gaze from the past, but to raise their eyes from the ground and look at what is coming toward them? Can he get them to look at the future? Can Rossiter's conservatism, unlike other brands, work with *change,* and not merely accept the changes that have already occurred and that other people have brought about? Can his conservatism, to be exact, be of use to America in helping it to face its problems?

No, it cannot. It cannot work with change any more than the conservatism of others, or any more than conservatism has been able to do in the past.

What is Rossiter's view of change? He tells us that the conservative is committed to a "discriminating defense of the social order against change and reform." That is, while he admits change is rife among men, he insists that it be "sure-footed and respectful of the past." He distinguishes this idea from stand-pattism, reaction, and revolutionary reaction. He also tells us that the essential difference between conservatism and liberalism in regard to change is one of mood and bias—one of the few times when Rossiter can be caught out in a contradiction, as we shall see. So far, according to his definition of change we are on very free, liberal, and open ground. Who does not discriminate when looking at change? But Rossiter goes on to say that change must never be undertaken for its own sake, that it must have preservation and if possible restoration for its main object, be limited in scope and purpose, be a response to an undoubted social need, represent a change for the better, be brought about under conservative auspices.

Things no longer look quite so free and easy. Indeed they look positively Kirkean, and we are even told that conservatism looks for the order that inheres in things rather than imposing an order on them. Man looks for social stability made up of unity, balance, authority, security, continuity, we are told by Rossiter. However, as we know by now, there is always another Rossiter to appear around the corner. He tells us in *The American Presidency* that by 1957 the American people had had their fill of moderate conservatism, and certainly his praise of Roosevelt and his quite remarkably severe criticism of President Eisenhower for not leading and for not moving in the direction of the future seemingly show a different Rossiter view of change. Yet this criticism of President Eisenhower only points up his concept of change since he is critical of Eisenhower because he stood pat instead of trying to draw the sting out of change. Rossiter believes that a conservative should be a gradualist.

[The conservative] must be a gradualist lest he be a liberal or radical; he must be active lest he be a standpatter or reactionary. . . . Change will continue to be the essence of American life, and the conservative, powerless and indeed unwilling to block it, should devote his best efforts to diverting it into channels of progress. . . . Many men on the Right, unworried or delighted about isolation, discrimination, and vulgarity, do not look ahead to a brave new world and a more democratic, cultured America. At least as many do, however, some with enthusiasm, and they will be the agents of the new conservatism in these three areas. Their mission in each seems clear and urgent: to *prevent* reactionaries and standpatters from exploiting the conservative urge in order to block normal progress; to *scrutinize, criticize,* and often *oppose* flatly the eager proposals of liberals and radicals; to *insist that change represent progress, keep continuity* with our past, and be worked by constitutional methods; to keep *an eye out for damage* to basic institutions and traditions; *to remind us* courageously of the strengths and weaknesses of the materials—American men and women—with which we are working; and to take command themselves at moments of decision and abrupt transition. It will not be easy, especially for those who wish the ends but are skeptical of the means, but the conservative mission is never easy.[31]

One other aspect of Rossiter's thought on change must be mentioned to complete the picture. In describing the conservative view of government he states that power should be diffused horizontally and vertically so as to put a brake on wholesale reform. Power should also be balanced so as to achieve the equilibrium that is the mark of a stable society. And government must be representative because representative government too "delays decision and frustrates whimsical change."

We are now in a position to evaluate the whole of Rossiter's thought, and more important, to understand why it is that, for all his efforts to create a progressive conservatism, his conservatism cannot face the problem of change any better than any other we have studied. Rossiter may have been able to "modernize" conservatism in regard to certain aspects of modern society such as the presidency, and even democracy. But he has not been able to "modernize" the conservative attitude towards change, because if he did he would cease to be a conservative.

It is apparent how Rossiter looks at change. He may accept the changes brought about by someone else. Or he may try to modify the changes brought about by someone else. Or he may quibble and try to block the changes brought about by someone else. But *he*, he the progressive, openminded conservative, *he* will not bring about change.

The clue is given by Rossiter's remark that "it is for the liberal to expand liberty, it is for the conservative to defend it." Under this rubric his seemingly contradictory views of change can be encompassed. He can accept the New Deal as the proper work of liberals, can even accept it as part of the American tradition.

---

[31] *Ibid.*, pp. 300; 296; 293. Emphasis added.

But an acceptance of the New Deal (for example) is a far cry from starting it, from bringing into being new methods of facing the problems of society. Hence, while Rossiter's New Conservative can accept what is, at the same time he must postulate the conservative attitude toward change, an attitude of timidity at best, of trying to divert change so that stability and equilibrium will not be shattered. The New Conservative will not initiate change. At the best he will watch it passively or watch it to see that it represents his version of progress.

What is, therefore, Rossiter's version of progress? The answer lies in the conservative values that he puts forward. These are essentially the values of the fixed stable society and are common to both the New Conservatism of Kirk and the Old Conservatism of Burnham, Morley, and Chamberlin. Whatever changes occur in the United States, Rossiter, like other conservatives, would see to it that they work toward the type of society represented by those values. Hence, his acceptance of the idea of the "welfare community." Someone else having brought about the change of creating the welfare state, Rossiter would accept it if he can bring it into line with his ideas of elite leadership and private enterprise. If he could not achieve that transformation then he would work with the results of someone else's initiative and prevent it from doing as much damage as possible to conservative values. Having done so, he would establish a stable society, i.e., a society in which change would be nonexistent or minimal, in which it would be low in priority—a society, that is, in which freedom would be restricted by stability. Rossiter's attempt to create a progressive, modernized conservatism crashes on the rock of the conservative inability to accept change in society. He takes it as far as anyone has before, or as it is possible to do. Such an animal as a progressive conservative may exist in the factual reality of daily life, although even so he is a scarce animal, a rare bird. But Rossiter has chosen to argue on intellectual grounds and on the grounds of political theory, and on such grounds it cannot be established that there is any fundamental difference between his conservatism and that of the other conservatives we have studied here. (It goes without saying, of course, that there is a very real and deep gulf between Rossiter and the wild men of the Right whom he so correctly spurns.) Even his acceptance of democracy will not help establish the case because the democracy he contemplates is democracy with such a strong mixture of elitism, private enterprise, checks and balances, and concurrent majorities that it can hardly be said to be a democracy in the sense of an open, free, equalitarian society.

Rossiter cannot break away from the conservative mold because there is an absolute gulf between conservatism and modern liberalism and because, therefore, mixtures such as liberal or progressive conservatism do not have any significant or real meaning. The gulf is the result of the key value which modern liberalism possesses, the value of freedom. Freedom *may* be *a* value for a conservative. For a modern liberal it *must* be *the* value. Thus the gulf that separates the two beliefs is revealed by the attitudes the two ideologies take toward change. Modern liberalism sees change as the very quality—good or bad—of human existence, and the ability to change as the meaning of freedom. The conservative may, by making a gigantic effort of good-will and stretching the logic of his creed almost to the breaking point, accept changes brought about by someone else. But freedom and change are not the key value of conservatism. Its key values are stability and order—eternal order if at all possible.

Can Rossiter's conservatism be of help to America today in facing her problems? He speaks of the need for conservatives "to take command . . . at moments of decision and abrupt transition." For what purpose would they take command? With what tools? With what aims and methods has conservatism, even that of Rossiter, equipped its proponents for moments of decision? We have tried to show what those aims and methods are. One can only wonder on what grounds the conservative believes that he is capable of dealing with moments of decision and abrupt transition. Do those moments call for stolid clinging to an eternal order? Or do they call for the imagination that is born from freedom and the acceptance of change?

7. The Public Philosophy of Walter Lippmann and the Quest for Order

PROFESSOR CLINTON ROSSITER is not the only one who is struggling to make conservatism into a significant guide for present-day America. While Kirk is laying down the law and the commandments, and while the Old Conservatives rumble and grumble over the horizon, Walter Lippmann in his brooding sort of way is dedicated to the proposition that America and the West are failing and must be shored up with a conservative society. His book, *The Public Philosophy*, is his most recent attempt to save America and mankind from folly, but what makes it significant is not the nostrum it peddles but the conservative ideas that are its ingredients. *The Public Philosophy* is a book that postulates the severest conservatism, one that differs little if at all from that of Kirk. The fact that Lippmann turned to conservatism in the 1950's does not necessarily reflect the influence of conservatism in those years; Lippmann is too independent to be influenced by shifting intellectual currents. But it does indicate the depth of the shift that had taken place in American life if Lippmann also could find conservatism to be his intellectual and spiritual home in the 1950's.

The question may be raised, of course, whether Lippmann

has not always been a conservative and whether he is not today, therefore, a sort of old New Conservative. It is an important question from the point of view of a study of the life and opinions of Walter Lippmann, but it is not one that is to the point here. The importance of Lippmann to this study lies in the conservatism of *The Public Philosophy* and in the concern and affection for conservative values which that book demonstrates. It is the most recent in his long line of works of high seriousness that have sought to clarify the dilemmas and problems of political life which he has seen about him. Their originality, and at times their depth, cannot be denied. But whatever may be said of the books as individual books, their total effect as a *corpus* is lost in the inconsistencies which one book displays when compared with another. One may say that Lippmann is a conservative, or a liberal, or a socialist at this or that particular point of time. But one cannot say that he is a conservative, or a liberal, or a socialist. Lippmann is the supremely inconsistent journalist. As such he is to some extent an asset to the Republic for which he stands, but it is impossible to reconcile the different positions he has taken throughout his long career as a writer.[1]

But if Lippmann cannot be nailed down to a label—and it should be made clear that changes in opinion are not to be deplored if there are logical reasons for them—his inconsistency

---

[1] Arthur Schlesinger, Jr., in Childs and Reston, *Walter Lippmann and His Times,* has made as much coherence of Lippmann's opinions as anyone can, but even he admits finally to being baffled by some of Lippmann's shifts and the logic which lay behind them—if any logic did lie behind them. Marquis Childs, on the other hand, ignores such problems in his haste to praise Lippmann and to let him off easily. D. W. Weingast, *Walter Lippmann: A Study in Personal Journalism,* also reveals Lippmann's inconsistencies and, one might add, his many mistaken judgments as expressed in his column, "Today and Tomorrow." For a debate between Archibald MacLeish and Lippmann on *The Public Philosophy* see *The Yale Review,* Summer, 1955. Lippmann's reply does not advance the position taken in his book.

has a significance of its own. Lippmann shows the mind of a man at sea and looking for a philosophy by which he can live. In this sense Lippmann's record of inconsistencies, the only consistent thread in his writings, is the honest revelation of the loss that the intellectual man of affairs has suffered in the twentieth century. But his dogged inability to be tied to a belief for the many years of his career shows not only the difficulty of belief in the twentieth century; it also shows his insistence on the supreme importance of having an ideology, of having an ideological framework into which the facts of public life can be inserted. The fantasy of life in the twentieth century is paralleled by the rapid changes of Lippmann's opinions, but he, like the rest of us, needs some way of making sense of that fantasy.

In view of the variety of his past political opinions is it just and proper to consider *The Public Philosophy* as a conservative book? We will see below that there is indeed good and overwhelming reason so to consider it, but it must be said here that opinion on Lippmann's recent conservatism is confused. It is interesting to note, for example, that there is no mention of the conservative opinions of Lippmann in Child and Reston, *Walter Lippmann and his Times*[2] even though the dust-cover mentions Lippmann's "judicious conservatism." It is seldom that a blurb writer is more perceptive than the authors of a book. But there are others who are more positive. Rossiter, for example, has high praise of Lippmann as a conservative, and a review in the *American Political Science Review*[3] makes no bones about the conservatism of Lippmann's thought in *The Public Philosophy*.

The Public Philosophy is treated here as a conservative book for three reasons. First, because Lippmann's values as stated

[2] Reinhold Niebuhr does, however, discuss Lippmann's elitist views, but not in terms of their implications for conservatism.
[3] *American Political Science Review*, March, 1956.

there coincide with those of the other conservatives we have studied, and especially with those of Kirk. Almost all of the themes brought forward in such majesty by Kirk can be seen in Lippmann's recent book. He is blessedly brief about his ideas, but they do not differ fundamentally from those of Kirk. Second, Lippmann is a conservative in *The Public Philosophy* because of his attitude to change. Third, and most important, his conservatism is revealed by his belief in, and insistence on, an objective order.

What is the source of Lippmann's conservative bias and his "public philosophy"? There are many sources but one of the most significant is the pre-World War I liberal-critical view of society which he has maintained. He still has many of the attributes of the typical intellectual of the years before 1920 and especially he still has a distrust of democracy and the public and a consequent need for a firm point of reference from which to understand the ever-increasingly dizzy changes of modern society. The Eastern seaboard intellectual of the days of Wilson and Theodore Roosevelt is displayed in both the contorted, fastidious, and painful prose of Lippmann, and in his despair that no one in a crude society will listen to the sensitive few. Lippmann is our last aristocrat, detached, aloof, and just able to bear the sights he must look upon. All of the ingredients of the myth that James Reston soberly and reverentially retails to the gawking many in *Walter Lippmann and His Times*, show the aristocratic image in which Lippmann wishes to pose. That it may be a bit off focus, somewhat contrived, does not mean that it is not a significant source of his opinions. Lippmann is dismayed, deeply and profoundly dismayed, to find the reasonable man overcome by so much unreason. Like so many people of the pre-World War I years and the years immediately after, he never recovered from his sense of shock at the "failure" of nineteenth-century liberalism and rationality in a new age. It was that sense of shock that set him on his long quest for some viable interpretation of man and society. It is that sense of shock, but now multiplied by the increasing dangers of the post-World War II period, that motivates and underpins *The Public Philosophy*. Although there is no comparing the intellectual endeavors of the two men, Lippmann returns us to the pre-occupations of W. H. Chamberlin—to the preoccupation with the coming, or present, ruin and decline of civilization. Thus, to understand his attempt to create the basis for a conservative society and political philosophy, we must look first at the fears he has for Western society. It is on his conviction that the collapse of Western civilization is a very real possibility and is probably at hand that he builds his theory of conservatism.

Lippmann's conviction that the decline of the West is in full process leads directly to a conservative conviction because the main trait of the decline we are undergoing is disorder. In the face of disorder we must save civilization by curing the radical disease of disorder itself. We must resurrect order, and to resurrect order we must establish a society based on fixed principles, on a public philosophy. The very idea of a public philosophy is itself a conservative idea, depending as it does on the assumption of fixed and eternal principles. But it is not only Lippmann's reliance on eternal principles that reveals his attitude. The very criticisms that he makes of modern society, the very reasons that make him think that disorder is the mark of our era, also show his conservative views.

Lippmann's belief in the decline of Western civilization is cast in the wide and general terms of modern doomsaying. When we see that *The Public Philosophy* opens with a section

called "The Decline of the West" we are afraid at first that
Lippmann has swallowed whole both Spengler and Toynbee;
after reading him we are convinced of it. In his latest incarnation he goes all the way with those who think that the end of
Western man is just around the corner, if indeed it has not already arrived. Whatever may be the causes of the decline, he is
in no doubt that it is the fundamental fact of Western society
in the twentieth century. This potential and/or actual decline
of the West is not a recent development, in Lippmann's view,
not the fault of one man in America or one administration, or
even of one world war. It derives instead from the very nature
of twentieth-century society: "We are . . . sick." Lippmann tells
us in discussing Western society before World War II that
"there was no mistaking the decline of the West." Presumably
these judgments still apply to society in the 1950's for otherwise
he would not have published his book in 1955. If anything, the
growth of the Russian threat, with its fulfillment of Toynbee's
requirements for a barbaric proletarian outside the gates of
civilization, has simply increased the threat.

It would be pleasant to be able to report that Lippmann has
some well-thought-out concept of decline in mind when he
discusses the subject with such assurance, but such is not the
case. Although it is possible to draw forth a sense of what he
means by the decline of the West from his general criticisms of
Western society, it is necessary to say that his failure to think
in terms that have conceptual validity destroys the basis of his
book as an intellectual endeavor. It is indeed ironical that one
who seeks eternal principles of public conduct should be incapable of establishing his work on concepts that extend beyond
the history of a particular civilization in a particular half-
century and that could act as more than a means of expressing
his particular likes and dislikes. For what is the decline of the

West to Lippmann but the decline of certain standards of civilization to which he is partial, the standards of nineteenth-century liberalism as he, and other conservatives, have dreamt of them? Thus, to Lippmann, the threat facing the West is more than a simple question of foreign policy or a problem of political, economic, and military power. It is a threat to the internal strength of the West, which will lead to decline through chaos. Such is the price the conservative believes will be paid by those who desert nineteenth-century liberalism.

The cause of that desertion is plainly stated in *The Public Philosophy*. Although Lippmann's fears for the West are cast in general doomsaying terms, in fact his fears concentrate on only one aspect of Western society—democracy. The decline of the West is equated with the rise of democracy in a one-to-one ratio; the more democracy, the greater the decline. Ostensibly he is not against democracy; he tells us in a sly aside that he is a liberal democrat and has no wish to disenfranchise his fellow citizens. We shall see why he feels it necessary to reassure us. But if he is not against democracy on the surface, his book carries the refrain that it is democracy that makes social order impossible. We are concerned only with an evaluation of this idea from the point of view of conservatism; but it must be said here that Lippmann's slanderous attack on democracy is presented without a shred of concrete, factual evidence. He finds it easier simply to assume the truth of his claim. Detachment from the hurly-burly of real life can sometimes do damage to intelligence.

Lippmann's assumption that democracy equals disorder is based on his belief that the democratic states have failed to maintain government, the word government standing in his mind for order. In part this failure became apparent in the West about 1938 when, in his opinion, the democracies failed to deal with the realities of the time. The defeat of the enemies of democracy after 1939 did not cheer Lippmann; his worst forebodings were realized when the liberal democracies failed to "make peace" or restore order after 1945. For someone so versed in international affairs it is strange that Lippmann should condemn democracy for failing to "make peace." He never defines the word *peace* in general or specific terms, nor does he tell us just what it is that he expected the liberal democracies to do. Thus he is able to ask, "could it be denied that they were sick with some kind of incapacity to cope with reality?" As a matter of fact it can be denied.

But a denial is beside the point for it would force Lippmann to discuss specific performance. What he is interested in is a general proposition.

There has developed in this century a functional derangement of the relationship between the mass of the people and the government. The people have acquired powers which they are incapable of exercising, and the governments they elect have lost powers which they must recover if they are to govern.[4]

How he can make such a statement in the face of the growth of executive powers in Western democracies is a mystery he never discusses.

How does liberal democracy sap the strength of government? In various ways. The executive is weakened because power is drained from the governing center down into the constituencies; elected officers become the mere agents of organized pluralities. Thus the public interest is determined, or perhaps one should say, not determined, by the voters. Do the voters have the ability to establish, or an interest in establishing, the public interest? By no means. The opinions of the voters are simply

[4] Walter Lippmann, *The Public Philosophy* (1955), p. 14.

the opinions of the voters; "they are not—as such—propositions in the public interest." All that a vote shows is what the voters are thinking about; the idea of public interest, therefore, degenerates into a mere accommodation between the executive defending the public interest and the opinions of the voters. Or, to spell out Lippmann's thoughts for him, the voters have no sense and can have no sense of what the public interest is; they simply must be tolerated as a rather tiresome group of busybodies. The voters are incapable of recognizing the public interest because the public interest is what men would choose if they saw clearly, thought rationally, acted disinterestedly; obviously Lippmann does not think the voters are capable of noble thoughts.

There are other reasons for the decline of government, one of which is the loss of power by the executive to representative assemblies, bosses, pressure groups, and the owners of mass communications. Lippmann is not very clear about what he considers the proper relation between the executive and representative assemblies; all he says is that there should be a dual relation in which neither side would encroach on the other, a fine-sounding, if useless statement. But in view of his belief that representative assemblies today have encroached on the executive, and in the light of his statement that the executive should be the active power, we may assume that the representative assembly is to be kept delicately but firmly in its place. The people should not, Lippmann says, be flattered. For there is a vast difference between the people as voters and as an historical community. The former does not necessarily express the latter. The voters should learn to accept their place in the historical community and no fooling about it. Lippmann, in short, makes it clear that he comes down solidly on the side of Burke as against Bentham, that "resolute nominalist" as he calls him.

Because of the discrepancy between The People as voters and *The People* as the corporate nation, the voters have no title to consider themselves the proprietors of the commonwealth and to claim that their interests are identical with the public interest. A prevailing plurality of the voters are not *The People*. The claim that they are is a bogus title invoked to justify the usurpation of the executive power by representative assemblies and the intimidation of public men by demogogic politicians.[5]

The question can be raised, of course, who is to determine the interests of the real community if the voters are not allowed to do so? It is a difficult problem, but Lippmann has written his book to give the answer. For now, let it be said that the voters are not the chosen vessel because they disrupt government and order.

The question that faces modern society, in Lippmann's view, is thus: "what . . . are the true boundaries of the people's power?" The answer is:

The people are able to give and withhold their consent to being governed. They can remove it. They can approve or disapprove its performance. But they cannot administer the government. They cannot themselves perform. They cannot normally initiate and propose the necessary legislation.[6]

The fact that this statement is hardly anything but a statement of the practice followed by normal democratic government does not occur to Lippmann. Has anyone ever suggested that the people should administer, initiate, and propose legislation (except for a few Progressives of his youth)? What, then, is he complaining about? What he is complaining about is revealed by the assumption that lies behind this statement of proper

[5] *Ibid.*, pp. 33-34.
[6] *Ibid.*, p. 14.

governmental practice. The assumption that Lippmann makes is that modern democratic states do not operate in the manner that he considers to be proper. He sees modern democracy not as a system of orderly freedom but as the scene of disorderly anarchy. It is the fact that Lippmann obviously thinks democracy is incapable today of the practices he describes as proper that makes his book so significant. He assumes that democracy will prevent government. He assumes that his standard of desirable governmental practice is not achieved by modern democratic states.

What enables him to make such an assumption? He is able to assume the failure of the modern democratic state because he believes it is in the hands of the masses, who obviously are incapable of order or government. (Naturally, Lippmann gives no definition of the masses, but we should be inured to such gaps by now.)

A mass cannot govern. . . . Where mass opinion dominates the government, there is a morbid derangement of the true functions of power. . . . This breakdown in the constitutional order is the cause of the precipitate and catastrophic decline in Western society.[7]

The transition from a statement of hypothesis—"a mass cannot govern. . . ."—to a statement that the hypothesis is true of Western society today—"this breakdown in constitutional order. . . ."—should be noted. We are in the presence of another of Lippmann's sweeping assumptions, that the West is in decline because of the masses—whatever the masses may be taken to mean.

Having told us that we are ruled by the masses to the detriment of government, he must next ask how that awful event came about. He tells us that the rule of the masses is a conse-

[7] *Ibid.*, p. 15.

quence of the Jacobin conception of an emancipated and sovereign people, and, more important, of the decline of natural law in the nineteenth and twentieth centuries. We are living in a plural and fragmented society; there is no rational order to hold men in their place once natural law is ignored. The masses have been given freedom from public, general, and objective criteria of right and wrong, a freedom, however, that often becomes insupportable to the masses themselves; hence their yen for dictators. But whether the masses turn to dictators or not the results are the same. When higher law is lost the masses have such an unholy freedom that they either ruin government by compelling it to do what it knows should not be done, or they throw government into the hands of a totalitarian dictator. In the first instance the result is anarchy; in the second instance the result is tyranny. The masses cannot govern, nor can their chosen instrument, the dictator (except by force, which is, of course, the absence of government). Only through the restraint of a higher law that is beyond the control of men can the two alternatives be avoided. Only through higher law can government be attained. Such is the dualism on which Lippmann takes his stand. It is a dualism that brings us back to his main concern; there has been a "devitalization of the governing power," a devitalization that is the "malady of democratic states." The executive and judicial departments "have lost their power to decide." The masses always say no; the masses prefer the easier way.

Is such a scene of anarchical rule by the masses the only possibility for democracy? Lippmann's answer, as an advocate of government as order, as a man who sees disorder all about him, is to draw a sharp and clear distinction between liberal constitutional democracy and totalitarian, Jacobin democracy. Where have we heard these terms before? We are back with the Old Conservatives gnashing their teeth over the end of the nineteenth century. Lippmann tells us that there is an orderly form of democracy, a form that assured stability and democracy. Liberal democracy would not allow the masses to take over government. By no means. Instead it would assimilate the newly enfranchised many to the governing class, the way it has in Britain. A Reign of Gentlemen, those careful Harvard gentlemen of the late nineteenth and early twentieth centuries, the old elite of American life when life was still good, would combine firmness with a courteous ear for the many. Like the Old Conservatives, Lippmann cannot get over the idea that once there was a perfect society, that it existed at some fairly well-defined point in the nineteenth century and that it provides the standard for all that has followed.

As we shall see, between Lippmann and the Old Conservatives there are divergences that mark him out as more of a New Conservative than an Old. But on the subject of nostalgia for a vanished liberal era they are as one.

The main cause of Lippmann's divergence from the Old Conservatives and the reason why he spends less time regretting the past than he does moaning over the present is his acute sense of catastrophe in the present. For whatever the liberal dream may be, he knows that it is Jacobinism that has a hold on man today. Jacobinism is revolution, the attempt of those who have been excluded from power to attain power, and therefore it is utopianism. Jacobinism comes into being whenever reforms are refused. But as Lippmann would be the first to admit, the West has not been chary about giving out reforms. Nevertheless, he thinks that the West is threatened today with a revolutionary upsurge from below. Not in any direct sense, but in an important indirect sense, modern man is Jacobinical. Or, as Lippmann puts it, "the future of democratic society has been staked on the promises and predictions of Jacobin gospel." And the seat of Jacobinism today is found in the theory of mass education!

This surprising statement is derived from Lippmann's belief that Jacobinism is a way of escaping from what is otherwise an almost impossible task, the task of educating

. . . rapidly and sufficiently the ever-expanding masses who are losing contact with the traditions of Western society.[8]

Jacobinism is nothing less than the promise of redemption once political power is seized. It is the promise that men, acting like gods, can establish heaven on earth if they assume complete power. Hence for the Jacobin the problem of how to govern does not arise, the place of civility is taken over by the new men, and in education "there is no such thing as a general order of knowledge and a public philosophy. . . ."

Thus Lippmann establishes his morality play. There is the nineteenth-century man of reason checking his appetites with careful thought, ruling society with no belief in utopia—what he did believe in we are never told—against the lustful mass man of the twentieth century who believes that utopia can come and soon, who believes that man can do anything and should try. The former would keep himself carefully within bounds; the latter would engage in "overpassing" bounds. It is a somewhat old picture now, rather quaint, and hardly relevant, redolent of the days of Lippmann's youth. But it provides him and other conservatives with what they need, a reason to return to tradition.

The most interesting aspect of Lippmann's vision of the two adversaries is his belief that once tradition gives way the road to

[8] *Ibid.*, p. 73.

Jacobinism is wide open. Once the masses lose contact with tradition they have nothing to rely upon but themselves; the only rule in public affairs becomes the instinctive rightness of the people themselves. And such reliance is Jacobinism, simple and unadorned. Once tradition is swept away everything is swept away but human will. Where there had been a tradition of civility and a public philosophy there would be only private belief. The result would be what we have today, a

". . . growing incapacity of the large majority of the democratic peoples to believe in intangible realities. This has stripped the government of that imponderable authority which is derived from tradition, immemorial usage, conservation, veneration, prescription, prestige, heredity, hierarchy."[9]

Once again we find a conservative faced with the shattering realization that modern man has nothing to depend upon but his wits.

What is man to do? Whatever man may do, Lippmann has his solution ready. The public philosophy of liberal democracy must be resurrected. There are elements of both Old and New Conservatism in this solution.

On the one hand it is an attempt to recreate the old nine-teenth- and eighteenth-century ideal of government.

I hold that liberal democracy is not an intelligible form of government and cannot be made to work except by men who possess the philosophy in which liberal democracy was conceived and founded.[10]

If that statement means anything it means that there must be a return to an earlier form of liberal democracy, away from the shattered form in operation today. For Lippmann himself tells

[9] *Ibid.,* pp. 55-6.
[10] *Ibid.,* pp. 160-61.

us that the form of "government" that exists in the West today is hardly adequate, is hardly government at all. He is quite clear about the need to return to the past. The public philosophy he suggests we adhere to today was "articulated before the industrial revolution, before the era of rapid technological change, and before the rise of the mass democracies." So far Lippmann is simply the oldest of Old Conservatives.

But he shifts into a new note that marks him as a New Conservative when he talks about the public philosophy itself. The Old Conservative does, of course, believe in the old liberal society and government, but simply as a society and government that once provided the best way of life. Lippmann, however, is as impressed with the facts of decline as he is with the goodness of the past. What is the solution to his problem? The solution he chooses is one that puts him squarely within the confines of New Conservatism. If it is not possible to restore the past as the Old Conservative wishes to do, it may be possible to fix man in a framework of eternal principle. Once this framework is established man will find his freedom to experiment, his ability to think for himself, curbed for good. However they might disagree on specific points, Kirk and Lippmann are as one in their conviction that man must be fixed by the restraint of a higher law. As for democracy, the voters will have to take their place in the queue of generations that have come before them and will come after them. Democracy may not be overthrown; as Lippmann says he has no desire to disenfranchise his fellow citizens. But it will be carefully restricted in what it can do and cannot do by eternal principle. And out of it all will come order and the salvation of the West. Disorder and decline will yield to a new public order.

That belief in eternal principle is the conservative core of Lippmann's thought; it is revealed as soon as we ask, what is the public philosophy? After so much talk about its necessity if we are to save ourselves we feel that it is important to know what the public philosophy means. But nowhere in *The Public Philosophy* are we given the actual *content* of that vital nostrum. Nowhere does Lippmann describe the actual beliefs that make up the public philosophy. His failure to do so seems rather odd until we realize that what he is really talking about is belief in fixed, eternal principle *as such*. The belief in a fixed philosophy of government and society *is* the public philosophy. Its content matters less than the idea that man should restrict his freedom with an unalterable higher law.

The failure of Lippmann to define the public philosophy is not complete. He drops a hint about its content, as in the following statement.

. . . The democracies are ceasing to receive the traditions of civility in which the good society, the liberal, democratic way of life at its best, originated and developed. They are cut off from the public philosophy and the political arts which are needed to govern the liberal democratic society. They have not been initiated into its secrets, and they do not greatly care for as much of it as they are prepared to understand.

In Toynbee's terrible phrase, they are proletarians who are "in" but are not "of" the society they dominate.[11]

However, we are never told with any precision what the liberal democratic way of life at its best is or should be in concrete, or, indeed, general terms. It is flattering of Lippmann to assume that our minds run parallel with his on this subject and that we all know together what the liberal democratic way is, but in view of the fact that the purpose of his book is to show the danger we are in because mankind has ignored the public

[11] *Ibid.*, p. 96.

philosophy he is being somewhat optimistic. If Lippmann had spent less time on eternal principles and more on a description of liberal democratic politics as it is and as it should be, we might have been in his debt. But eternal principle has a mysterious and fatal attraction for those of the conservative persuasion. It is one of the signs by which we know that we are dealing with a conservative.

The Public Philosophy, thus, is not a concrete sense of politics and law and institutions. It is the principle of principle—eternal principle. It is the idea itself of natural law; "the public philosophy is known as *natural law*. . . . This philosophy is the premise of the institutions of Western society. . . ."[12] Lippmann's return to the eighteenth century in an effort to avoid the problem of today also leads him to the statement that the

rational faculties of men can produce a common conception of law and order which possess a *universal validity*.[13]

Having a universal validity it is obvious that the natural law is not something invented by man; it exists already before man; it is superhuman.

Is there a body of positive principles and precepts which a good citizen cannot deny or ignore? I am writing this book in the conviction that there is. It is a conviction which I have acquired gradually, not so much from a theoretical education, but from the practical experience of seeing how hard it is for our generation to make democracy work. I believe there is a public philosophy. . . . It does not have to be discovered or invented. It is known. But it does have to be revived and renewed.[14]

[12] *Ibid.*, p. 101. [*sic*].
[13] *Ibid.*, p. 105. Emphasis added.
[14] *Ibid.*, p. 101.

It is important to note that public-philosophy-cum-natural-law is essential in order to make democracy work. The freedom of being without fixed principles having failed, in the place of freedom we must erect that which exists without and despite man's arbitrary caprice, that which exists above and beyond man's freedom, that which can enclose his freedom.

The conservative, as we have seen, in full flight from the ugly realities of today, turns in the direction of his last hope—stopping man from acting. And how can man be prevented from acting? One way to prevent action is by balance. We have seen how Morley and Burnham conceive of the question; there is no reason to believe that Lippmann thinks any differently. Given man's search for power, he asks, as good old John Adams asked, how can government, in the sense of order, come into being? How can men be governed and their desire for freedom and action be negated? By balance, by pitting one power against the other.

True to form Lippmann tells us little about what he means by the phrase, balance of power, except that a balance of power makes it possible for reason to be heard. One must frankly say that the concept of a balance of power as a solution to social and political anarchy is today absolutely untenable. It assumes a totally unrealistic rationality on the part of men, an odd assumption for conservatives to make. It assumes that men can know when there is in fact a balance, that a balance can be more or less permanent. It is shocking to see a publicist of Lippmann's stature depending on such a naïve idea. But perhaps the one thing the balance of power does achieve will explain why he and other conservatives look to balance as a solution to social problems. The balance does create fear by making brute force, economic or military, the only criterion of power. It makes men fearful because they are provided with the minimum of government, are as near to being in a state of nature as they can be without going back to the woods. Ironically, the very thing Lippmann hopes to achieve, the end of social disorder, is furthered by the means he suggests, a balance of power in society. But the balance of power concept attracts the conservative-in-search-for-order for a good reason. When men are fearful they are ripe for conservatism, clinging to the last shreds that remain to them and listening to what their superiors tell them.

Is not this conservative belief in the balance of terror as a means of holding disorder within tolerable limits a contradiction of the conservative belief in the public philosophy? It is. The conservative oscillates wildly between the two extremes of believing that man must be held down by terror and believing that he must be held in with a public philosophy. The fact that the conservatives can hold two opposite opinions at the same time, as Lippmann does in *The Public Philosophy*, indicates the desperate nature of their quest for order. They cannot trust man to choose correctly; some force must make him choose correctly. In one mood it may be a balance of power and in another mood it may be the public philosophy. But in either case man is not to be allowed to choose in freedom.

The need to keep humanity in check is as clear to Lippmann as it is to any conservative. Although he hates to admit it, he does admit as he must, that man is a free animal, that he is capable of doing anything. Indeed, it is just because human nature is so adaptable and plastic that it must be checked and that Lippmann must write his book. Being adaptable and plastic, human nature is also "mal-adaptable and mis-educable." Lippmann tells us that everything good man does is acquired; hence he may reject everything good too. The issue is always in doubt. How can one escape doubt?

We are now face to face with the issues presented by *The Public Philosophy*, with Lippmann's attempt to establish a fixed order for the rule of man and society. His conservatism lies both in his attempt to resurrect the eighteenth-century concept of the state, and, more important because he never really discusses the nature of such a state, in his attempt to revive the eighteenth-century concept of the higher law, natural law, *fixed* law. It lies in his belief that in the interests of self-preservation man must restrict his freedom not by self-restraint but by restraint from a power outside of himself. As we have seen, that attitude is fundamental to conservatism. Lippmann in *The Public Philosophy* is conservative to the core, whatever he may be elsewhere.

The meaning of his faith in higher law emerges most clearly when he faces the problem of how to put that law into operation. Is this high-flying idea really feasible? Or is it simply the fruit of the midnight musings of a tired sage from the class of 1910? Lippmann has no doubts about the difficulty of the enterprise. Modern man, being the irreverent Jacobin he is, will not believe easily in higher law. Can a positivist believe, Lippmann asks, in what he cannot see? No, he cannot and will not, ungrateful sceptic that he is. In the good old medieval age men did believe. The men of the medieval age agreed

. . . that there was a valid law which, whether it was the commandment of God or the reason of things, was transcendent. They did agree that it was not something decided upon by certain men and then proclaimed by them. It was not someone's fancy, someone's prejudice, someone's wish or rationalization, a psychological experience and no more. It is there objectively, not subjectively. It can be discovered. It has to be obeyed.[15]

[15] *Ibid.*, pp. 174-175.

Hence the crucial question for our age: can man and will man believe in and experience a reality beyond himself? More precisely, although Lippmann does not state the problem in this manner, can man accept values that he has not made himself?[16]

Belief in an objective order is the essential need if the public philosophy is to be resurrected, if the decline of the West is to be halted. To establish belief in an objective order it is necessary to destroy the belief that man is free to do anything he wills, good or bad. Here Lippmann runs headlong into Jean-Paul Sartre, the modern logician of man's freedom. The few pages in which he takes issue—vainly—with Sartre are a revelation of the profoundest feelings of conservatism.

Lippmann looks upon Sartre as the devil's own advocate because Sartre, he tells us, by doing away with God, has struck the ultimate and crushing blow at the public philosophy or whatever the self-appointed agents of God wish to put on men. Lippmann sees only too clearly the implications of Sartre's act. Man must now make his own meaning. Therefore, objective meaning that exists above and beyond man and cannot be touched by man, has either been destroyed or has been shown never to have existed. God, to Lippmann, is the personification of objective meaning and once He is destroyed the hope of fooling the masses into accepting the public philosophy is dim indeed.

Man must now *invent* values. Lippmann, like all conservatives, shrinks from the truth that man today cannot find any values outside of himself. There must be, Lippmann pleads, another source of values than man himself. For if there is not, man will not and cannot believe that "beyond our private

---

[16] Lippmann never discusses the question of who is to discover values. Is it to be all men? Or a selected few? But perhaps the question is too concrete for a public philosophy.

worlds there is a public world to which we belong." Sartre's philosophy, according to Lippmann, would destroy any hope of a public life, because it destroys any hope of an objective order based on an objective public philosophy.

Lippmann is wrong in asserting that because man must create his own values he cannot create a public life; the task may be of a different order from what it is if man looks to an already existing set of values, but it is one that is capable of achievement. And since there is actually no alternative, since even the public philosophy is a figment of man's imagination, it might be well to recognize the truth and admit that man in his public as well as private life has no one to depend upon but himself. Once he makes that act of recognition he can come to grips with the realities of the task to be performed. If he fails to make that act of recognition, as Lippmann would have him do, he will not even know what it is he must accomplish.

Of more significance, however, than Lippmann's misreading of Sartre is the reason he has misread him. If man is free to invent values, then man can invent any kind of public life that pleases him. He can, in other words, innovate in the social realm. And it is the fear that Sartre's value-inventing man will innovate that shatters Lippmann. Lippmann's whole struggle is against innovation. He wants man to return to an "independent reality that can be known and must be recognized" because in doing so we will return to the security of the known, will have put aside the adventure of the unknown. The harsh yoke Lippmann wishes to put on man's freedom is hardly concealed by the old-world phraseology of his summary.

I have been arguing, hopefully and wishfully, that it may be possible to alter the terms of discourse if a convincing demonstration can be made that the principles of the good society are not, in Sartre's phrase, invented and chosen—that the conditions which must be met if there is to be a good society are there, outside our wishes, where they can be discovered by rational inquiry, and developed and adapted and refined by rational discussion.[17]

If a convincing demonstration could be made . . . . ! It never occurs to Lippmann that such a convincing demonstration has not been made today because it cannot be made. What Sartre is saying may be unpleasant—Sartre finds it unpleasant too. But it cannot be denied, despite the unsuccessful attempts of totalitarianism to do so, that man is indeed free.

Lippmann does not like the fact that man is free. He shows his dislike of freedom when he stresses the need for "significant objects that are *given*."[18] If our aims could be "given" to us by something outside of ourselves, then our troubles, in Lippmann's view, would at long last be at an end. Then man would possess fixed aims that would compel him to act according to right truth insofar as it is possible for man to act in right truth. Lippmann cannot trust man to choose public order. Man must be *given* a public order, and he must restrict his freedom so that he may act within the bounds of the order that comes to him from outside of himself.

There is, of course, no such thing as unlimited human freedom in Sartre's world or anyone else's world; man must restrict his freedom by the very act of making a choice; indeed the restriction of freedom is the essence of choice. But freedom may be restricted by the human being involved in choice or it may be restricted by mankind refusing to admit that he has the ability to choose. Since Lippmann cannot trust man to restrict his own freedom, cannot trust man to choose his own limits, he

[17] Lippmann, *op. cit.*, pp. 179-80.
[18] *Ibid.*, p. 180. Emphasis added.

must not allow man to know that he is in fact free. Hence Lippmann tries to prove that man must not choose but must acknowledge and bow down to an eternal law, an eternal essence, a higher law, a god—or a public philosophy. Whatever it is called, the purpose is the same—to prevent mankind from knowing its freedom and using its power to choose.

Lippmann's search for the perfect box for man is part of a long search, as Arthur Schlesinger, Jr., makes clear in *Lippmann and His Times,* for essence and the realm of essence in the manner of Santayana. It is a search that saved Lippmann from being a pragmatist, but it has led to some odd places. Like Rossiter, and unlike the Old Conservatives and Kirk, Lippmann looks at the American government in pro-executive terms instead of pro-legislative terms. So pro-executive is he that he cannot conceive of the executive, the "officials" as he calls them, making a mistake. What went wrong after World War I, for example, was public opinion, not the executive, the officials. True, they are human, but the big mistakes were not theirs.

Public opinion, having vetoed reconciliation, had made the [Versailles] settlement unworkable. . . . In the crises [after 1919] democratic officials—over and above their own human propensity to err—have been compelled to make the big mistakes that public opinion has insisted upon. . . . Even when there is no deliberate distortion by censorship and propaganda, which is unlikely in time of war, the public opinion of masses cannot be counted upon to apprehend regularly and promptly the reality of things. There is an inherent tendency in opinion to feed upon rumors excited by our own wishes and fears.[19]

In this cheap and nasty misreading of history, Lippmann finds what he seeks, the conviction that if the masses can only be subjected to the public philosophy the decline of the West

[19] *Ibid.,* p. 23; pp. 24-5.

The Futilitarian Society

from lawless disorder will come to an end. Or as he puts it, freedom of speech is a fine thing but only if everyone agrees on the public philosophy. The idea that the free speech is even better when there is no agreement is not one to commend itself to Lippmann.

What is the itch that has turned a seemingly sane individual like Lippmann into a raving conservative? We have already pointed out that his opinions today bear a close resemblance to the fashionable pessimism of his early days as a writer, the years just before and following World War I. But one may be more precise. Lippmann's *Public Philosophy* is based on the fear of the Great Society that was the rage around 1920 and is still the rage among conservatives today. The term *Great Society* is Graham Wallas' phrase for the typical large-scale, urban society of the twentieth century. Wallas was no conservative, but he expressed deep and uneasy concern over the nature of such a society. Was it viable? Could the principles of nineteenth-century liberal government operate in such a society? Or would the phenomena of the masses overcome reason and rationality? Lippmann takes up these concerns—many of which are, of course, justifiable—and raises them to a new pitch of intensity on the basis of the supposed failures of Western society since the end of World War I. He does more. He erects a conservative philosophy on what he sees as the ruins of the Great Society (something Wallas was careful not to do). How can a heterogeneous, large-scale society be ruled? Only with "rational order," a public philosophy.

Alexander had discovered empirically what Zeno was to formulate theoretically—that a large plural society cannot be governed without recognizing that, transcending its plural interests, there is a rational order with a superior common law. This common law is "natural" in the sense that it can be discovered by any rational mind,

182282

that is it not the willful and arbitrary positive command of the sovereign power. This is the necessary assumption, without which it is impossible for different peoples with their competing interests to live together in peace and freedom within one community.[20]

What was the embodiment of the public philosophy that Alexander found so necessary to his rule? The Roman Empire. Back to Alexander and the Roman Empire.

Lippmann's desire to return to Rome not only indicates his conservative urge to establish a final order, but also his conservative concept of freedom. Lippmann would not have us believe that he is against freedom; by no means.

[There are] the laws of a rational order of human society—in the sense that all men, when they are sincerely and lucidly rational, will regard them as self evident. . . . They are the terms of the widest consensus of rational men in a plural society. . . . It is possible to organize a state and to conduct a government on quite different principles. But the outcome will not be freedom and the good life.[21]

But he does not face, as we must face, the question of whether or not his concept of freedom is compatible with the whole basis of his thought, the idea of the public philosophy, or the question of whether his concept of freedom is not simply another form of conservative order.

In his view the problems that the Great Society must face are so overwhelming that they can only be solved on the basis of what Lippmann calls self-evident, rational principles. Once agreement has been reached on those principles freedom will be possible, for then freedom will have been enclosed, will no longer be a threat. A Great Society, by virtue of its inherent instability, cannot allow freedom leading to consensus, and

[20] *Ibid.*, pp. 106-107.
[21] *Ibid.*, pp. 123-24.

freedom questioning consensus, which then leads to further consensus and further questioning in infinite progression. In Lippmann's pessimistic view man must build his consensus on eternal principles that are outside of himself if the consensus is to survive. There are "laws of a rational order of human society. . . ." There is *one* consensus, not a perpetual series bound up in freedom and made by freedom. The Great Society is too fragile to stand the questioning of its basis, and thus freedom must be made a result of consensus, not a cause of consensus.

Lippmann never tells us how freedom is to result from the consensus that will come to man from the rational order that "must be met." He does not tell us because freedom under such circumstances would cease to exist; freedom would have ceased to exist because it could not question the consensus itself. It could not question the consensus because it would be the true, the only, the final consensus, not the consensus that is the best possible at the time and would have to be changed later and might have to give way to a new consensus, to innovation.

The conservative root of Lippmann's thought is his desire for a fixed essence external to man to which the consensus of the Great Society would conform. Then the Great Society would be saved. But only on the condition that man was not free to question the one consensus, the "true" public philosophy.

Lippmann in his *Public Philosophy* reveals more clearly than either Kirk or Rossiter the quality of fear that is so important to the New Conservatism. It is a fear of the Great Society that has come into being in the twentieth century, a fear of what is modern. The Old Conservatives fear it too, and make a quick return to the safe haven they know. But because they are more sensitive to the degradation and decline of modern society from the time of Rome and Burke, the New Conservatives are more horrified than the Old. What is the answer of the New Conservative to the problems and threats of the Great Society in which we live? It is not to use man's freedom to make it a better society or to make a new and different society, to innovate. It is to enclose man's freedom in order to prevent man from doing more damage than he has already done. The best way they know to enclose man's freedom is to make him subservient not to his own freely chosen limits but to the limits of a law higher than himself and outside of himself.

The conservative answer to the horrors of the Great Society —and certainly they are many—is appealing. If man has done so much damage by having been given so much freedom why not bring his freedom to an end? It is a quick and not very difficult conclusion. But what if the trouble is that man has not been given *enough* freedom?

8. The Businessman and Conservatism

WE HAVE SEEN that there is an uneasy, distrustful, and some-what despairing relationship between conservatism and the businessman. On the one hand the businessman cannot be de-scribed as a conservative because of his technological daring, because of his innovating impulse. By virtue of his ungoverned desire to tear down old buildings and to see to it that the bull-dozer leaves no stone unturned, he destroys the very symbols of conservatism; the ruins he makes are not exactly what the conservative means by ruins. Yet, as we have also seen, there is a certain tenderness on the part of the conservative for the businessman. They view him almost as a child gone astray, one whose intense concentration on the joys of his Erector set has led him to forget his civilized good manners. It is not just the fact that the conservative needs a constituency to which to appeal—although such considerations are not unimportant—that leads him to view the businessman as a potential ally. More important is the undoubted fact that the businessman likes conservatism too. He may not be very clear what he means by conservatism, but he shows a distinct tendency to display himself as conservative, to support himself as conservative in the ideological wilderness that howls outside his offices.

Yet the problem he presents is not a simple one. It is not a question that yields to the confused rhetoric of the conservative ideologists or the clear but one-page summary of the businessman's staff assistant. Its complexity reverberates through almost all of American history and life; the businessman is not only the kingpin of the American economy, he is also the kingpin of any interpretation of American society. So magnificent a figure is he in the old tradition of the Venetian doges and so involved in his role in America that he bursts the bounds of this study and would force us, unless we stayed a respectful distance from him, to follow him into areas far removed from the question of the nature and use of conservatism. This book cannot devote itself to a discussion of the thought of businessmen because it is a separate subject of study and because businessmen spend most of their time thinking about questions other than conservatism.[1] Nevertheless it is possible and necessary to consider the logic of the relationship of the businessman to conservatism and to suggest some hypotheses concerning that relationship. In doing so we will not only learn something of the ideological necessities of the businessman and his deep need for conservatism; we will also discover another way in which nineteenth-century liberalism can be used—and is used—to achieve conservative ends.

First, some of the complexities of the relationship must be suggested briefly. One of the major problems presented by the businessman is his refusal to tell us or himself what he thinks about politics and society. Reading books by businessmen is

---

[1] Some of the books that give a sense of how businessmen and their allies think on political and social questions are: Gordon Harrison, *Road to the Right* (1955); Henry C. Wallich, *The Cost of Freedom* (1960); Russell Davenport for the Editors of *Fortune, USA: The Permanent Revolution* (1951); Roger Blough, *Free Man and the Corporation* (1959); and F. Hayek, *The Constitution of Liberty* (1960). See also the writings of Peter Drucker.

a dreary process in which one must wade through all-encompassing clichés. Except in one respect, the businessman has little to say about political and social thought.[2] One must add, of course, that such inability does not reflect on his intellectual qualities since his role is to produce goods, not thought. And it must also be added that there are some books by businessmen that show their ability to think lucidly about society; one such book is James Worthy's *Big Business and Free Men*. But the businessman's refusal to be articulate does make it difficult to know where to place him in a spectrum of ideological thinking—a fact that will make him smile with pleasure.

The one exception to this refusal to think clearly about society is related to the well-known addiction of the businessman to profits. It is an addiction that is entirely justified and one that rapidly brings the businessman down from his cloud-cuckoo-land of happy platitudes. It is also one that might imply a view of society, and has often been taken to do so. But it raises the second difficulty presented by the businessman.

Does the addiction to profits imply a conservative view of society? The conservatives whom we have discussed have said No, an addiction to profits is not enough to make a conservative. Indeed, it may even be detrimental to conservatism, for there is no question but that profit-making may upset an established order. And in their more emotional and religious moments such conservatives would even claim that profits and conservatism are absolutely incompatible. One can see their point. But are they consistent in maintaining their point? Or do they weaken before the lure of filthy lucre? And are they correct in thinking that profits and conservatism do not mix? Arthur Schlesinger,

[2] For an example of the masterly prose of inaction favored by so many businessmen, see *Free Man and the Corporation* by Roger Blough, president of the United States Steel Corporation.

Jr., has told them in quite specific terms that they should become defenders of business and the business community, that the business world should be to American conservatism what feudalism was to European conservatism.[3] Is he correct in seeing a close and logical tie between the two? We shall see that there is good reason to think that he is, but before we do so it is necessary to look at another difficulty of the relations between conservatism and business.

One of the reasons, and perhaps the main reason, why the conservatives in America have such a distrust of the businessman is his devastating record in the nineteenth century. And devastating is the word. What the businessman did to the rather plump and somnolent society of the eighteenth century is the one thing that the conservative cannot tolerate with comfort. It is of no use to plead that today things are different, that businessmen now are well-bred gentlemen. So they are, but the cost of producing those gentlemen, the conservative moans, was the destruction of everything held dear—order, stability, tranquility, peace, quiet, and a hierarchy of country gentlemen. Even worse, it was all done in the name of liberalism. This energetic giant a conservative? Not according to Burke, he isn't.

More significant than the opinion of conservatives themselves —for they are not noticeably clear about their own past—is the opinion of those who feel that America is a liberal nation rather than a conservative one because the businessman is its representative figure.[4] This theory runs as follows. The businessman either in his petit- or grand-bourgeois incarnation is the dominant figure in American life; he is found at the beginning in,

---

[3] Arthur Schlesinger, Jr., "The New Conservatism in America," *Confluence*, December, 1953.
[4] See Chapter 9 for a more complete discussion of this idea.

say, Benjamin Franklin, and he is found today in, say, Roger Blough. As such he is always and everywhere a nineteenth-century liberal, a man dedicated to the principle of high profits through *laissez-faire,* and dedicated to swift change in all spheres of social life. Hence it is impossible for conservatism to exist in America because America is a nineteenth-century society based on business activity. This theory, in other words, not only makes conservatism the idea of a coterie, but postulates that the businessman is a liberal because he seeks the free society of Smithian economics.

Leaving aside some of the manifest difficulties of such a theory, e.g., its simplistic version of business politics (is the businessman always devoted to *laissez-faire?* Does a devotion to profits necessarily lead to a liberal society?), it is necessary to state that this theory together with conservative complaints about what the businessman did in the nineteenth century constitute the nub of the problem business presents to conservatism. It is time to unravel some of these complexities and to show that although the marriage between business and conservatism is an uneasy one it is nevertheless at least a marriage of convenience and perhaps of affection.

It is necessary to recall that a marriage does not destroy the identity of the partners. The businessman can go on his rollicking way while conservatism tends to its knitting, and the marriage can still subsist. More exactly, the businessman can engage in his technological buccaneering and yet strive to be a conservative; his identity as a businessman is not lost simply because he is a conservative. As we have said earlier, the businessman exists as a businessman; it is his existential role. But in that role he can be a conservative (or any other ideologue) and use conservatism to support his role.

When he does so, is conservatism ready to receive him? How deep is the conservative antipathy to the rough and ready manners of business? Oddly, although the conservative complains a good deal about the businessman, there is not only nothing incompatible between his ideas and the role of the businessman but, indeed, the two are positively at one on many questions.

Let us recall that the Old Conservatives in particular are essentially nineteenth-century liberals, that what marks them as conservatives today is the fact of their attempt to apply nineteenth-century canons to the society of the mid-twentieth century. Certainly, there is nothing incompatible between what the Old Conservative thinks and the urge to profit-making that must obsess the businessman. Quite the contrary, although a Felix Morley may be ueasily aware that those who cannot compete are also men, he has nothing to suggest that would in any way disturb the profit-making of, say, General Motors. Indeed, the kind of society that he suggests is ideally suited to the pursuit not of happiness but of profits, and insofar as the business world has had any ideas on the ideal society it has usually taken the form of a Morley-esque society. The Old Conservative, it is clear, is solidly in the corner of the businessman even though he may not shout the fact to the officetops. It is true that such an answer does not solve the problem of the relationship between technological vigor and the conservative's desire for a changeless society, but we will return to that question later.

What of the New Conservatives? They complain more loudly and with more exactness about the businessman. But for all their complaints do they show themselves at odds in any significant way with the business world? They do not. Each time they complain about the businessman they hasten to add (a) that it is necessary for conservatism to ally itself with business, and (b) that the businessman is really a conservative in his heart. Kirk and Rossiter especially, as we have seen, are particularly insistent that businessmen and conservatives recognize their common interests. And as for the good old liberal doctrine of *laissez-faire,* why Messrs. Kirk and Rossiter would not have us give up one iota of it. Further, their thoughts on leadership in the America of the twentieth century are certainly not incompatible with a business society; while Kirk would prefer us to be run by Scotch lairds, he will obviously settle for the lords of General Motors. Rossiter is even more precise on the subject of business leadership. Neither has seriously contemplated a society not dominated by business. One may safely say that the conservative society of Kirk and Co. would be a society in which what was good for General Motors really was good for America. The very object of Kirk and Rossiter is to make such dreams come true.

Not only, therefore, are the proposals of the conservatives, New or Old, compatible with the business-run society of today; they would make it a society even more to the liking of the businessmen. It is particularly noticeable that the conservatives have proposed many weird and wonderful things for mankind, but the one thing they never propose is regulating or restricting business. Is such a lacuna due to their other-worldliness, to their myopic concern with original sin and all that? Partly, but only partly. It is also due to the deep and profound coincidence of view between the business world and conservatism. The businessman is, so to speak, the natural ally of the conservative. Neither may recognize it, but the marriage between them is viable and long standing. It is no mistake that the conservative treats the businessman with great tenderness.

What is the tie that holds them together? Let us look a little more closely at the implications of those technological innovations that so ruffle the normal good nature of the conservative. Certainly he is correct in saying that it sweeps old landmarks away; the technological fantasies of the businessmen are the cause of profound social changes. But does the businessman desire those social changes? Is he even aware of the results of his activities? With his eyes glued to the balance sheet, is he capable of seeing what social change his technology involves? Once upon a time he was; once upon a time he did desire a profound social change. When he was driving hard for the creation of an industrial society in the place of an agricultural society he was indeed a revolutionary force. But those days have been gone these past one hundred years.

What happens when the industrial society is achieved? Is the businessman still eager to carry forward social change as a result of his technological developments? Or is he rather intent on preserving the society that has given him what he wanted? Is "business as a system of power," to use Robert Brady's excellent phrase, revolutionary in any social and political sense once it has achieved power? Does it not rather desire a fixed society in which it can play with its technology and its power undisturbed by social and political change? It would be passing strange indeed if the latter were not true.

It may well be that what the businessman hopes for is unreal and naïve. But that is no reason for believing that he does not have such hopes. As a way of viewing his society it is quite possible for the businessman's vision of technological change and social stasis to exist simultaneously in his mind, if not in fact. The businessman loves his technological change, of course, because it is the means of realizing ever greater profits. But the more he sees the profits that accrue the less anxious he is for any social change that would interfere with his profit-making activity. From his own point of view he is quite right to hold

such an attitude. But in social and political matters it is nothing
if not a conservative attitude. His desire for social and political
fixity, the very heart as we have seen, of conservative doctrine,
is in his mind the essential condition for profits. True, there may
be a difference between a conservative ideologist and the businessmen over the exact outline of the ideal society. But they
are both conservative in their opposition to social and political
innovation. The conservative ideologist may be more logical
because he opposes all innovation. But although the marriage
is uneasy, such differences do not necessarily disrupt it. Besides,
ideologists are always more logical than the facts warrant; in
one sense the businessman is more realistic than the ideologist
because he knows that you must have both bread and circuses
to keep society in a condition of stasis.

The businessman, once he is faced with the results of his
deeds, therefore, refuses to acknowledge that they entail a
different kind of society, and as a result he fights every proposal that the "radicals" bring in to redress the things he has
done. "Radicals" are in fact so busy bringing about the social
and political changes made necessary by the businessman's
activity that they seldom have time for anything else, for any
kind of long-range revolution. But the businessman does not
see what the radicals are driving at because he does not want
the social and political change he has made necessary. One may
take as an example of his inability to see the consequences of
his acts the recently introduced compact cars. Having created
a situation in which urban life has come to a condition of near-
crisis through the overproduction of automobiles, what is the
businessman's solution to the problem he has created? It is not
to contemplate the creation of a new kind of urban existence,
of new social and political measures to deal with the failures of
city life. No, his solution is—to produce more but slightly

smaller cars! Did every family have one big car? Now they should have one big and one small car. As a solution to urban congestion it leaves something to be desired, but one can see the point, the point being (a) that there was profit to be made from compact cars, and (b) a real solution would mean social innovation.

The businessman is certainly an asset to the Republic but even he would agree in his more secure moments that he has no solutions to the problems that his technological drive creates. He has no solutions for two reasons. (1) He is, as we have said, a businessman and as such he is not a social thinker. (2) But when he does think about society he thinks about it as a conservative. He is incapable of concepts of social and political change because his role as a businessman is bound up with social stasis. It is not just that he likes social stasis. It is a necessity to his very existence as a businessman in a business-dominated society.

This gross generalization requires, of course, various kinds of qualifications, one of which is that this society is not as business-dominated as might appear from the advertisements —a fact, however, that is not calculated to please the businessman. Still it comes as close to it as any society has except for Venice. One must also say that one is grateful to the businessman both for his ability to maintain and create a high material standard of living and for his instinctive sense that his job is to produce goods and stay out of politics. Yet it is difficult and even impossible for him, as a member of a power group, to stay out of politics. He must of necessity—the necessity being to sell more goods and to prevent alternative ways of existence from arising—impress the nation with his vision of the good society. And not only must he impress the nation with the idea that it is good to buy goods, but he must impress them with the idea that those goods can only be produced and sold in a certain way. One must note here the anger with which such business organs as the *Wall Street Journal* have pursued Professor Galbraith's suggestion that society reorient itself around other ends. The mere suggestion that Mad. Ave. may after all be truly mad is hardly palatable to those who gain by its madness. The businessman is, after all, engaged upon a difficult and treacherous enterprise, and one can quite understand that he does not want to have his delicate operations disrupted by social and political change. But please, let us stop saying that the businessman is not a conservative. He is *both* a businessman and a conservative. And it is time that the businessman and the ideologists of conservatism recognize the fact.

Anyone who has ever talked with businessmen must know the immense fatigue with which they receive any suggestion that social and political change is necessary as a result of what society has become. And they are quite right to be weary of such suggestions. Business is bad enough as it is. They are right because social and political change will upset the apple cart even more. Does one really expect General Motors to stop producing so many cars because there is no need for them, because they are a positive detriment to "better living" (as duPont likes to put it)? It would be a logical solution to the problems of the cities. It is even a quite feasible solution. But not in a fixed society.

Hence the businessman's liking for a liberal society of the nineteenth-century variety, for that society favored by Felix Morley and James Burnham, and also by Kirk and Rossiter. Such a society—decentralized, *laissez-faire*, and powerless—is the perfect venue for the work of the businessman. Within the ring of fixed rules he can pile up his profits to unimaginable heights while everyone else stays passively in his place. Profit-making as an activity is not disturbed. The hierarchy of business domination is not disturbed. And business as a system of power is not disturbed. Nineteenth-century liberal society can not only be made into a fixed conservative society by the theoreticians of conservative beliefs; it can also be made into a fixed conservative society by the businessman. For it is one in which there is no change except bigger and bigger profits, one in which the businessman does not have to face the consequences of his acts. Nineteenth-century liberalism could yield in the nineteenth century and can yield today the same fruit to both the conservative ideologist and the businessman. It gave and gives both what they are looking for, a society in which the rules are fixed, in which significant social and political change cannot therefore take place, and in which men are not allowed to make social innovation. The difference between the businessman and the ideologist is that the former by the nature of his function creates technological innovation and hence social changes that he does not desire but must be faced sometime by somebody. Hence the businessman breaks with his own hands his conservative dream. The pursuit of profits and nothing but profits is not as pure and innocent an activity as he thinks.

Yet the conservative dream is always with the businessman. It *must* be with him, for otherwise he would be forced to contemplate a society in which the pursuit of profits would be subordinated to other considerations. If it is possible for society to change, to innovate in the social as well as the technological realm, then a different, a new, type of society may come into being in which other and alien norms would (by definition) operate. In the nineteenth century the businessman reached his social goal, a society in which he could pile up profits without regard for the consequences of such activity. It was a goal reached under the aegis of a particular form of government, the bargaining model of nineteenth-century liberalism. It was an excellent model for his purpose because it could be used to enclose man's freedom through the use of mandatory natural laws.[5] Those laws could be used to say that such-and-such was proper and such-and-such was improper, that the form of society was fixed. Within that form bargains might take place but by the very nature of bargains they could not result in any fundamental change; i.e., the weak could not overthrow the strong. Hence nineteenth-century liberalism *could* be—not necessarily *had* to be—used for the purpose of negating change then and now. It could be used for conservative purposes, and through such use became the distinctively American form of conservatism both for the ideologist and for the businessman who had to find some means of negating the effects of his own technological fertility.

The businessman's affection for conservatism runs far deeper, therefore, than mere expediency. His conservatism does not and cannot differ in any fundamental respect from that of the ideologist. In order to preserve himself and the society that he dominates he must prevent change from taking place, he must strive to establish a fixed society.

The attempt to establish such a society fails and must fail by the logic of the situation. But the consequences of the attempt and its failure are enormous. They serve essentially to make for a society that is out of control because the businessman as the dominant force in that society refuses to face the fact of change. Hence they help create the irrational society of which the businessman and the conservative ideologists complain so bitterly. Who has created the mass society of today?

---

[5] See Chapter 13 for a more complete discussion of this point. See also John Dewey's comments on natural law and fixed order, *The Quest for Certainty*, chap. VIII.

Was it the modern liberal with his rather starry-eyed visions of the "better life"? So one would think to read how the conservatives have interpreted George Orwell's *1984*. Or was it the businessman with his technology and advertising, his thrust toward change and his refusal to contemplate new ways of controlling and ordering change? The conservative and the businessman when he is acting as a conservative find the irrationality of the mass society repugnant. Yet what is its irrationality but the irrationality of technology gone mad? And why has that technology gone mad except for the fact that the makers of technology today refuse to contemplate those innovations that would lead to the control of technology? They cannot contemplate such innovations because to do so would be to admit the possibility of a different kind of society. It would be to admit the possibility of change, to admit that the fixed society is not feasible.

Thus the businessman turns to conservatism both to protect his position as the leader of his society and to protect himself against the results of what he has done. Is it claimed that his product produces lung cancer? He must react as the cigarette companies in America have reacted, not by allowing some new innovating form of social control, but by simply adding a filter tip and spending more money on advertising. The society, if not the health of its citizens, will go on undamaged and will not have admitted innovation into its system. It is true, indeed, that there is a profound fissure in the conservatism of the businessman; compared to the conservative ideologist he finds it much more difficult, as a real human being living in a real world, to be a conservative, since he is always destroying the fixed condition he strives to erect. But it is just because his activities are a threat to order and fixity that he needs conservatism so much.

9. The Conservative Mood: Louis Hartz, Daniel Boorstin

IN THE 1950's a widely-shared impulse created what might be called the Conservative Mood of that decade. They were quiet years, the 1950's, years when the forces of history were preparing new surprises beneath the placid surface of things. They were good years too, good for introspection. Many therefore turned to introspection on a large scale, and yielded passively to the impulse that promised them relief from knowledge of evil. It was an impulse to look inward and backward, to search for the essence of America and to find once and for all what America Stood For. The search for the Real Meaning of America, for the thing that could unite the variety and the vast, confusing sprawl of American life and history into one grand thought, one all-encompassing essence, was a profoundly deep desire of those years. (It was a desire, needless to say, much abetted and aided by the profit motive of Madison Avenue.) If the American essence could only be captured and fixed, then there would be the security of the known.

Once America was pinned down to a known quantity, then the fact that one could not see what the future would bring, and was not sure about what to do in the present, would not matter quite so much. One would at least know what America had been in the past; one would have a secure base from which to operate. Much uncertainty would thereby be removed. Even better, by knowing what the essence of America had been it would be possible to know what the essence of America is and should always be. The guideline would have been laid down to the future; that treacherous moment when one hesitates before choosing the next step into the future, before creating anew in the midst of nothingness, would have been abolished. Assurance about the past—it is important to know this lesson—is assurance about the future too. Know thyself! was therefore made a maxim for the practical purpose of telling Americans how to defeat the future by acting as they always had in the past. The object of turning inward was to grasp a hard and solid essence so that all the unpleasant variety that can disrupt security and finality might be sloughed off. Obviously, if one knows what America has been, then to be a good American one need only go on doing what has been done before. Indeed, not to do what America has always done is to be positively un-American. The study of history—of a certain type, of course—can truly be an excellent discipline.

But it can be even better if certain conclusions are drawn. Merely to look inward and backward—and, naturally, one cannot look inward without looking backward since the past is the only hard fact we find when we introspect—is not enough. There is something else that must be sought to make the inward search a good thing. Obviously neither the tentative conclusions of scholarly research, nor the efforts of those who would seek to show America as the place of significant and important conflicts, whether the conflicts be political or ideological, satisfies the conservative urge for security. The whole point of the inward search is to get away from conflict and to

grasp that shiny essence that stands above and beyond conflict, the essence[1] that those lesser mortals who insist on en-
gaging in conflict should obey but which they fail to see. That
there is such an essence is never doubted, of course, by those
involved in the search. Thus the object of the search is to get
rid of conflict by showing it to be meaningless, by finding the
essence of America—the unity of a changeless society. If that
Great Truth can be discovered then the sting can be drawn
from change. The changes of history, all those tiresome differences of opinions in which men will engage, can be viewed
with a tolerant and amused glance and with the certain knowledge that the disputants of the past were wrong, were even
debating the wrong issue. As one of the practitioners of this
art of the amused wink and nod, Professor Louis Hartz says
in his discussion of American Progressivism, the "Progressive
historians . . . fortified with a mass of erudition all the misunderstandings the average American . . . had about himself." He
goes on to say that "there is more than a touch of comedy in
this, ..."[2] because "fundamental value struggles have not been
characteristic of the United States."

Once we agree with Professor Hartz that all the changes and
arguments of the past are waste we are in sight of the promised
land. The impulse that has steered the inward-backward search
is also an impulse to find a fundamental and overriding unity
that can cancel out change and confusion by participation in
the Great Unity that flows from the Great Essence. There must
be a unifying rubric that will tie up the whole messy affair of

[1] Obviously, to describe the essence of a thing is not necessarily to take a
conservative attitude towards it. But it is to take a conservative attitude if no
other possibility than the essence is postulated. As we shall see, it is because
Hartz and Boorstin do not postulate any other possibility and indeed make it
difficult to do so that they can be said to fall into a conservative mood.
[2] Louis Hartz, *The Liberal Tradition in America* (1955), pp. 248-49.

the past. It will be, by its very nature, a rubric that will show that the American people are not merely one people—such an assertion is too obvious even for those in the Conservative Mood—but that they are one people because they are united on one set of values, a set of values that is so important that other values become meaningless. Conflict and change exist, to be sure. But the values that override them make conflict the work of comedians, of comedians who cannot see that they are in agreement with their enemies. Such methods of interpreting history, such big general theories of history, really do turn Marx on his head. But more important than showing that those who lived in the past were comedians, such interpretations demonstrate (or attempt to demonstrate) that those values that unify America make it a unity *without any other possibility*. By displaying an America that has never changed, by describing an America that has always had the same values, such interpretations tell us that since our nation has never changed it is fundamentally the same today as it was in the eighteenth century. Hence it follows that America is not a place where change and variety can take place; it is instead a nation that, because it has always been the same, must therefore always be the same in the future. To attempt to make important changes in American life would be to destroy the mold that *is* America. In any realistic sense, therefore, America cannot change, find a new form in the future. Further, if America has not been able to break out of the mold that was set in the eighteenth century it is difficult to believe that it will be able to do so at this late date. Seldom has any nation been clamped into such an excruciatingly tight box. Seldom has the conservative view of change been thrust so brutally upon the American public. And seldom has a nation been so stripped of possibilities.

LOUIS HARTZ

Professor Louis Hartz is the dean of this new school of historical interpretation. His *Liberal Tradition in America* (1955) is an attempt to prove that the unity of America is so profound and so deep that it overrides and has overridden all other considerations and conflicts, and to show that this unity has always existed; no matter what the issue, no matter what the historical period, America has been united on one set of principles, the principles of Lockian liberalism. Hartz would acknowledge that there have been conflicts in American history and differences of political opinion. He might even admit, although he does not in fact, that those conflicts and differences were important and significant to those living at the time. But in his eyes they all fade to ashes, to insignificant battles fought by deluded pigmies, because the really important features of the American past as he sees it and as we should see it, looking back from our comforts of today, is the fact that the participants in the arguments really were united by sharing the same values of Lockian liberalism. He can only wonder that they did not understand that what united them was so vastly more important than that which was at issue. Looking back we can know now that America is a fixed and single unity running from its beginning right up to now. The lesson of *The Liberal Tradition in America* is clear. Lockian liberalism is all there ever has been in American history; America has been closed and impervious to any other set of values. There have not even been significant differences of interpretation.

Hartz's general thesis can be simply described. He takes off from where Rossiter stopped, for the fact that has determined our history from its beginning is that Americans were born free, that they did not have to struggle with a feudal system to attain freedom. From then on the blessings began to flow, and first among the blessings was the absence of a revolutionary and reactionary tradition. Or, as he puts it, the outstanding feature of the American Revolution was not the freedom to which it led but the feudal system it did not have to destroy. If such a statement sounds peculiar it is because Hartz sees the nation not in American terms but in exclusively European terms. One of the fatal weaknesses of his book is his postulate that because we did not produce the equivalent of Bonald, we had no conservatives; that is, what is left, as he would say, after you subtract a Bonald from the American scene where he did not exist, was John Locke. It is all very confusing, but designedly so, for otherwise it would be hard to show that America was *only* a unity. He does not hide the perspective he adopts.

If the American are "realistic" when they celebrate their solidarity in London or Paris, can they also be "realistic" when they forget it in Philadelphia? What happens, of course, when the Americans come home is that they lose their comparative perspective and plunge themselves into the shadow world of their own social conflict.[3]

Certainly no one will accuse Hartz of having lost his "comparative perspective." Not after referring to American social conflicts as a "shadow world."

Thus, for Hartz there is no conservatism in America and no radicalism because we have never had the European feudal system to be conservative and radical about. We started out as Lockian liberals and so shall we remain. All we had to do was to conserve the freedom that we had. As for our domestic struggles, those deplorable shadow worlds of conflict, they can easily be explained as simple variations on the theme of Locke.

[3] *Ibid.,* p. 81.

Both sides in the various struggles, from the beginning to the end, were simply delightful but fuzzy-minded Lockian liberals, their only fault being that they didn't know it.

To explain this happy state of affairs Hartz has to invent a *deus ex machina*—Horatio Alger. It is Alger who saves the day after the demise of Hamilton and the Federalists, who, of course, were Lockian, too, but refused to admit it. As Hartz puts it, there is a difference between feudal pessimism and liberal pessimism about man, an awesome thought that he never quite develops. However, after the Federalists the Horatio Alger mechanism swings into full operation. Because the American "left" is simply the European petit-bourgeois tradition of liberalism and the American "right" is the European big-property tradition of liberalism, the two sides could come together in a celebration of Lockian liberalism while pursuing the fortunes of Alger. Thus America was bound to become both capitalistic and democratic, although the irony of our early history is that the two "seemed" to conflict with each other rather than complement each other. But still, the American democrat was as much an Alger liberal as the men who opposed democracy. Thus those who denounced the American democrats cannot be considered or called conservatives. By no means, because, as we recall, there is no feudalism here. No, the opponent of the democrat had better be called a Whig, for the term Whig will rid American history of the suspicion that the quarrels of Democrat and Whig were of significance. For, as Hartz never tires of telling us, the American Democrat was no threat to the Whigs; he was the same kind of Liberal as the Whig who opposed him. The fact that neither side saw it that way is one of those comical episodes of history. As Hartz says, in the early years and almost up to the Civil War, there was a "massive confusion" in American political thought. Indeed there was.

But the confusion can be dispelled for us at least if we concentrate on Horatio Alger, for he combined Hamilton's vision of capitalism with the Jeffersonian vision of equality; he united the two great traditions of the American liberal community. It was a successful unity because all Americans were of the same estate; the Whig was simply a wealthy middle-class capitalist and the Democrat was a small propertied farmer, practically the same thing you might say. As for the worker, he was, of course, a potential entrepreneur.

One might complain here about Hartz's simplistic, Chamber of Commerce, version of American class structure, but suffice it to say that he shows no recognition of the real and significant existence of class in America, that he swallows the nineteenth-century myth of happy equality among the Algers without a glance at the facts of sociology. And, of course, it is necessary for him to ignore class,[4] if he did not do so his Lockian unity might not present such a smooth surface to the world. His object, he tells us, is to contrast the reality of American social freedom and social equality with the misrepresentations of the past by Americans who see our nation only in terms of oppression and struggles against exploitation. This cheerful view of things is shown in his treatment of Shays' Rebellion, Shays being another deluded agitator. To Hartz the reality of the rebellion is clear; those who rebelled were men of kindred spirits with those they rebelled against, they were both inside, not outside, the liberal process of American politics.

Thus the joke of American politics, this comical shadow world, goes on. The gigantic figure of Horatio Alger strides across the scene, uniting democracy and capitalism in the

[4] It is interesting to note, in this connection, that Berthoff's "The American Social Order: A Conservative Hypothesis," (*American Historical Review*, April, 1960) finds class conflict to be the very stuff of *American* social history.

happy fusion of Lockian liberalism. Does it seem that after the Civil War capitalism became more capitalistic and democracy became less democratic? It is not a problem Hartz discusses, but he does say that even though the financially successful people—not the Robber Barons, the successful people—saw a vast difference between themselves and the crowd below them, they were nevertheless at one with the nation as a whole because they were not and could not be European aristocrats. The Lockian liberal synthesis is still sound despite a few creaks and groans from those holding it up. Indeed, what characterized the successful people, or Whigs, after 1865 was their "wild" devotion to Locke. Quite so.

But there is always a malcontent around the corner. The Progressives were an unpleasant fly in the ointment. It was, to be sure, a "sporadic Progressivism," not one calculated to disturb Alger and his Lockian synthesis. Still, it did present us with a nasty moment or two. It did so because the Progressives, like poor old Daniel Shays, missed the whole point of their solidarity with their enemies. How often the delusion of conflict appears in our history! The Progressives were victimized by the fact that their enemies were not European Tories and Socialists. Thus they were no more able than their old friends the Whigs had been to perceive the nature of their own liberalism, to perceive their basic agreement with the Whigs on Lockian liberal principles. Instead they insisted that their enemies were conservatives with whom they had some important and rather pressing differences of opinion. "With the whole scheme of liberal unity blacked out, Whiggery became for the Progressives a frightful 'conservatism,' whereas it itself became 'progressive' or 'radical' . . . ."[5]

[5] Hartz, *op. cit.*, p.29.

But we can know today that they were not fighting a frightful conservatism because, first, there is no such thing as conservatism in America (there never having been a feudal system here) and second, the liberal reform movements were "enslaved" along with the Whigs to the dream of Horatio Alger and democratic capitalism. The fact that the dream was more rewarding to some than to others is not, of course, a consideration that enters into the abstract speculation of Hartz's political theory. This "pathetic enslavement" of the Progressives to Whig beliefs was an "expression of the dogmatic Lockianism of the nation. . . ." Thus, the futility of the Progressives along with everyone else.

The Progressives failed because, being children of the American absolutism, they could not get outside it, and so without fully seeing that Locke was involved *everywhere,* they built their analysis around a titanic struggle between "conservative" and "radical" which had little relevance to Western policies as a whole.[6]

Hartz adds:

"There is more than a touch of comedy in this. . . ."[7]

The reason the whole thing is so humorous is that the Progressive critics did not tell the American petit bourgeois about his "solidarity with the Whigs." Maybe they were afraid of being lynched.

The New Deal is a tougher nut to crack because it had the audacity, as Hartz admits, to deviate to some degree from Lockian liberalism. But Hartz and Horatio Alger come through in the end. For it turns out that the very deviations of the New

[6] *Ibid.,* p. 236. Emphasis added.
[7] *Ibid.,* p. 249.

Deal from Locke proved their devotion to Locke. The logic here is close and even subtle, but well worth appraisal, for if Hartz's description of the unity of American life fails to encompass the New Deal it fails totally and completely. The New Deal must either fit the pattern of Lockian liberalism that Hartz has laid down for us, or the pattern must be discarded as irrelevant today, whatever it may once have been.

What was the New Deal? On the one hand it was a "movement within the framework of the liberal faith . . . which sought to extend the sphere of the state and at the same time retain the basic principles of Locke and Bentham." (This mention of Bentham is the first time he has entered into Hartz's discussion; although he is suddenly coupled with Locke we are not told whether or not there might be or is any difference or conflict between them. Can Bentham be treated as a simple appendage of Locke?) On the other hand the New Deal "involved substantive departures from the Liberal faith of a considerable kind." Are we faced with the first break in the seamless web of Lockian Liberalism? No, because the New Deal—and here is where the logic becomes breathtaking—really was liberal deep down in its innermost beliefs. The reason Hartz thinks the New Deal was really liberal is that it did not spell out its philosophy since there was no challenge on the left and right to force it to do so. We are back with the study of American history as the study of what it does not contain.

In other words, the crucial thing was that, lacking the socialist challenge and of course the old corporate challenge on the right such as the European conservatisms still embodied, he [F. D. R.] did not need to spell out any real philosophy at all. His "radicalism" could consist of what he called "bold and persistent experimentation," which of course meant nothing in terms of large social faiths and was indeed perfectly compatible with "Americanism." Good Americans like Edison and Alexander Graham Bell were experimenters. So were the pioneers. When asked concerning his social philosophy, Roosevelt once said that he was a Democrat and a Christian, which meant, needless to say, that he was as good an irrational Lockian as Grover Cleveland.[8]

Thus while it is true that the New Deal was an antagonist of property it was true only because there was no one of importance to the left of them. If there had been they would have revealed their liberal faith. As Hartz sorrowfully says,

Alas, as always, there was nothing to bring to the surface this last-ditch Lockian spirit because the leftist challenge was inconsequential.[9]

Alas, the New Deal and Roosevelt are just further examples of Americans not knowing what their own thoughts were. And that being the case Hartz can have it both ways. The New Deal did depart from the "national liberal scheme."[10] But the unity of America, the static timeless quality of American life, its eternal essence, cannot be allowed to slip from our fingers at this last and crucial moment.

What emerges then in the case of the New Deal is *a liberal self that is lost from sight:* a faith in property, a belief in class unity, a suspicion of too much state power, a hostility to the utopian mood, all of which were blacked out by the weakness of the socialist challenge in the American liberal community.[11]

[8] *Ibid.*, p. 263.
[9] *Ibid.*, p. 269.
[10] *Ibid.*, p. 249.
[11] *Ibid.*, p. 270. Emphasis added.

In summary, there were no socialists in America because ours is a liberal community; because there were no socialists the New Deal did not have to demonstrate its liberal faith; thus, the New Deal was a liberal movement in the same tradition and of the same kind of Lockian liberalism as all the other movements in the American past. In the nick of time American unity, complete and final, is saved.

It is easy to criticize Professor Hartz's work. The reader for example, is often curious to know what he means by the term *Lockian liberalism.* He never defines it, but he does not have to do so, because whatever the Americans have thought is Lockian liberalism. The reader may also feel that poor old Locke, for all his originality and profundity, is hardly a suitable vehicle to explain everything in our history from George Washington to Franklin Roosevelt. Further, Hartz is more than somewhat naïve about the reality of social class in both Europe and America; his view that "class and ideological forces were at the heart of European politics, feudal as it was in origin" may be worthy of Marx but is hardly worthy of modern scholarship on eighteenth- and nineteenth-century Europe. It is, to be quite exact, an out-of-date textbook image. He also makes the comparative method of history a sad joke by his misuse of it; he tells us, for example: "remove Wellington from Macaulay, and you have in essence Alexander Hamilton. . . ." He adds, "the link between the latter two is not at first easy to see." Indeed it is not, because if you remove Wellington from Macaulay, a neat trick in itself, you have nothing at all. You have nothing at all because you have destroyed the whole historical context in which those three gentlemen lived. In fact, you have destroyed history. But to destroy history is what Hartz aims to do, what he must do, because history is the record not of eternal essence, but of change and innovation, of new and unique events and ideas.

But criticism of Hartz is beside the point,[12] the point being the support he gives to the conservative belief that change and innovation can be stilled, that the eternal essence of Kirk and the public philosophy of Lippmann are to be found in the history of America. Hartz himself is no conservative, of course, but he reflects the Conservative Mood in his search for timeless unity, for the higher law that has ruled America.

He gives his aid to conservatism in a variety of ways. First, while he has some interesting insights, even they reveal his effort to twist history into the shape of a perfectly round and finished ball. He sees, for example, the liberal character of the Progressives, their attempt to create a world of small business, of local control, to avoid the consequences of bigness in industry, farming, and politics. He is correct in saying that the trust-busting aims of the Progressives were part of a liberal program. (To claim that their liberalism was Lockian, however, is to make a meaningless statement; Locke never thought much about trusts.) But what he misses, and for a good reason, is the fact that there was a real conflict between big and small property, a conflict that can not be done away with by saying that both sides agreed on property and that therefore the conflict was a comical misunderstanding.

The Progressives, whom Hartz misunderstands himself, (for he makes no mention of the variety of beliefs in Progressivism

[12] Eric Goldman in *Political Science Quarterly*, December 1955, after pointing out that Hartz never comes to grips with the fact that there were deep-seated conflicts in America before 1900, says that his thesis is less open to attack in regard to the years after 1900 and especially in regard to the 1950's. He concludes his review of *The Liberal Tradition in America* with the following comment: "Not the least of the fascination of Mr. Hartz's volume is the way it raises the eternal question of historiography. Could it be that historians and political scientists of the 1930's frame of mind, thinking amid such strident ideological warfare, overemphasized the degree of cleavage in previous decades? Could it be that a later generation, thinking amid rampant middle-roadism, is overemphasizing the extent of agreement in the past?"

regarding size[13]) were engaged in a serious and significant conflict—one that was significant for them and us. They may have been wrong in thinking that their methods could achieve what they wanted to achieve. But they were not wrong in believing that a conflict existed between the owners of the trusts and those who were owned by the trusts. To say that John D. Rockefeller and a shirt-tailed farmer in the Dakotas were both Lockian liberals because they both liked property and therefore had no real differences is to reach new heights of distortion in the reinterpretation of the past. It is also to give comfort to those today who are on top of the heap, because they can be assured that we are all good fellows together, all Lockian liberals, and that there are really no vital conflicts between Americans. Just a few unfortunate misunderstandings.

The significance of Hartz's refusal to see that when men fight they fight over something important to them and that the fight is not just a misunderstanding of deluded men is seen in his treatment of conservatism in America, or rather, in his refusal to treat it. He refuses to admit that there has been conservatism in America because, as we know, there has been no Bonald among us; that is, there has been no movement in America similar to that of European conservatism. And he is right (more or less; in fact the question does not yield to such simplicities). There have been no Bonalds in America. But does the nonexistence of Bonalds mean that there has been no *conservatism?* Is it not possible that we have developed our own form of conservatism within the unity known as the United States of America? And that that peculiarly American form of conservatism has been productive of real conflicts between its adherents and their opponents past and present? Have not other nations developed their own unique forms of conflict in

[13] See Eric Goldman, *Rendezvous with Destiny* (1952).

which their own unique conservatism plays a part? Is there a Bonald in Britain?

Hartz's use of the name Whig is inadmissable because it smears out the real conflict between conservative and radical in America, a conflict over social control and a conflict—Locke notwithstanding—of philosophy. It was a conflict over the nature of social freedom, and while our good friend John Locke may have provided arguments pro and con, the argument took place in an historical context that created a unique debate. Hartz makes his bow to the facts of conflict in America when he tells us that to stress liberalism in the United States is not to deny that wide variations take place within liberalism, that one can still emphasize the differences between Taft and Bryan.[14] But, as we have seen, that emphasis is exactly what Hartz is at pains to avoid. And the question can be raised; if one insists on seeing conservatives as Whigs and Progressives as Alger-types, can one even discern significant conflict? On the evidence of his book the answer is No.

Hartz's refusal to see that America could and did produce its own form of conservatism is, of course, necessary to his vision of America as a seamless unity. But in the process of creating a seamless unity he has not only destroyed history but made a meaningless unity. As we have already seen, conservatism in America is a form of nineteenth-century liberalism. One may call this conservatism Whiggish if one wants to do so, but to miss the conservative feature of nineteenth-century liberalism, both then and now, and especially its conservative view of development and innovation, is to miss the point about political thought in America in order to postulate a unity that never existed in reality. Nineteenth-century liberalism was and is today an effort to establish a timeless political system in

[14] Hartz, *op. cit.*, p. 26.

which political and social—as distinct from technological—innovation would have come to an end. It is, of course, derived from the mechanistic world of Locke, from the eighteenth century with its antihistorical concepts and its belief in eternal laws. Hence Lockianism can be easily used for conservative attempts to bring history to an end. To call the nineteenth century liberal then and Whig now, may or may not be legitimate, but it is not legitimate to confuse the nineteenth-century liberal with (a) the modern liberal with his emphasis on historical development and change, and (b) the enemies of the nineteenth-century liberal, past and present, whose wish was and is to make such wide and significant changes in society as would disrupt the present distribution of social power that the nineteenth-century liberal, past or present, has wished to preserve.

One may grant, certainly, that American political battles take place within a unity that transcends the battle; if they did not there would not be, by definition, an American nation. But other countries also have their fundamental unity that overrides their battles. To understand any nation it is essential to grasp both the nature of their unifying forces and the nature of their battles. To miss the nature of their conflicts is to miss the very quality of a nation. In the case of America the conflict has ranged under many rubrics; to try to squeeze them into one category is to obscure and distort the point of historical change. But one rubric is that of conservative *vs.* radical, conservative having in America its particularly American sense of the nineteenth-century (or Lockian, if one prefers) liberal with his particular view of social and political change, his particular view of what is the good society for America, and his particular set of enemies who disagree with both his attitude to change and his view of the good society. We have seen not only what those views of change and the good society are; we have also seen that there is little fundamental difference between what the Old Conservative and the New Conservative thinks on such questions. Names, of course, are arbitrary; Lockian liberal, Whig, nineteenth-century liberal, Old Conservative, New Conservative—they can all be used. But reality is not arbitrary, and the reality behind all the tags is the particular ways of looking at change and the particular set of values that make not a European but an American conservative. Therein is the reality of social attitudes, and not in a simplistic version of history that seeks to show that nothing happened in American history just as the eighteenth century tried to show that nothing happened in the Middle Ages.

The question can be raised, did not the American nation agree mainly with conservative-Whig-nineteenth-century-Lockian liberalism? The answer would, one supposes, require a Gallup Poll of the dead, but even without such a poll it would seem that there have been some rather fierce conflicts in America, that unanimity has been decidedly lacking.[15] However, the Conservative Mood requires that such conflicts be blacked out, to use Hartz's favorite word. Hartz gives aid and comfort to those who fight against change, who desire to find a timeless essence in which they can immerse themselves, when he shows not only that America is such a timeless essence, but when he shows that ideological arguments among us do not matter because they have not mattered. Those in the Conservative Mood have what they are looking for, an excuse to avoid the discomfort of ideological thought, and an excuse for not being con-

[15] We have not discussed Hartz's view of the Civil War because, as he says, his analysis cannot throw light on the Civil War since it was the one unique event in American history for which there is no comparative material. Hartz, *op. cit.*, p. 19.

cerned. Hartz is aware of the virtue possessed by his analysis; in his words, he who believes that America is simply one huge Lockian liberal unit "tends to criticize and then shrug his shoulders. . . ."[16] True enough.

Indeed, so true is it, that Hartz himself, who aspires, it would seem, to better things than conservatism of whatever name and variety, is bothered and worried over the vast unity he has created. One of the persistent themes that runs through his book, as a sort of counterpoint to his theme of liberal unity, is the threat that that unity holds for America, the threat of what he calls liberal absolutism. For Hartz writing in and around 1955 the facts of political life pose a problem for America that his interpretation cannot solve and cannot explain.

The problem is McCarthyism and the wave of decidedly anti-liberal opinion it engendered. Even Hartz has to admit that Locke never thought of a McCarthy. But if the thesis of *The Liberal Tradition in America* is correct, all manifestations of political life in America are Lockian; they must be, for if they were not the seamless unity of America would be torn past mending (or if it could be mended, it would certainly not be seamless). Therefore Hartz develops his countertheme of liberal absolutism to explain the fact not only of McCarthy but also of a nation that in almost two hundred years of existence has never had a serious argument.

What he calls "the problem of unanimity" in America derives from his theory that the nation is of the same mind on the liberal formula. America therefore does not face a problem of majority tyranny, as so many have thought, but a problem of virtual unanimity. Once there were dreams of diversity; as Hartz puts it, adding and subtracting people in his usual way, if there was no Burke in America there was an Adams. But

[16] Hartz, *op. cit.*, p. 32.

sometime before the Civil War, when everyone turned to Horatio Alger and democratic capitalism, the nation developed a common ethic. Hence the phenomenon of "Americanism" is the other face of Lockian liberalism in America. This absolutism is not always present, but there are moments when it rises to the surface in a Rousseauean tide. Thus, the threat of unanimity in America comes from liberalism, a remarkable feat on the part of both Locke and Hartz.

Hartz is even more remarkable when he tells us that the same force that produced a McCarthy was "fated" to produce a Wendell Willkie, and the same force that produced an A. Mitchell Palmer was "fated" to produce a Woodrow Wilson.[17] We are never told how or why the fates work to produce these opposites. Nor does he explain why it was that a country that was born free and has its whole history determined by that fact of its birth, should immediately clamp down upon itself this new despotism. Nor does he ever distinguish between liberalism that works for freedom and liberalism that is used to work against freedom by conservatives. For, of course, there are no conservatives in America and no significantly different varieties of liberalism. Thus liberalism must take the rap for our faults; if it did not, Hartz's vision of the total unity of America would fall to the ground.

Yet the unity, the liberal absolutism, that he has created bothers him when he looks upon its finished and perfect form. He believes, must believe, that McCarthy (and others of that ilk) are the product of that unity. Yet, as the undoubted man of good will that he is, he would like to dissent. But can he dissent?

No, he cannot dissent. As he himself has already admitted, all he can do is to criticize and shrug his shoulders. In fact it

[17] Hartz, *Ibid.*, p. 287.

is doubtful that he can even criticize, for he has deprived himself of the weapon of both criticism and dissent—ideological conflict.

Hartz is caught in the trap of the Conservative Mood, a trap he has had some part in making. By refusing to identify a conservatism with which modern liberalism is in significant disagreement, even though it is not willing to destroy America over its disagreement, Hartz has made it impossible to take a stand not against the McCarthys of America—that is easy to do on plain, old-fashioned, horse-sense moral grounds—but against the forces and the kind of civilization that lurk in the background of the McCarthys and are opposed to freedom.

Thus he tells us at the end of his work that we must transcend American, Lockian liberalism. But how can we transcend it when Hartz's analysis has stripped us of the essential weapon and means for transcendence—a belief in possibilities, a belief in innovation, change, variety, conflict? We have been told that America has never had any political thought except one, and that conflict has never existed here on any significant scale. How then can we realistically expect transcendence to take place? It has not done so for almost two hundred years. Why should it do so today? We may hope that transcendence will occur. But if we follow Hartz, we will have no means to bring it about because American political thought in his hands presents no basis for an alternative set of values. America is one set of ideas, according to Hartz. It follows that to transcend it is impossible without destroying it.

In fact, of course, the human being is more free than Hartz would have him be, and since America is not one set of ideas, transcendence is possible today as it has always been. But not on the basis of the theory of Hartz, not on the basis of the Conservative Mood. He sees the need for transcendence but all that his theory presents is the basis for repetition. In order to transcend a situation or environment one must believe that change is possible, that innovation is a worthy risk, and that conflict can lead to valuable new ideas. American history can give support to those beliefs. But it can also be twisted to show that change, innovation, and conflict are impossible, have never existed, and indeed must not exist on peril of destroying the America that has existed from the beginning till now as a complete and fixed unit.

Hartz's theory and his *Liberal Tradition in America* may well have in the 1960's the look of a historical curiosity, for even the most obtuse among us today recognize, six years after the publication of Hartz's book, that conflict is a meaningful thing in the United States and that such things as conservatism and conservatives are with us and have been with us for some time. But the ideas presented by Hartz are a fitting memorial to the days when we needed desperately to be told that we were one nation, indivisible and united. They performed the same therapeutic service for those who wanted to be in a Conservative Mood as Eisenhower did in uniting all of us above the messy arena where politics, change, and conflict are the reality of national existence—and the necessity of national existence.

DANIEL BOORSTIN

The Conservative Mood of Oneness and Unity through Essence seeks to avoid the fact and consequences of change— of adventure—through a re-evaluation and reinterpretation of American history. A new age calls for a new history, and the old view of America as a place where significant conflict of a peculiarly American variety takes place and has taken place has been modified to present a nation in which conflict is stilled into insignificant and meaningless murmurs beneath the vast arch of unity that spans our country from sea to shining sea. This new history puts the historians of the 1930's themselves in historical perspective and sees them as a part of a political movement that today is considered not so much wrong as merely and simply irrelevant.

The 1950's were, as the phrase goes, a time to rethink the American past, to rediscover the nature of America. No nightmares for these historians, no fears that perhaps the essence of America like the essence of man is that it has no essence. The search for that quality which *is* America and has always been such is based on the assumption that the new history will discover what America really is, that there is a particular unique *thing* that America really is. It is an important quest because it follows that once the quality of America has been captured, then the task of the future is to maintain and perpetuate that quality. In this mode of belief, one does not look back to the past to understand the process of social and political change or to grasp the way men have faced their problems in order to understand where we are and what new things we must invent for the future. Instead the past is conceived as dictation —nothing less—to the future. It must be dictation to the future, for, if America has an essence that is embedded in the past, to destroy that essence is to destroy America. The ways in which men will seek to end their freedom are curious and frightening.

If that *real* America could only be found! If we could only sink ourselves in what others before us have done! Then no matter what happened we would be safe. For those who are engaged in this search the stakes are indeed high, and they make the petty arguments, the tiresome differences of opinion look like childish pouts. To know what America is! What grander task awaits the historian? To know what America is would quiet argument in the present, and, even better, would quiet it in the future, make it puny beneath the grand arch that is the unity of America.

If Professor Louis Hartz has given us the most sustained effort of the 1950's to create a total unity, Professor Boorstin has driven the point home with a different interpretation of that peculiar essence that is America. It might be said here that one of the more discouraging aspects of the quest for the real nature of America is the fact that different historians find different essences. There cannot be two essences for the same subject. In an area where so much is clouded over with high purpose that much is clear. The essence of America can be this or it can be that. But it must be one or the other. Somebody is going to have to make up his mind.

Boorstin's *The Genius of American Politics* (1953) introduces us to the ideology of anti-ideology. Since its publication, anti-ideological thought has been carried to new heights of sophistication by Daniel Bell, but Boorstin will serve both to introduce us to the logic of the anti-ideologists and to tell us what he thinks the essence of America is, as well as to show how neatly conservative attitudes flow from the preoccupations of the Essence Seekers.

What is the "genius" of America? It is the idea of "givenness," a somewhat recondite concept that Boorstin invents in order to describe that particular quality that is America. Givenness has three aspects. First, it is the approach that Americans have made to their life that stresses the preformation, historical aspects of our nation. The American people—how the generalizations roll out from these writers—have a belief that "we have received our values as a gift from the *past*; that the earliest settlers or Founding Fathers equipped our nation at its birth with a perfect and complete political theory." [Emphasis added.] The essence of America, in other words, is its confidence that it has an essence. America does not need to think, or to face the problems of conflict that thought so often produces, because it needs only to uncover what it is. Second, the idea of givenness is the "notion that in America we receive values as a gift from the *present,* that our theory is always implicit in our institutions." The choice of the word "gift" is a good one; it too relieves us of the necessity of thought and conflict over ideas. Third, the idea of givenness is a "belief in the *continuity* or homogeneity of our history, . . . so that our past merges indistinguishably into our present."[18] The unique quality of America, its genius, is thus the belief that values are in "some way or other [!] automatically defined: *given* by certain facts of geography or history peculiar to us."

The result of this happy-go-lucky view, one which the Eisenhower administration enshrined in its political practice by refusing to think about values except on the level of the cliché, is the American belief, as described by Boorstin, that "explicit political theory is superfluous precisely because we already somehow [!] possess a satisfactory equivalent." The equivalent is the sense of givenness.

Having put us in the lap of the gods, Boorstin teaches us how to look at our past and find that it has always manifested the values of no-value, a belief in givenness. The Puritans soon came to terms with the fact of givenness for they quickly dropped their cantankerous Puritan values and sought standards in their own experience; they made what they accomplished the standard of what they should accomplish. The American Revolution, too, was no innovating occasion but

[18] Daniel J. Boorstin, *The Genius of American Politics* (1953: Phoenix Edition), p. 9.

merely a "revolution without dogma"; indeed, it was hardly a revolution at all, and certainly it was not a democratic revolution. It was just one of the "few conservative colonial rebellions of modern times." How dull American history is after all.

And thus, we are told that Americans were born free, that all they had to do was to preserve their freedom, and that they were therefore conservatives. Jefferson and the Declaration of Independence, of course, become pillars of conservatism in this view. As for the Civil War, it too was an outburst of conservative feeling; neither side pursued a new vision of society, no basic political issues were raised, and the conflict was a simple normative one that took place within the framework of legal argument and of the federal system. The Civil War, contrary to the Beards, who got the whole thing wrong just as they got their interpretation of the Constitution wrong, was an illustration of the continuity, not the discontinuity, of American history.

And so it goes. American history becomes a series of dogged, not very interesting, and certainly not very significant legal debates. These new historians are certainly determined to destroy their own subject.

But it is in a good cause, the cause of anti-ideology. More explicitly than Hartz, Boorstin spells out the meaning of the new history. He admits that Americans have argued about values in the past; as he says, it is easy to multiply examples of the characteristic attempt to be articulate about national values. But the arguments were, of course, mere posturings, for the agreement on national values was there all the time. Much of what passes for debate, he tells us, in the United States, is simply an attempt to tell everyone what they think already, for Americans slur over differences and refuse to sharpen definitions. To Boorstin disagreement is un-American,

since it is characteristic of Europe, not America—of a disintegrating society. Hence, the possibility that there could be a
sharp difference over ends in a society without the society
disintegrating is not one that Boorstin considers. To equate
disagreement over ends with social disintegration—and especially to do so without defining one's terms—is indeed to make
controversy of any significant kind impossible.

It is also to postulate that conflict is of no value, is positively
a threat to society. But that is the way of the Conservative
Mood. If values are automatic, there is no need to argue about
them. Nor is there any need for politics to become the scene of
important encounters between distinctive ideas. The Conservative Mood would have us blur all ideas together in an easily
digestible pablum and Boorstin's theories are no exception.
The politics of the United States for him is a low temperature
disagreement over means between two parties who share the
same basic values. Hence ideological distinctions between the
two parties are "small," for each party shares the "same vision
of the kind of society there ought to be in the United States."
There are few in the United States who do not accept the predominant values of its society; hence the lack of political
theory, for who wants to explore what everyone agrees on?
Since Boorstin does not tell us what he means by ends and
means, or consider how the one can be separated from the
other, or examine the reality of parties in the United States, his
belief that the two-party system is a gentlemanly contest of no
particular meaning is not, perhaps, as important as he might
like to think.

But the point is clear. The genius of American politics is that
America has no politics. The new historian looks upon parties
with an amused and tolerant eye and a shrugging of shoulders,
but he cannot see that it really matters whether one or the

other party achieves office. It is important, however, to understand this approach of the Conservative Mood, because their downgrading of parties, their attempt to create apathy on the subject of party politics, is basic to the ideological crusade against ideology.

It might strike a reader of *The Genius of American Politics* as odd that in a book on politics only four pages out of 189 would be devoted to a discussion of parties. (Political parties find no place in Hartz's book.) The reason is clear and important. Parties, by their very nature, are the means and fomentors of conflict and differences of opinion. Their role in constitutional and democratic government is to present alternatives, significant alternatives, to the electorate. Naturally they do not always perform their role; naturally they often smudge differences. But when they do they fail. And it is exactly when parties fail that the conservative likes them best. Hence he mounts an attack on the political party as it should function by glorifying it when it functions least effectively. As we have seen, the conservative aims for, desires, lusts after, a position of total stasis, complete rest, final truth, essence. There is nothing so disturbing to his aims as a brawling, argumentative, and aggressive political party that insists on shouting another opinion in his ear. Essence and the Higher Law will never be discovered by a political party; on that point we can all agree. The political party disrupts, and designedly, the total unity that the Conservative Mood hopes to find. Working at its brutal best it gives comfort to no one; it forces the electorate to think on this issue and that. It *puts into question* the whole enterprise once again; will there never be a rest? No wonder parties are so disliked. And no wonder they are so important.

But the conservatives would not have them be important. Some conservatives would like to have them vanish. Others,

somewhat more sophisticated, see that the two-party system of
the United States is not only here to stay—one might even say
it is a tradition—but that given its peculiar traits, its ability to
obscure differences of opinion and to shy away from ideas, new
or old, it is not a bad weapon for those who prefer to see the end
of ideology. The genius of American politics being the absence
of politics, the more the party system muddies the waters the
better it is. And the more American it is too, for everyone knows
that it is in Europe that parties divide on ideological lines
whereas in America they destroy ideological distinctions. As
Boorstin says, "to talk to the people [of Italy] is an education
in the variety of concepts which a sane people can hold of the
proper ends of society." True. But it never occurs to Boorstin to
ask whether such conflicts may not serve a function in that
society or if conflicts over different issues may not serve a function elsewhere, too. It does not occur to him because our two-
party system provides him with what he wants—rest. Why look
further?

Boorstin feels no need to look further as far as the two-party
system or any other aspect of America is concerned. His theory
of the givenness of American life has provided him with the
prescription that he and others in the Conservative Mood want
to find.

But, like Hartz, Boorstin is uneasy because he has proved too
much. What an awful thing it would be if our sense of givenness should vanish. And that seems to be what is happening. He
tells us that the sense of givenness has been weakened in
America since the end of the nineteenth century. The American
people are no longer so impressed with the easy and eternal
verities of givenness since they seemed to be of such little value
when the real world thrust itself upon us. As Boorstin puts it,
today we feel that

. . . we are cast in a great role, but for the first time, we begin to wonder if we ourselves may not have some responsibility for composing the plot.[19]

This stunning reversal of form, this sneaking suspicion that America may have to accept responsibility for its actions, is leading to even more dangerous thoughts.

From the notion that . . . the common experience was enough, Americans moved to the fear that if they did not discover where they were going, they might find themselves going nowhere at all, or even in the wrong direction.[20]

At this rate we will soon be no better off than the Italians with their frequent discussions of political ends, for, as Boorstin darkly points out, the result of such thoughts is an effort by certain liberals to organize American society around a "well-articulated, comprehensive, and defensible social philosophy." It is hard to believe that in this happy land of Lockian liberalism and Boorstinian givenness such things could occur, but so it is. Once the rot sets in. . . .

What is one to think about this relatively recent desire of the American people to know where they are going, what they are doing and why? It is possible to approve of such eccentric behavior, of course, but not if you are in a Conservative Mood. For the very fact that such behavior is a new way of behaving is a break with the past as that past is seen by Boorstin (and Hartz), is enough to condemn it. By breaking with the past, by destroying or rejecting the sense of givenness (or Lockian liberalism) the people will be destroying America. A nation, according to this theory, *is* its past because the past embodies

[19] *Ibid.*, p. 163.
[20] *Ibid.*, p. 166.

essence and because the past is the only solid thing there is.

Boorstin is in no sense ready to welcome thought and inno-vation on the part of the American people. What, according to Boorstin, is to be done about our weakened sense of givenness? He suggests two possibilities. We might answer the demand for a democratic philosophy by making one. This straightfor-ward approach does not appeal to Boorstin because he has demonstrated that Americans, by the essence of their being, cannot do such a thing; it would be innovation, and innovation would destroy the past instead of preserving it. Besides, Boorstin points out, the attempt to think out what we would do in the future would create discord. Thus we are left with the second possibility, namely, to bring to the surface the ideas latent in the idea of givenness itself. The only real difference between this suggestion and those of Messrs. Kirk, Rossiter, and Lippmann is that they would reach up to a Higher Law, and Boorstin would reach down to Givenness.

But Up or Down we are back with Burke, discovering all those ancient virtues by which we have always lived. We have no ideological idols like those poor and deluded Italians. (Are they poor because they are ideologically deluded or are they ideologically deluded because they are poor? It does not much matter; we are out of it.) We have shown that the "romantic" illusion that men could change their institutions at will is indeed an illusion. We have a seamless culture. We have risen above utopianism.

How can we reach down to givenness? We should reassert the seamless quality of our life in order to preserve it. By doing so we will find a guide to behavior. Thus the seamlessness of our culture shows our society to possess both an organic "na-tional character" and a canny pragmatism that enables us to seize our unique opportunities. Boorstin never discusses the possibility that there might be a conflict between a pragmatism reaching for new opportunities and a given, organic national character because the second aspect of our seamless culture negates it.

The second aspect of the principle of "seamlessness" asserts the historical continuity of institutions. This is the counterpart in *time,* [*sic*] of the organic concept in space. . . . It is not surprising that we have no enthusiasm for plans to make society over. We have actually made a new society without plan.[21]

Is Boorstin suddenly giving way to a sense of innovation instead of givenness in his remark that we have actually made a new society? No, for he immediately reaches the higher law. He continues.

Or, more precisely, why should *we* [*sic*] make a five-year plan for ourselves when God seems to have had a thousand-year plan ready-made for us?[22]

Overlooking the unfortunate reference to a thousand-year plan, any suspicion that Boorstin is making a dubious joke is dispelled by the prescriptive conclusion he draws from his vision of history and the seamlessness of American culture.

From this point of view, the proper role of the citizen and the statesman here is one of conservation and reform rather than innovation.[23]

And what does the word reform mean to him? The answer is given by the way he couples it with conservation and opposes it to innovation. It is reform in the Kirkean-Burkean sense; it is a reform that will conserve what is. Thus his statement that the citizen and statesman will "occupy himself with the means of improving his society" because there is "relatively little disagreement on ends," is either meaningless—improvement and

[21] *Ibid.,* p. 177.
[22] *Ibid.,* p. 179.
[23] *Ibid.*

means cannot be divorced from ends and disagreement on ends—or it is simply the Kirk-Burke attempt to castrate reform in order to make it a eunuch in the service of conservatism.

That Boorstin means the latter is also indicated by his nervous flirtation with the idea of conservatism itself. He is a man in a Conservative Mood, but would not have us confuse him with conservatives. However, it is a fine line he wants us to draw. He tells us that the attitude he suggests for the citizen and statesman need not be smug, uncritical, or unprogressive. But he also tells us that "the American past fits us not only for a skepticism of doctrinaire politics but also for a lively sense of tradition." He goes on to point out that a "wholesome conservatism" must know what is worth preserving. And he concludes his book by saying;

We must refuse to become crusaders for conservatism, in order to conserve the institutions and the genius which have made America great.[24]

He has unwittingly given us a wonderfully precise definition of the Conservative Mood. The Conservative Mood would conserve the American genius (read essence) but not crusade for it, the nature of the Conservative Mood being a rather heavy feeling of fatigue.[25] The Conservative ideologist would con-

---

[24] *Ibid.*, p. 189.

[25] Another manifestation of the Boorstinian view and one of the oddest manifestations of the Conservative Mood can be found in Samuel P. Huntington's "Conservatism as an Ideology," *The American Political Science Review*, June, 1957, which tells us with more candor than logic that the American liberal of today should give up his liberalism in order to preserve it; "only by surrendering their liberal ideas for the present can liberals successfully defend their liberal institutions for the future." Thus the "liberals must be the conservatives in America today," for there is "no necessary dichotomy . . . between conservatism and liberalism" (pp. 473; 472; 460). There is no dichotomy for Huntington because he never considers the different points of view on freedom held by conservatism and liberalism.

serve the American genius and crusade for it. Neither would innovate.

There are other differences than the question of To Crusade or not To Crusade; the New Conservative is more oriented toward Europe and a shaking-up of the soul, while the Conservative Mood tends to look lovingly upon America and conclude that history came to a stop when the Pilgrims arrived or soon after. But they agree on the heart of the matter, on the need to enclose man within the finished globe of the past and keep him there. They agree on getting man out of time, and above all, they agree that there is an essence, above and beyond change, that can fix man and must therefore be conserved at all costs.

For what, when all is said and done, is America to Boorstin? The result of his theory of givenness is that America need not create, must not create, and cannot create new values or ends, because America is the refusal to create new values.

10. The Conservative Mood:
Daniel Bell and the End of Ideology

IF BOORSTIN INTRODUCES us to the ideology of anti-ideology,
Daniel Bell, in his *End of Ideology* (1960) makes it the official
belief of the disillusioned Left. The phenomenon of those who
Once Believed but now No Longer Believe was a common sight
in the 1950's. The roots of this disillusionment lay deep in individual psyches, and the nature of the Left in America, but our
concern here is not with an analysis of those who left the Left
but with what they contributed to the Conservative Mood.

They contributed a good deal, as Bell's attempt to sum up
the decade shows. Hartz and Boorstin have shown us that
America cannot invent new values because its essence, like any
essence, is fixed and eternal. America is not, according to their
point of view, and by definition, a value-inventing nation. Bell
takes a different tack to arrive at the same conclusion. He
shows that the attempt to create values is both dangerous and
futile. It is both dangerous and futile because ideology is
dangerous and futile. He does not distinguish between ideologies, it might be said here; the idea that some might be
dangerous and futile while others might be useful and important is not a possibility that he considers. But if we must avoid

ideology, what remains? Does he offer us an alternative? Does he tell us in what manner we can otherwise create new values and innovate? Does he even consider the problem of how we can innovate if we have no ideology? No, we are put into limbo, where forces outside of ourselves, with more sense of purpose, work their will on us. We are left without an alternative except to watch passively while the society that we have turns end-lessly and somewhat senselessly in its daily round. We are left, in short, in a Conservative Mood.

Having given up on ideology, Bell does not present a very consistent or significant analysis of American society as a whole. He describes it as one in which ideology competes with interest as the motivating force of American life. As a result, a book that was written to show the "end of ideology" shows instead the increasing, or at least continued, importance of ide-ology, an ironical conclusion that Bell refuses to acknowledge. His belief that modern American society is a place where in-terest and ideology are in conflict is demonstrated in his treat-ment of American labor unions. He tells us that laborism among the trade unions is their ideology and has acquired a political force of its own, one that "conceives of unionism as a social movement, and . . . as being opposed to the employer class as a whole." But this laborism on the other hand is faced with another point of view held by the unions, the idea of market unionism in which the union becomes an "ally of 'its' industry." It becomes, as he puts it so neatly, the "capitalism of the prole-tariat," and in doing so raises the question whether the AFL-CIO will use its political power to protect its interests or to become a social movement. His point is carried to a higher degree of abstraction when he says:

A public opinion which claims to reflect a public interest is in-herently, therefore, an unstable compound of ideological and market

335

decisions. The question whether such opinions can lead to action, and of what kind, depends upon the degree of tension between the two types of motive and upon the degree of identification with one or the other.[1]

Bell's analysis of American society, unlike Hartz's or Boorstin's, is unimpeachable. His descriptions of the changes in American socio-economic life and the resulting anxieties and tensions, especially those of "the 'small-town mind,' which tries to locate its own place in an increasingly amorphous society," are keen and sensitive contributions to anyone's understanding. As an analyst of the American scene he cannot be bettered, a fact that makes it all the more regrettable that in his hurry to get away from ideology he proves the opposite of his thesis.

For what does he conclude from his description of the tension between ideology and interest? Far from showing the end of ideology, he suggests the growing importance of ideology.

In a mass society, where public opinion is king, various groups are more than ever forced to assume some coherent identity and to clothe their aims in national or general interest terms.[2]

Thus he goes on to speculate briefly as to "what will be the political and ideological content of this new unionism" that he sees arising among us. Ideology is evidently going to win out over interest after all. He is, however, uneasy about this role of ideology for he believes that the "public," which is so synthetic in a mass society, may use a "mask" of consensus to hide the conflict of interest, which in truth continues to go on.[3]

Can such a statement reconcile the contradiction between his analysis and his theme? Perhaps, but in fact he does not attempt such a reconciliation. One can only say that his refusal or in-

[1] Daniel Bell, *The End of Ideology* (1960), p. 192. Italics in original omitted.
[2] *Ibid.*
[3] *Ibid.*, p. 220.

ability to make his own statements square with each other reflects the high cost of repudiating ideology as such. For having repudiated the very idea of ideology, he can hardly fit the fact of ideology, which he discovers in American society, into any theoretical framework. Bell, like many others in his situation, can be brilliant in analysis but cannot give his analysis any broad meaning, cannot make it serve a point of view, since a point of view comes close to or is an ideology. That failure is the particular quality, in fact, of the Conservative Mood. To be in a Conservative Mood is to want not to push one's analysis "too far."

Bell's anti-ideological view emerges, however, from more than the contradictions in his thought and the title of his book. The reasons for his mistrust of ideology derive from his attack on the 1930's, which one would imagine from his pages to have been a time of unmitigated disaster not because of depression and slump but because of those who tried to think about what depression and slump meant. He looks back on his own past with a profoundly jaundiced eye. His generation, he cheerlessly tells us, today "finds its wisdom in pessimism, evil, tragedy, and despair." Who are these somber souls from the underground? Those who came to political awareness in the depression, like Bell himself, today an old man indeed at the age of 42. What is it that seared them so? "The loss of innocence." And what caused them to lose innocence? The answer is breathtaking in its simplicity. Dogmatism. It was dogmatism, i.e., ideology, that corrupted them. (It should be pointed out that this charge, whatever it means, is assumed to be true by Bell; no evidence is given to substantiate it.) Such efforts to confess the past are not original, of course, with Bell; Leslie Fiedler was first to find that the effort was balm to the soul with his *An End to Innocence* (1955).

What does it mean, this turning on one's past impulses, impulses that Bell himself describes as "generous." What Bell and the others think it means is a frank admission that the radical generation of the 1930's failed because they were ideologists.

> In the end, the generation failed. . . . The seed of the corruption was the *hubris* of the "possessed." Generous of impulse, it sought the end of justice, but in the single vision the dogmatism grew hard and the moral sense cynical, so that, when reality proved the vision false, all that was left was the hardness, or the despair.[4]

The statement is impressive in its sincerity, and those who were not at the storm center in the 1930's are not, of course, in a position to cavil at it. Yet there are several things wrong with this repudiation of the past, several ways in which it creates an unnecessary burden for those too ready to assume it. First, those who came to political awareness in the 1930's were still young and hardly in a position to influence events; a small consideration, but one worth recalling since these old men today seem to feel that theirs was the only moral burden. Secondly, did the generation fail? At least it aimed at something, it had some object in view, which, *hubris* or not, is better than squatting on one's rump like primitive man. It is worth recalling that *hubris* is what distinguished the Greeks from the higher apes.

Most important, however, of what is wrong with Bell's statement of disenchantment, sincere though it is, is his assumption that ideology and a moral sense are opposed. Even Bell seems to shy away from it, for he suddenly drops the reference to ideology and takes up the word dogmatism. But we know and he knows what he is talking about. He is talking about the radicals of the 1930's, who became immoral as they became ideological. As he says, "This may well have been the *last* radical generation for a time—the last because it was the first

[4] *Ibid.*, pp. 291-92.

that tasted power and became corrupt." But Bell's theory of causation is wrong. Even assuming—a most dubious assumption—that the radical generation of the 1930's was corrupt—and the exact meaning of the word is not defined by Bell—certainly their "taste" of corruption in the 1930's will not prevent a later generation from tasting it again. To believe that one generation can learn so much from another's experience is to be optimistic, indeed. But it is true that another radical generation will not arise if today we assume that those who chose in the past were wrong not because they made the wrong choice but because they chose at all. If morals and ideological choice are put into opposition to each other, then indeed there will not be and cannot be another radical generation.

Bell's whole discussion of the Loss of Innocence has a dubious quality about it. When did Bell lose his innocence? In the 1930's? Or in the 1950's? Did he lose his innocence when he was a radical or when he turned his back on radicalism? Did he lose his innocence when he sought to improve society or when he decided that there is no alternative to today's "unheroic, day-to-day routine of living"? Did he lose it when he attacked injustice or when he wrote in 1957,

Today, intellectually, emotionally, who is the enemy that one can fight?[5]

One may, of course, approve of the loss of innocence. It is, after all, a normal part of growing up, and hardly need call for self-accusations of *hubris* and corruption. It may be wrong to say that life begins at forty, but Bell and those who think as he thinks must be among the first to tell us that life ends at forty. Yet, if it is conceded that the loss of innocence must be followed by pessimism, evil, tragedy, and despair, then its loss

[5] *Ibid.*, p. 288.

is indeed a grievous one for Bell and others like him. But the problem Bell and his fellows present for those who do not so concede is not their loss of innocence in the 1930's but their refusal to know anything but pessimism, evil, tragedy, and despair today. They may do what they want with their own innocence; but they should know what they are doing with it. What they are doing with it is to throw it away now, not in the 1930's. And they are throwing it away now by proclaiming that they threw it away when they were radical, when—and this is the important point—they say *today* that it is impossible for another radical generation to exist.

It is certainly true that Bell himself, whatever may be the case with his generation, is caught in a tragic impasse. On the one hand he tells us that for those who wish to forgo the sin of pride the proper role should be to "reject all absolutes and accept pragmatic compromise." In this frame of mind his hero is none other than Theodore Roosevelt. One can certainly understand why he must reach back so far for a model. But unfortunately, Bell is not content with pragmatic compromise or even Theodore Roosevelt. Not only, as we have seen, is he acutely aware that that old devil—ideology—is still with us, but he himself has a profound antipathy to the whole economic system in which he like the rest of us must play a part. His essay "Work and its Discontents" sounds almost like a utopian tract of those long lost days of innocence. But it is not, because, although there is profound discontent with our system of work in his essay, he has no suggestions to offer for reform or change. We are left with a skillful analysis of what is wrong with the way men work today, and a long-drawn sigh of helplessness. He cannot even tell us what William Whyte told us, that we should cheat the corporation, because he understands the modern corporation better than Whyte. You cannot cheat an automatic production line or an IBM machine. They know you are going to cheat before you start.

Bell knows they know and he fears his knowledge. Yet, given his refusal to be radical because he also fears ideology, what can he do but end in a long sigh? He has not solved the contradictions of his own thought, and thus he is, as he says, pessimistic and despairing. At times, to be sure, he comes very close to an ideology; ironically, on the page facing the final chapter, "The End of Ideology in the West," he tells us that to solve the problems of the work place "what is needed is a change of fundamental attitude" to the whole problem of workers' control.[6] But he gives us no idea of what the new innovating attitude would be that could achieve his surprising and utopian suggestion. Imagine reviving the old syndicalist dream in 1960! But at least it provides welcome relief from the political fatigue that informs so much of Bell's writings. It is indeed, an admirable idea.

Yet his suggestion is a wayward one, and he quickly mounts his full attack on ideology. He poses the problem by stating a distinction between "two ethics." Is ethics, he asks, a purpose or a limit? Can politics be an ethic of responsibility and an acceptance of limits, or must it be an ethic of conscience and dedication to absolute ends? The question itself assumes, as he points out, that in modern society there is a separation of ethics and politics. He argues his assumption only briefly by saying that whatever the case in the past, today "no group can, through the civil arm, impose its moral conceptions on the whole society; . . . ideology—the façade of general interest and universal values which masks specific self-interest—replaces ethics."[7] He goes on to equate ethics, which is purpose rather than an

[6] *Ibid.*, p. 368.
[7] *Ibid.*, p. 110.

acceptance of limits and the rules of the game, with ideology, since it transforms politics into an all-or-nothing struggle. The consequences are fatal to a nation, since ideological politics as distinct from interest politics polarizes groups and divides society.

The tendency to convert concrete issues into ideological problems, to invest them with moral color and high emotional charge, is to invite conflicts which can only damage a society.[8]

He tells us that "ultimately" one comes to admire Theodore Roosevelt with his scorn for intransigents like Godkin, and that "democratic politics means bargaining between legitimate groups and the search for consensus."

But his case against ideology goes beyond a reiteration of the Madisonian view that politics is factionalism. Ideology holds a horror for Bell, and it is derived from its chiliastic nature. Ideology is action, passion, the means to domination, the "conversion of ideas into social levers." It has today the ugly imprint of revolutionary action, "not mere social change," left on it by Marx, an imprint that cannot be erased. Hence Bell greets with relief his conclusion that the age of ideology is finally at an end.

In the Western world, therefore, there is today a rough consensus among intellectuals on political issues: the acceptance of a Welfare State; the desirability of decentralized power; a system of mixed economy and of political pluralism. In that sense, too, the ideological age has ended.[9]

Or has it ended? Alas, his next sentence shows Bell despairing in his doubts once again, for no sooner has the West cured itself of this virus than the new states of Asia and Africa are catching

[8] *Ibid.*, p. 373.
[9] *Ibid.*

342

it. Even worse, the West is suffering from the desire of its own younger generations to find new purposes; "in the search for a 'cause,' there is a deep, desperate, almost pathetic anger." The young intellectual is unhappy once again because the "middle way" is only for the middle-aged, "is without passion and is deadening."

Thus, what can Bell say? He can only say that "one's commitment is to one's vocation," and that the present belongs to the living and not to the future, a sound but not very helpful statement.

Bell's hope for restoring the present to those living today is not very helpful because it avoids the question: who among the living today possess the present? All of us? Or is it possible that not everyone possesses it in equal and fair measure? Further, is it possible to make such a sharp break between present and future? More exactly, unless one is contented with what we have in the present the problem is not so much how to turn it over to the living, but how to get out of it and into something better. Naturally, if one is actually contented with the present it will be sufficient to hand it over to the living and do as Hartz suggests, namely, shrug one's shoulders. Bell is not a shoulder-shrugger, but he is in the Conservative Mood because he presents no alternative to the present. He is also in a Conservative Mood when he admits that America is a society that undergoes change, but refuses to allow men to direct that change by a conscious choice of values. There is, he tells us, innovation built into the structure of American society, but he never answers the question of how that innovation can be controlled to achieve what men want. We know that Bell is, for example, disturbed by the social meaning of automation. We also know that he feels unable to do more than record his regret, because he fears ideology as a destructive force.

It is time to come to grips with this distrust of ideology because, as we have seen, it lurks behind Hartz's formulation of American history and behind Boorstin's theories of Americanism.[10] It is one of the symptoms of being in a Conservative Mood, since to reject ideology absolutely is to relax into political futility. Certainly, ideology is a dangerous weapon; certainly it has destroyed and can again destroy nations—along with the operation of other factors; a simplistic interpretation of history will not help us now. Certainly it can posit the choice described by Bell in his idea of the "two ethics." But, alas, futility is equally dangerous, can equally destroy nations, can equally posit a choice between the ethic of ends and of responsibility. (What end has one chosen by futility? To whom is one responsible?) One cannot avoid the problems of the present by saying that once we were corrupt because we were ideological and if we cease to be ideological we will not be corrupt.

The search of those in the Conservative Mood for a way out of the problems posed by ideology leads to futility by various roads. First, it leads to a version of government and governmental practice which like all simple versions of reality contains some elements of reality, omits many other important elements, and solves nothing. As we have seen, having repudiated ideology, Bell turns back to a version of politics that sees government as a place where "bargains" take place. As a description of how government works and as a statement of value, this theory holds some truth. But we need not be blind to its inadequacy on both levels. More important, it need not

[10] The impulse to shy away from ideology is, of course, a complicated one; David Riesman and Michael Maccoby in their "American Crisis," *Commentary*, June, 1960, point to other aspects of the problem.

blind us to its conservative meaning. Such a theory means that those will get the best bargains who have the most power to bargain with, e.g., General Motors, which already possesses that power. Further, it means that we have returned to the endless round, the fixed governmental universe, of static government. The picture is not unlike that presented by Morley and Burnham, in which a fixed set of balances swings eternally around a fixed center.

Naturally, if one feels that the present is fine the way it is, or that there is nothing one can do about the present, this model of government will be considered as the supreme perfection and aim of government. And in truth it is an excellent model for the *status quo,* since government itself on this model is passive, a market place where an auction is held. It is also an excellent model for allowing the operation of what Gunnar Myrdal calls backwash effects.[11] But what happens to such a model in a mass society? Is it still viable even in its own terms? Although Bell hints at this question, he nowhere faces it and we are left with his picture, on the one hand, of a mass society in which consensus is manipulated, and his desire, on the other hand, for a bargaining process in which consensus arrives from the bargain each side gets.

The truth of the matter is, that while the bargaining model of government postulates many essential features of democratic government, it is an inadequate model. The fact that it is inadequate is exactly the reason a problem of democratic government exists today. (It needs to be said, too, that the model has nothing to contribute to a solution of such problems as race relations in the South, for example.) Thus to put it forward at this time is to avoid the real problems that exist today

[11] Gunnar Myrdal, *Economic Theory and Underdeveloped Regions* (1957).

345

in favor of futility. One may justly desire to limit the destructive effects of ideology but that desire is no reason to engage in a process of self-destruction.

The second way in which the attempt to avoid ideology leads to a Conservative Mood of futility is demonstrated by the misunderstanding such an attempt creates of the nature and role and impact of ideology. The remarks of Professor H. Stuart Hughes on this subject are so much to the point that they deserve quotation. Admitting the historical truth of Bell's description of the problems faced by Bell's generation, Professor Hughes goes on to say that

. . . it is not the whole truth. It is a parochial version of recent history betraying the myopia of the New York intellectual . . . . A wider view of the past thirty years would include intellectual biographies which do not fit into Mr. Bell's mold—those of professors in the "provinces" who followed the ideological debates of the 1930's only from a distance, and who sometimes had a clearer view of the permanent significance of events for the very reason that they were not concerned with short-range tactical decisions; of men who spent long years in military or government service and whose ideological reflections necessarily matured at leisure since they could not be expressed in the public prints; of people who never became so disillusioned as those Mr. Bell writes about since they never were so *engagé*—who had committed themselves only in part to Marxism and hence had nothing to apologize for in later years; of intellectuals who saw no reason to give up their ideology because the one they had was sufficiently flexible and non-dogmatic to confront without flinching or becoming discouraged even the squalid realities of the 1950's. I think if Mr. Bell had broadened his view to include people of this sort, he would have found that the older members of his "twice-born" generation have not been quite so influential as he imagines. He would have seen that it is rather the "once-born"—the generation of Dewey and Brandeis—who despite all change of circumstance have remained the mentors of twentieth-century America.[12]

As a result of his myopia, Bell sees ideology exclusively as chiliastic, revolutionary, neo-Marxist change. It cannot, by his definition, be a vehicle of social change. It can only disrupt and destroy. But not only is such a statement untrue. To propose it as true is also to turn the game over to those who do have an ideology, who do know what they want, and to let them make the rules by which the rest of us should abide. They will, of course, be glad to do so.

The third way in which the avoidance of ideology leads to futility is to confuse the content of an ideology with that abstraction we call an ideology. Bell makes such a confusion when he poses an ethic of end and an ethic of responsibility against each other. Essentially he is making the old and impossible distinction between ends and means in which "responsibility" becomes an attachment to means in order to achieve reconciliation. Hence he sees a "tension of ethics and politics." But tension is not fruitless; on the contrary, it is the norm of human existence and in social life can have a vital function to perform.[13] Indeed the model of government for which Bell has formed such an attachment, the bargaining model, postulates the importance of conflict and tension; Locke himself assumed the existence of conflict and if he hoped to reconcile it—as any society, by definition, must do—he also did not shrink from the fact of it. It might be recalled that he assumed and stated a right to revolution, a part of the Lockian thesis which, for some reason, seems to be neglected today by

---

[12] H. Stuart Hughes, "End of an Epoch," *Partisan Review,* Summer, 1960, p. 567. See also the comments of Professor Dennis H. Wrong on Bell's book, *Dissent,* Summer, 1960.

[13] See Lewis Coser, *The Functions of Social Conflict* (1956).

the neo-Lockians. An attachment to an ideology may not be an act of irresponsibility. It may, on the contrary, be an act of the highest responsibility. It depends on what the ideology is about.

To succumb to futility, i.e., the Conservative Mood, is an act of irresponsibility. It is to withdraw from the struggle, to sit by, while others carry on. One might bring up in this regard, since Bell has raised the issue of the 1930's, the depression of 1929. Who was responsible for the depression of 1929? Was it the ideologists? Quite the contrary, it was the futilitarians. There were many individuals who were responsible for 1929, but among them one might point, just for the sake of illustration, to Harding, Coolidge, and Hoover. Bell assumes that there were disastrous choices of ideologies in the 1930's, and he is correct. He is also correct in assuming that those who chose wrongly were responsible for their choice; their failures were not the responsibility of Harding, Coolidge, and Hoover. But we might once in a while wonder just who got us in the mess to begin with. The fact that we seldom do wonder, and spend most of our time condemning those who made mistakes in trying to get out of it, in itself indicates the profoundly Conservative Mood of the United States today.[14]

No one, it must be repeated, should deny the dangerous effects of ideology, both on the individual who is being eaten by it and the society that is victimized by it. But ideology can be something else than chiliastic writhings. It can also be a point of view, a means of analysis, and, most important, a means of forming the future. As such it may not be the world-maker that the chiliastic ideologist wants it to be, or the world-shaker that Bell always sees it as being. But at the very least, and in a mass society especially, it can be a means of personal

[14] A notable exception, of course, is Arthur Schlesinger, Jr., in his *Age of Roosevelt*, Vol. I. (1957)

autonomy by which one is able to say what he thinks rather than what someone else thinks he should think. At the very minimum it enables him to say No. Ideology can also be the means by which a group can form a political force that will not go around and around on the weary treadmill of government-by-bargain, the treadmill that leads, for example, to more cars, then to more roads to hold the cars, then to more cars for the roads, etc., etc. Ideology can be—although it will not necessarily be—the means to break out of the timeless shell of essence in which the Conservative Mood would encompass us. Indeed, when one stops to think about it, there is hardly any other way to break free. Certainly it will not be done by bargaining with General Motors, because they will win, as they have been winning now for some time.

Thus the Conservative Mood. Hartz tells us to shrug our shoulders. Boorstin tells us not to be crusaders for conservatism but to be conservative. What does Bell tell us? Bell, as the acuteness of his descriptive essays show, will not give up his radical streak. Thus he tells us that it is necessary to criticize the existing order. But how? On what grounds: Is it enough to say as he does say that "one's commitment is to one's vocation"? Especially when he also says that an outlet for intellectuals in science or university vocationalism is "often at the expense of narrowing . . . talents into mere techniques. . . . "? That someone with the intellectual skills and radical instincts of Bell should end in futilitarianism is sorrowful evidence indeed of the victory that the Conservative Mood enjoys today.

11. Subtopia and the Conservative Mood

THE CONSERVATIVE MOOD involves more than the ideas of those writers we have discussed or the ideas of those in the 1950's who wrote novels or works on religion, sociology, economics, and politics in order to express their fall into acceptance, fatigue, guilt, complacency, or simple pessimism. Hartz, Boorstin, and Bell are simply the most intellectual of the many who have found release from the complexities of modern society and the tensions of conflict through the Conservative Mood. As intellectuals they present what might be called the theory of the Conservative Mood and thus enable us to understand the ideas that sustain it and their relation to the beliefs of the conservatives themselves.

But the Conservative Mood has roots that strike deep into American soil, or, to be more precise, if more paradoxical, into the deracinated soil of the American suburb. The Conservative Mood is not just a set of ideas floating aimlessly but a set of ideas that fulfill a function for the society of today, the society of suburban "living." The suburb and the Conservative Mood cannot be divorced from each other because each is necessary to the other, because each is derived from the other. The cancerous proliferation of the suburbs in the postwar period and the recognition that they had become the typical form of social life for America coincided with the growth of the Conservative Mood. It is impossible to imagine the present Conservative Mood without the present subtopian existence of America, just as it is impossible to imagine subtopia without a Conservative Mood. When the American middle-class man faces his weary self toward the suburb at the end of a hard day in the city he is once more trying to re-experience his Conservative Mood, to realize his conservative dream. He is leaving the world of conflict—conflict with his superiors, with his inferiors, with his equals, and with himself—and is looking to the green land where the dream of finality and fixedness can be achieved. There he will find "Tea for Two," "Blue Skies," "Someone to Watch over Me," and all the other accouterments of bourgeois bliss.

Or will he? Alas, it is not so simple as he once thought. The suburb is in fact a bloody battleground on which men oppose each other to win status. The same bourgeois values that inform the suburbanite at the office motivate his life and that of his family in the suburbs; indeed, the suburb can most realistically be viewed as a well-designed factory for the production of status achievement. Yet the suburb is at the same time and because of the high cost of status achievement a place where the Conservative Mood is enshrined as a means of transcending and stilling the struggle for status achievement by holding out the promise of a condition of fixedness above the painful daily battle. The suburb is indissolubly connected with the Conservative Mood because both are attempts to establish a fixed, timeless universe apart from conflict, change, and uncertainty. And yet the suburb is a direct contradiction of that dream because it is where the struggle for status takes place. Hence the paradox of suburban life today, one based on the reality of conflict between men, women, and even children, in the search for status achievement, and the desire to escape from that conflict.

It is no wonder that the suburbanite dreams a conservative dream of a quiet society in which he will find the freedom that comes from the cessation of conflict. But the American bourgeois in his newest incarnation as suburbanite is as confused as ever about the meaning of freedom. The Conservative Mood and a hope for freedom are inextricably mixed in the suburban mind. Having to pay so heavily for the status competition in which he engages, the dweller in subtopian halls aches to realize his dream of freedom-as-the-end-of-conflict by the conservative dream of a fixed society, a dream that takes the concrete form in the suburbs of a house, lot, and family placed and fixed. The idea that freedom is the need to make continual choice is not one to commend itself to those engaged continually in the making of the nerve-racking choices necessary to status achievement. Instead they think of freedom as the conservative thinks of it, as the end of conflict, as the quelling of change, as the attainment of essence. This Conservative Mood may be a naïve dream, but it is the only one subtopian man has, the only one that promises to get him out of the awful situation he has created for himself. Any other way of escape would thrust against his value of achievement-as-status, would force him to think again, to conceive of social change, to innovate. No, it is better to have the conservative dream, to drift in the Conservative Mood.

To understand that mood and its potency in America today, the America that is one huge disorganized subtopia, we must understand the despair and anguish to which it is a response. We must look at the battleground itself and see what the issues are and how costly the struggle is. Only thus can we know what the Conservative Mood involves and how deeply rooted it is in the daily desires and concerns of so many Americans today.

Subtopia and the Conservative Mood

SUBURBAN DREAM*

Walking the suburbs in the afternoon
In summer when the idle doors stand open
     And the air flows through the rooms
     Fanning the curtain hems,

You wander through a cool elysium
Of women, schoolgirls, children, garden talks
     With a schoolboy here and there
     Conning his history book.

The men are all away in the offices
Committee-rooms, laboratories, banks,
     Or pushing cotton goods
     In Wick or Ilfracombe.

The massed unanimous absence liberates
The light keys of the piano and sets free
     Chopin and everlasting youth
     Now, with the masters gone.

And all things turn to images of peace,
The boy curled over his book, the young girl poised
     On the path as if beguiled
     By the silence of a wood.

It is the child's dream of a grown-up world.
But soon the brazen evening clocks will bring
     The tramp of feet and brisk
     Fanfare of motor horns
     And the masters come.

—EDWIN MUIR

And what do the Masters find? How are their wives and children living in the utopia designed for them? Anyone who has lived in a suburb at one time or another can tell something of the life there—of the daily round of travel to and from the house, of that part of the "community life" they happen to touch, of the quasi-friendly neighbors, of the financial and physical burden of being a householder. These are the small change of suburban complaints, but behind them there presumably lies a greater reality that distinguishes the suburb from the city and the suburbanite as a species from his fellow sufferers who live in different places.

But does anyone really live in a suburb? Are they not rather resting places where one stays for the night until the possibility of moving elsewhere offers itself? The phrase "flight to the suburbs" is a misnomer; the suburbs are as much fled from as they are fled to. Here is the first distinguishing feature of the suburb. It is not the terminus of movement but rather a stage in movement. It is a vast mart where land and houses are transferred from one hand to another, where families are moved from one neighborhood to another, and where the concept of living some place has to give way to a desire to get on the smooth upward curve in a search for status achievement. The suburb looks like a place to live, the city like a place to work. But like the city, it is a place where necessary transactions of prestige and material satisfactions are carried out; if these transactions are in terms of land, trees, glass-houses, or what have you, they differ only in degree from the city's transactions.

No, the reality of the suburb does not lie in providing a place to live and in providing a focus of loyalty. Who can imagine loyalty to a suburb? To a city, perhaps; state, possibly; country, certainly; church, maybe; but suburb!—the question puts itself out of court. The inhabitants—one can hardly call them citizens—care, of course, a great deal about the conveniences of a suburb; party talk is incessant—and incessantly dull—about tax rates, garbage disposal, schools, streets, etc., etc. But whether one lives in this or that suburb matters not at all. To maintain a sense of loyalty to a suburb is one sure way of marking oneself as queer, and anyone who is so misguided by his childhood as to think that because he grew up in a suburban spot he has a tie to it will be soon disabused by the demands of his own desires to get on that rising upward curve. To be loyal to a suburb is to insult "the American dream."

Despite its appearance of fixedness and place, the American suburb is the institutionalization of mobility, much more so than the city, which, perhaps because there is so much granite lying around, seems to represent the principle of immobility. It is to mobility that the middle-class American turns when he goes to the suburb. Here he can freely take up the game of shifting himself from one place to another, and can work at realizing his belief in the rising upward curve. In the suburb social mobility can penetrate his whole life, and not just his working life; it can involve his family as well as himself. Nowhere else can middle-class man achieve so perfectly the isolation he seeks from the rest of mankind—the isolation necessary to mobility. In the desert of the suburb, community life has lost whatever vestiges of meaning it ever had for Americans; if any community life exists at all, it exists frantically on the synthetic level of club and church; it has a tinny quality betraying a lack of conviction on the part of all concerned. Nowhere is there more consciousness of the need for community; nowhere does this consciousness of need reveal more clearly its hopelessness. For how can community be built in a place the purpose of which is to escape the smothering effect of immobility? It was not Kafka who invented "the hero as the lonely man" but the

suburbanite. And if today the periodicals directed to the suburban way of life prattle like infant minds about "together-
ness," this simply shows an acute vision of what the American
suburbanite is not.

Marquand saw this clearly when he described Clyde, Massa-
chusetts, as an historical survival—a town with a living plan
that was natural and had a place for everything and everyone—
and contrasted this with the formlessness of the suburban life
of Charlie Grey. Yet there is a sort of living plan, too, in the
suburbs. The American middle class has collectively inhabited
the place long enough to create a suburban way of life, one
which has been described by a group of sociologists in *Crestwood Heights*.[1] It is a perceptive work, and it gives a true and
unpleasant view of what it means to live in the upper-middle-
class suburbs of America today.

What is the living plan of Crestwood Heights?[2] Above all else
it is a place for women and children. It is to these women and
children that the "Masters"—we will see how masterful they
are—come home, for whom they work, and for whom the whole
suburb is supposedly created. (If any woman doesn't believe
this statement, she is quite correct, but more of that later.) The
family thus finds its venue here; the idea is that, given a place
with a house, open areas, and schools, the wife and child—for
many of the "Masters" the difference between the two is not
absolutely clear-cut—can grow into beautiful and intelligent
things that it will be a joy and pride to possess. The effort
would seem to be to create a home as distinct from a house so
that this growth into wisdom and beauty—the kind seen in

[1] John R. Seeley, R. Alexander Sim and E. W. Loosley, *Crestwood Heights*
(1957).

[2] Crestwood Heights is a recently developed suburb on the edge of a big city
in Canada; the sociological description of it, however, applies equally to the
American suburb.

House Beautiful, for instance—can go on apace. Since creating a home is the reason for the suburb, it is legitimate to ask how successfully this is done.

The answer, according to *Crestwood Heights,* is not very well, if at all. If one thinks of a home as a sort of fortress where the self can be attained then the suburban home as distinct from the house is a marvel of inefficiency. Family privacy is broken into by every conceivable gadget known to the middle-class mind; its activities are so time-regulated by outside agents —clubs, schools, TV, etc., etc.,—that it virtually ceases to exist at all. The authors of *Crestwood Heights* go even further: these agents intruding and thrusting themselves upon the family have an interest in the family that is purely impersonal, catering to things rather than people.

But one need not blame some outside force as a scapegoat; subtopia is created in the image of its creators and the fact of the matter is that this is what the creators want; those who are intruded upon when they are in the suburbs help create the intrusion. More: the family in Crestwood Heights is not concerned with the passing on of a tradition—about society or itself—but is rather dedicated to its own disintegration. "Father, mother, brothers, sisters, kin, friends, and neighbors are seen as necessarily expendable" in the demand for social mobility, in the need to get on that rising curve. The need of the members of the family to seek outside the family thus reveals the essential dynamics of the suburb; it is not really a place where the family can grow, but rather it is a place where the family can disintegrate in the most efficacious way possible. The purpose of the suburb is to break the family in the interests of the rising curve.

The suburb, then, is not a place for the nurture of the family as the bourgeois likes to pretend, but a place for a particular kind of socialization. The child's "childhood" in which he struggles to find his place in the amorphous and shifting society of the suburbs (the authors of *Crestwood Heights* record that one high school student became so disgusted that he went to live in the Channel Islands; one raises one's hat) reveals the importance of the suburb as the place where the career is started, taught, and carried on. The suburban home turns out to be a hotel from which the businessman emerges to do battle in the race for success, and the child emerges to learn to do battle in *his* race for success. Around the careers of both revolves the whole system of subtopia.

The career of the parent is the mainstay of life in expensive subtopia; it pays the bills. And the career of the child is the object of life in subtopia itself, which is there to provide the climate, means, and incentive for riding the rising curve. The suburb is both the reflection of upward mobility achieved and the training ground for further mobility to be achieved. Thus the symbolism of the modern school where all is open glass (except for the toilets and the office of the principle), so that no one can develop by any chance a tendency toward inwardness. The school in *Crestwood Heights,* the authors say, is concerned with outer reality, not with what might go on inside the student. Values of success, happiness, and health are accepted as God-given and passed on in the same way. And if religion is so rash as to question these truths, it is made to conform; in practice it has become the happy eunuch of the school system.

One should not conclude from this that the Crestwood student is driving hard to success. No: safety comes first. The student in Crestwood hopes for a lot from his career but doesn't expect much. He is prudent, therefore, and anxious not to destroy the possibility of a career by foolishness (always with the honorable exception of the young man in the Channel Islands).

It is out of this cautiousness that the personal relationships of the suburb grow, those "quasi-intimate relationships with people in impersonal situations." Human contacts are not for pleasure but for a purpose, and the same status struggle that takes place in the business world takes place in the suburb, where instead of the secretary there is the wife and instead of the junior executive there is the son. There is the same wearing of masks and the same tension between equals. The businessmen meet face to face in the suburb just as they do in business and a slip of the tongue or a drop of the mask can mean disaster. Here is Marquand's description of social life in subtopia.

The trouble with dancing with Molly Blakesley was that since that situation had arisen at the bank they each knew too well what the other was thinking. He suspected that her dress must have come from Bergdorf's and must have cost at least a hundred and fifty dollars, which Roger could afford because the Blakesleys did not have children. He wished that he did not keep putting their lives into terms of dollars and cents and that he did not always seem to be going over expenses whenever he danced with Molly Blakesley. It was necessary to be careful with her, too. She had a way of remembering everything one said, accurately and usefully. She was a very good wife to Roger.

What of the woman in this maelstrom of social climbing, social knifing, and social anxiety? Surely she is the kingpin— rather loose at times, perhaps—of family life? Not exactly. Because the family is disintegrating beneath her feet she must perforce aid in its disintegration. And not only is the purpose of the family to throw the children out of the family and into society; the wife herself is taught to flee the family as a deadly and constricting thing. Wives, too, are career-oriented because they are taught to be, because that is all they can be. The wife's job at home is that of a manager concerned with schedules: the husband gets off to work at 8:10, the girl to junior high at 8:25, the boy to grade school at 8:35. "Time is the master." But once a wife has met the time schedules set by the outside forces she faces her own personal vacuum, which must be filled somehow.

The crux of the problem of the wife in the suburb seems to lie in the fact that the woman is trained with men, to compete with men. Speaking of woman's education in *Crestwood Heights* the authors say that "in some respects it seems that sexual differences have been eliminated . . ." (the power of the suburbs is awe-inspiring). The woman is driven into two markets at once; the marriage market and the money market, and this dichotomy continues after her marriage with the additional burden that now she has as many careers to further as there are members of her family. It is her job to balance the various aspects of the suburbs (clubs, schools, church) so that a combination will come about that will maximize the benefits the family can receive. Along with this devotion to the career interests of the family she cannot forget her own self, for this is what she was taught, that she too is a person with career interests. And if she doesn't succeed in both roles her failure will be a threat to her husband. No suburban woman can afford to be devoted to the family as such. Her job is to get the family out, to get out herself, to represent the family before the world, and to place the family in the world. In short, she has to *maintain a house, destroy the family,* and *flee the home*. The only thing that maintains her sanity is that at some stages in her life these needs do not occur simultaneously. The thing that threatens her sanity is that at some stages in her life they do occur simultaneously.

And what of the man in the suburb? It is his life, his activity, that creates the suburb and sets the standards and activities, the goals and functions of suburban existence. If the children and the wife have become "future-oriented, voluntaristic, individualistic, control-aspirant, rationalizing, organizing people," it is because the man has created the suburb as an expression of his way of thinking. But the man is in, not of, the suburb. He lives there temporarily; his house is for him a sort of supermotel and his scale of activities and scope of action lie in the outside world, in the big city. The suburb is only a fraction of his existence. But it is an important fraction, for it is the place where his system of values, his ultimate aims are to be realized. More than any other spot on earth, the suburb is the place where the bourgeois is to make himself what he wants to be, to come to the realization of himself as embodied in his values. Here he will find himself. The suburb is simply the ultimate expression of the bourgeois value system; here at last can be achieved—absolutely, irrevocably—the things for which all the bitter striving and infighting exist in the city. But can these values be realized in the suburb? Can the bourgeois find himself in the suburb, break free from the heavy hand of the city, find his ideal made real? Or is his hope impossible?

For the Master as well as for his family, the suburb is a necessity. It is the place that is to prove finally and conclusively that not only he personally, but his whole scale of values, his whole activity and class, can produce the good life. The suburb is the testing ground—the display case—for middle-class life; if it doesn't produce good fruit here it never will. But what are those values and goals?

Achievement is the word that best sums up the combination of personal success, social mobility, and public esteem at the heart of the middle-class value system. The life of the middle-class American is permeated with this concept; it involves his status in the city, his personal relations, his family position, and his particular role in the many shifting subclasses of American culture. The word *achievement* has many meanings: the authors of *Crestwood Heights* point to one connotation, the authors of such novels as *Executive Suite, The Man in the Grey Flannel Suit,* and *Sincerely, Willis Wayde* point to others. But the word never suggests achievement for the sake of achievement or for the individual's own satisfaction. Rather it stands for some kind of success as measured by society; the middle-class American is nothing if not a public figure. He stands before society hoping for the best possible verdict. To try to hide achievement would indeed be crazy, for then it would be a contradiction of terms. Achievement exists only when others think it exists, and there can be no achievement if it is not public and displayed.

Yet the outpouring of novels on the businessman at work makes it clear that the pursuit of his achievement is so costly that the business world as the arena of achievement is as much fled from as it is sought. Achievement and the attempt to escape the costs of achievement are the fundamental conflict in which the suburbanite is caught. He is driven into a race for achievement, yet in the process he must flee from what he has done. Don Walling in *Executive Suite* transforms himself into God to escape; Tom Rath flees back to the womb; Willis Wayde is too dumb to know what he has done. The brutality of business is too much, it seems, even for the businessman to stomach. Hence his flight from achievement.

But if the achievement is a failure so is the flight. And nowhere is the failure of the flight more apparent or severe than in the suburb. It is in the suburb that the utopia, the basic

escape, is to be created. Here of all places is where the middle-class American can realize his aims[3] and where the brute reality of what has to be done to achieve achievement can be forgotten. But once again he fails.

The suburb provides the perfect setting for escape. Outside of the filthy city, full of greenness and light, it has everything the city lacks. And most of all it has property, property that can be owned individually and not collectively as in the city. Here is the homestead where an individual can—after having sacrificed himself in the city—realize, if not himself, then his creed for himself. As *House Beautiful* put it in a celebration of American suburbia: "Everbody Can Own a House." Or more profoundly:

> No man need be common
> No life need be ordinary.

The age of the Common Man belonged to the first half of America's 20th Century. The Age of the *Un-Common* Man is now opening before us. More and more our architects, our builders, our designers, our manufacturers, all those who are closest to the new needs and new desires of our millions are aware of this as a fact to be coped with, not a theory to be argued.

People are aspiring upward in varied and individual ways.

Or:

Any direction you take—if you are good—leads you to success and self-fulfillment. That's why Americans are happy.

---

[3] Robert C. Wood in his *Suburbia: Its People and Their Politics* (1959) points to the conservatism of the suburbs as an attempt to resist twentieth-century reality and ideals and to maintain the past values of small-town life. He also shows how the suburbs are an expression of a fear of change and how they work against freedom. See especially pp. v; 9; 11-19; 197; 275-6; 282; 285; 301-302.

This paean of praise to "The People's Capitalism" reaches its peak in a spiritual apotheosis.

The American search for the spiritual is even greater than the increasing numbers of people newly going to church and to synagogue indicate. As God's first temples were said to have been trees so today His first temples might be said to be man's home among the trees—on its own plot of land, independent, individual, and in harmony with the restoring rhythms of nature.

That is the inner content of these houses. That is the meaning of this statistic:

Today 60 per cent of our families own their homes.

Yes, a suburban property can do wonderful things for the mind, soul, and body. The material shell of the escape is gratifying to the eye; never has the American suburb been more slick, never the picture windows so large. And if such a cocoon can enable, say Tom Rath, to forget his fears, or his mistress in Italy (fortunately she has grown fat now, so *that* problem is solved) why, then, it has fulfilled its purpose.

Still, it isn't quite so easy as the editors of *House Beautiful* and Sloan Wilson would have us believe. The illusion that the home in the suburb is the final resting place this side of the grave is a powerful one, but it is an illusion. Yet, where else is there to go? No place. The suburb is the last escape route and if the cost has to be paid it is just too bad.

"Will the Middle Class Inherit the Earth?" Thus the headline in the *Boston Sunday Globe*. There seems to be some doubt, as a matter of fact, and the *Globe* is afraid that automation will reverse "the promising trend toward moderation" and "turn the middle class into a proletarian horde more vast, more fierce than ever before. And the radicals would inherit the earth."

There are others who have even graver doubts; not about whether the middle class will inherit the earth, but whether they are now inheriting the earth. The news is getting around that subtopia is not all that it was hoped to be, that the suburbs are, to be exact, a rotten place to live in, and that they are a rotten place to live in because of the values they represent. *Crestwood Heights, The Exurbanites,* and *The Organization Man* all hammer at the point that the values found in the suburbs are so distorted and contradictory that the best that can be hoped for is a deadlock. It is in the conflict between the suburbanite's goals of achievement and his Conservative Mood, his dream of freedom-as-peace, that the failure of the suburb as an escape from the costs of bourgeois existence becomes manifest.

If achievement in the city is an impossible accomplishment or too painful to contemplate, then achievement-achieved can be caught, fixed, and founded in the suburb. In fact, however, it is the place where the failure to gain achievement-achieved is made manifest. The suburb for the particular species of suburbanite Spectorsky studies—the communication "boys" of New York City—is the place where the "rat race" of the city can be left behind, where a symbol manipulator can act like a "thing manipulator" and where he can find that vague hope for which all Americans yearn so earnestly, "roots." Whatever may be collectively produced by the communication industry of New York City, nothing is achieved by the individual despite his frantic efforts; worse, far worse, is the fact that the collective achievement has a high cost in insecurity and competition. The inevitable flight is away, away from the scene of the battle to the little house in the suburb. But the house is not so little, the bills pile up, and worse, far worse, the competition to achieve continues its merry, if slightly more drunken, pace. With all the money that the exurbs exhibit, it would seem that a few roots could be put down. What if they are ersatz roots? Better an ersatz root than no root. But no. The standard of living, i.e., of achievement, the "boys" have set themselves is too high and the pressure cannot be reduced.[4] And why such a high standard of living? Because the communication "boys" have been taken in by their own deceit, have sold themselves their own product: material goods as a symbol of achievement. So:

He moved to the exurb to escape the rat race; now, like as not, he looks forward to the morning train to New York as an escape from the trap which he perceives his limited dream has become. Hide in the exurb from the insecurities of the rat race, hide in New York from the frustrations of the trap.

Life in the suburb is to be a symbol of achievement that has been achieved *once-and-for-all.* It is to be the place where what has been achieved is to be set down, is to be there in that spot, and it is to be in the form of things, like a House and a Yard, two healthy Children, and a Slim, Sociable Wife (she must be slim). Unfortunately, this dream of achievement is not the reality of achievement.

Still it is the only dream the suburbanite has. And it finds its expression not only in things but in attempts to realize freedom as freedom from the ugly reality—for once the cliché is justi-fied—of the city. Hence the suburb is to be the place where an ideal freedom for the individual is to come into being. And once again the result is failure. In the city competition is open, acknowledged and brutal; in the suburb toleration, permissive-ness, and individual choice are to rule. The child is to be brought up as an "autonomous, spontaneous individual": thus

---

[4] Spectorsky estimates that his particular victims spend $32,000 a year with a yearly gross income of $25,000. This 30 percent overspending he considers par for the course.

the open glass school. The suburb will provide the arena in which the family and especially the children can emerge as "free" and "responsible," ready to take their place in the world. So it is in Crestwood Heights, and so it is in every suburb.

It is the dichotomy between the first goal—the suburb as the place of mobility and achievement—and the second goal—the suburb as the place of free development—that turns the suburb into the arena of a headlong and even tragic clash. For the achievement value must continue its work and the attempt to escape from it must of necessity fail because the whole system is built on it. To be crude: no achievement, no money. The suburb is tied to the reality of achievement by an indissoluble union despite the fact that the purpose of the suburb is to escape this reality. Thus in Crestwood Heights,

The child must be free in accordance with democratic ideology; but he must, by no means, become free to the point of renouncing either the material success goals or the engineered cooperation integral to the adequate functioning of an industrial civilization.

But it is not only the industrial civilization that provides the drive behind the overmastering of individual choice; it is the urge to go from status to status, for the members of one generation to achieve in the eyes of their peers what their elders could not, which is the motive force of suburban living. The child, thus, is "forced into the position of having to choose those competitive means which will assure his ultimate entrance into an appropriate adult occupational status." Since it is a choice made on the sly through an omnipresent culture, the child "sees no authority figures against which to rebel, should he feel the desire to do so . . . the child has, therefore, only one recourse . . . to turn his attacks against himself." A pleasant society this, a new society, in which freedom is institutionalized, in which choice is dictated.

The manifestations of this conflict can be found in any suburb. All suburbs like to call themselves Garden suburbs, yet it is a fact plain to the eye that they are being eaten up by modern slums, that they are incapable of planning for themselves, that they are being cut to ribbons by super highways. There is no planning for freedom or the space that makes freedom possible; for who in the suburb will rise up to defend planning? No one, since no one lives there. The planners prattle gaily about community spirit. But there is no community. What is a suburb to a suburbanite? A display case: and if it is ruined by outside developers, he will move a little further out to a newer suburb. It is easier that way. Besides he means to move anyway in a couple of years. *House Beautiful* was wrong; anybody can own several houses.

Yet all the movement is vain, for it does not signify change and innovation but simply status achievement. The suburb is a closed society. Those who can transcend it need not think they can bring anything to it. Locked within its own conflicts the suburb will admit nothing alien, nothing new, nothing startling. *Crestwood Heights*, that compendium of revolutionary thoughts, must be quoted again:

Within Crestwood Heights itself, few, if any, alternative cultural patterns present themselves. Unless he is extremely fortunate in being sent abroad to school or university . . . the Crestwood boy has virtually no choice but to enter the business or professional life of Big City and to live subsequently in Crestwood Heights or other suburbs like it.

A sad picture. No actual suburb could be as bad as the description given above. It is only a model, as they say today, or we would all have gone mad by now. This writer has, all through this recital of woe, felt the urge to say something good about the suburb. But he could think of nothing good to say.

The suburb looks so placid, so clean, and so green. It looks the way Edwin Muir describes it. But it is the middle-class man's last stand, the place where he refuses to admit the reality of what he is. When a glimmering of his reality comes to him in the city he runs to the suburb to avoid it. But it doesn't work. This is the failure of the suburb. It is the place to which the Man in the Grey Flannel Suit, the Man on the Train, Organization Man—call them what you will; we all know them—try to run from the ruins behind them, the place to which they run to escape from what they have done and have allowed to be done to them, the place where they play at being free. But the ruins return to haunt them.

In the suburb the middle-class man thought he could build his ideal world for which he was working. But what has he done? He has created instead a symbol of his failure. In terror of himself yet fascinated with his own power, he flees from his city, from himself and from his power, to what he hopes the power will make possible—freedom. But as he flees he brings his power with him and kills the freedom. Back and forth, from city to suburb, from office to family. The suburb is indeed a masterly symbol of his perpetual *oscillation* between his values-in-conflict. Impregnated with his own belief in achievement he kills the thing achievement is supposed to achieve; achievement-achieved carries within itself its own death and the death of freedom. For when the Master comes to the suburb he thrusts his values on wife and child, and they too are caught in the frenzy of achievement. But this frenzy of achievement is not what he meant at all; so back to the other failure in the city while during the day in response to his demands and values the wife and child flee the failure of the home to make his achievement all the greater.

369

Oscillation. It is at the heart of the twin failure, of the very existence of the suburban-city nexus. The Master dreams of establishing himself some place, of finding his fulfillment *some time.* But he breaks his dream with his own hands and then runs away from it—too dishonest to want to know what he has done. So he oscillates: he would be a comic figure if the consequences were not so sad. The failure of bourgeois values is nowhere seen so clearly as in his own life and in his own life nowhere so clearly as in his own ideal, the suburbs.

What is the suburb indeed? It is the attempt to flee from the cost of bourgeois values as they are found in the reality of the city to the ideal of bourgeois values as they would be found in the suburb. But the flight is a failure because the real values of the bourgeois life as they are in the city haunt the suburbs and are reproduced there. Hence the flight away from and then back to the city. The man at least has that consolation; the woman cannot do even that for she is caught in the trap made by her Master.

The suburbs are an attempt to found a gigantic illusion—that flight is possible, that the costs of bourgeois values can be avoided, that bourgeois means will not contaminate bourgeois ends, that a bourgeois utopia can be built out of bourgeois cruelty. These are dreams, and only dreams. Middle-class man will not see that there is no escape from the costs of his achievement, not even (or rather, least of all) in his lovely suburb.

The suburbanite has everything he needs except one thing— a capacity for confronting his sense of futility. And it is in the suburb that his attempt to flee his futility hurts him the most.

The circle that the suburbanite draws around himself is complete. He flees to the suburb to escape his existence as a status achiever. What does he seek in his flight? He seeks the conservative dream that change should come to an end; he seeks to found himself once-and-for-all as a finished object. It is true that the very thing he is running away from, the tempestuous, unfinished, constantly changing life of the status achiever, destroys and must destroy the dream he is trying to erect because the suburb itself is the scene of status achievement. But in his reaction against what he has become and against the senseless change he has thrust upon himself he turns to conservatism, to the belief that man and his history can be brought to a stop. The hope is futile. And so are its results, a playing with trinkets, with the childish counters of suburbia. But what else is there to do but to pursue futility? Subtopian man is lost in meaninglessness because the conservative hope that stasis is possible offers him nothing—literally nothing since its belief that man should stand still is simply a statement that in the place of creativity there should be nothing, an absence. No wonder the suburbanite turns his habitat into a toyland of noisy and absurd things.

The suburbs demonstrate the costs of conservatism and the source of conservatism. Thus it is that the suburbs are a place of refusal in which conservative beliefs find a rich humus and in which flowers of uselessness push up through disordered soil. The city at least produces something even if senselessly. The suburb does not and cannot because it is dedicated to the principle of noncreation and to the principle that man can husk off his freedom and fix himself.

12. Conservatism Finds Its (National) Purpose: Beyond Survival with Max Ways

SINCE THE EARLY part of 1959 the American people have been subjected to a new promotional scheme, the "debate" on national purpose that *Time* and *Life* have tried to arouse. Like most promotional schemes, the public did not ask for the product.

However, Time, Inc., rather obviously prodded by Henry Luce, has become worried about America. There is a feeling on the part of Mr. Luce and his team that America has fallen down on the job, whatever the job may be. But that is the point: what is America's job? Or, more elegantly, what is the purpose of America? The question is breathtaking in its simplicity and awesome in its scope. What is the purpose of America! It does set one to thinking.

As one might have expected the members of the team at Time, Inc., all nineteen of them, thought that the product needed endorsement, and they thereupon set about creating a "debate" that was duly published as *The National Purpose: America in Crisis: an Urgent Summons* (1960). This "national debate," as Mr. Luce calls it, thereupon overestimating his product as advertisers will, was not very productive of anything beyond evidence of the fact that the one thing Americans cannot agree upon is the national purpose. Indeed, the only two participants who agreed were Billy Graham and a John K. Jessup, one of Mr. Luce's editorial writers. They at least were as one in claiming that timeless beliefs and moral law are more important than democracy. The others[1] went their own way, some, like Adlai Stevenson and Archibald MacLeish, writing in commonsense terms that freedom was something to use,[2] others grappling more or less successfully with specific problems—Wohlstetter's essay was by far the finest in this respect—while others turned to a panacea like strong leadership (Reston), or platitudes like the pursuit of excellence (Gardner), or self-advertising (David Sarnoff). In short, as an attempt to show Americans the nature of their national purpose *The National Purpose* is a failure.

But one need not assume that the "debate" was a failure from the point of view of Mr. Luce and Time, Inc., for if no one else knows what the national purpose is, they do. One may assume that their attempt to create a debate was the soft-sell phase of the promotional campaign, a phase designed to open up the way to the hard sell of what Mr. Luce and Time, Inc., think should be our purpose. It is the mere idea of national purpose they are trying to peddle now, not a particular brand. Yet the brand has been developed; it has even been put on the market

[1] The contributors were John K. Jessup, Adlai Stevenson, Archibald Mac-Leish, David Sarnoff, Billy Graham, John W. Gardner, Clinton Rossiter, Albert Wohlstetter, James Reston, and Walter Lippmann.

[2] There is, of course, a possible liberal form of the idea of national purpose, although it has not yet been articulated. It is implied, however, by Stevenson, MacLeish, and Wohlstetter in *National Purpose*, and also in the articles by David Riesman and Michael Maccoby, "The American Crisis," and Hans J. Morgenthau, "Our Thwarted Republic," *Commentary*, June, 1960.

in the form of Max Ways's *Beyond Survival.* And it has a distinctly conservative flavor.

The conservatism of Mr. Luce's national purpose takes various forms. As Robert V. Daniels has pointed out,[3] the whole "debate" (and not just the contributions of Mr. Luce and Co.) has in large part resulted in simple reaffirmations of old American traditions, in calls for a "retreat to tradition." He goes on to point out correctly, that such a retreat will only make it more difficult for America to face the problems of today since many of the traditions of America are no longer adequate to the reality we face. More exactly, the reavowal of individual enterprise, states' rights, and national sovereignty-cum-supernationalism, will simply not do today. Yet those traditions are essentially what have been reaffirmed by most of the national purpose debaters (although not all). It need not be pointed out at this stage of our inquiry that such values are essentially the values of Old Conservatism, that the whole emphasis on tradition is a conservative enterprise.

But conservatism has more than one face. It is traditionalist and in favor of that quasi anarchy that goes under the name of *laissez-faire* government, but it is also capable of strong government and powerfully organized super-nationalism. That these two alternatives have important points of conflict is not to be denied. And neither is it to be denied that what Mr. Luce and his spokesman, Max Ways, suggest as to the national needs of America will go against the grain of many conservatives. For Time, Inc., is as impressed as Lippmann with the threatening decay of the United States and in its panic is ready to grab at anything, even a strong national government. (Time, Inc., is not at peace with itself on this question; *Fortune* is still for

---

[3] Robert V. Daniels, "Do We Need a National Purpose?" *The New Leader,* September 5, 1960.

weak government and never mind the consequences, but it has its own peculiar subscription problem to worry about.)

The ideas of *Beyond Survival* might be best described as conservatism finally faced with the recognition that it must do something and must attempt to solve a problem. What is significant about the proposals of Time, Inc., is the fact that when Mr. Luce and his team see the need for a national revival, when they feel an urgent need for a change in American life, they can only think in terms of a fixed society based on higher law. That solution is the significance of their suggestions. When the need for change in America becomes so overwhelming that it can no longer be neglected, when even Time, Inc., has to admit that a flaccid government and leadership will no longer suffice, they turn to the most conservative of social and political structures, a society based on plebiscite and one supreme moral law. Such a solution may and will shock conservatives although there is no reason to believe that it will shock such conservatives as Kirk and his crowd or Lippmann when he is feeling gloomy. (It might be pointed out here that Lippmann in 1960 felt that the Soviet threat to the United States was a blessing in disguise, for he was "sure" that without it America would decline.)[4] But whatever the feeling of conservatives may be, the brutal fact is that authoritarianism is the conservative's answer when all else fails, when he can no longer avoid the necessity to act. This is true not just because such a society enshrines elitist values, but because it is the very embodiment of a fixed society which has discovered its essence. Certainly, those conservatives who believe that the particular essence of America is Lockian, nineteenth-century liberalism will break with conservatism when it goes to this desperate length. But that refusal is a reflection on their inability to understand the nature of their conserva-

[4] Walter Lippmann, "National Purpose," *The National Purpose*, p. 134.

tism, not a reflection on conservatism itself. If such Old Conservatives—and some of the New Conservatives—do make such a break perhaps they will then learn where liberty really is defended and what liberty really means. Perhaps they will learn then that man is not free when he ties himself to an essence of any kind.

Vigor surges through our own society, through our allies (when last had France this look of hope?), through our enemies, through the "uncommitted" lands that are passionately committing themselves to the future. Yet in the midst of all this energy, the policy of the United States seems to be swirling into an eddy, a dead end.

Max Ways, *Beyond Survival*

Time, the Weekly Newsmagazine, like every good weekly news magazine, is acutely sensitive to both the fears of mankind and the trend of the market. It has therefore now come to realize that, as an ex-editor of *Time* has put it, behind the barbecue pit stands a man deeply troubled about the state of America. Or if he isn't troubled he certainly should be, for the United States is weaker now than it has ever been before, and certainly than it was in 1952. This admission, that Republicanism has failed by simply wasting the past eight years of American life, is the astounding conclusion one must draw from the most recent statement of belief by Time, Inc. Henry Luce and *Time* are not the *National Review;* they are not rabid or hysterical, and they keep a tight check on their emotions as well as their facts. It is not from the crackpots of either the Left or the Right that one hears of the collapse of Republicanism. It has come instead from the house organ of Republicanism itself. The accusation is clear: the United States is "swirling into an eddy, a dead end." As Joe McCarthy would say, there has been a betrayal some place. But who has betrayed whom?

The question of blame—whether Eisenhower betrayed Luce or Luce Eisenhower—can be left to the two gentlemen themselves. To an outsider, Luce's denunciation of the Republican failure is disturbing enough just by itself. One had hoped that somebody had been made happy by the Eisenhower administration. And, more important, one must agree that, while the country is throbbing with energy, if it has not swerved into a dead end, it has at least skidded dangerously and without direction.

Naturally, *Time,* being a responsible news magazine, does not parade its disenchantment in its columns. Quite the contrary, as a responsible news magazine it feels the obligation not to frighten or unduly depress the American people as a whole. But Time, Inc., behind the cheerful façade of *Time, the Weekly Newsmagazine,* has been doing a lot of thinking and worrying, and has gallantly presented the American public with a glimpse of its worries, and what it thinks should be done about them. *Beyond Survival* (1959), by Max Ways, is a book by a lifelong journalist who has occupied various seats of high influence in Time, Inc. It is recommended by Henry R. Luce—one of the few occasions when the Great Man himself has spoken directly to us. Even more significant is the statement by Mr. Ways that his book first existed in an "early version intended for internal Time, Inc., circulation and not for publication." In view of these facts one may consider the usual statement that Time, Inc., is not responsible for the book as more formal than real. *Beyond Survival* is a product of the thinking of Time, Inc., and a very candid one, too. We should be grateful for the warning it sounds.

Warning is the word. Mr. Ways is so concerned, his anguish is so real, his commitment so deep, that the further one reads in his book the more uneasy one feels. Granted the mishmash of politics and policy under the Eisenhower administration—and who now would not grant it?—must that fact necessarily lead to a rejection of the structure and meaning of the American political system? For that conclusion, whether Mr. Ways knows it or not, is the end to which his argument leads. His book is ostensibly about instilling a national purpose into American life; but under that formula some very strange ideas are put forward. Indeed, his ideas about what America must become are so strange that one is inclined to be more scared of Mr. Ways and Time, Inc., than of the failure they are trying to remedy.

Mr. Ways, clearly, is convinced that the "problem" of America today goes far beyond the failure of an Eisenhower. Indeed, Mr. Ways prefers not to discuss Eisenhower and his specific policy deeds and misdeeds, not only because *Time* does not discuss them (whatever Time, Inc., may discuss behind its closed doors), but because the reconstruction of America needs to be an almost total reconstruction—personalities are not, he thinks, at issue. In short, there is no real distinction to be made between Harry S. Truman and Dwight D. Eisenhower.

What is at the root of our drift to a dead end is something Big. It is nothing less than "Part II. The World Situation," certainly a Big subject. In fact, one of the problems this book raises is whether Time, Inc., does not think in terms that are *too* big. A little more concrete thought about the hard facts of "the world situation" might have led to some less anguished, and less dangerous, conclusions. But, as Mr. Ways says, we must not indulge in "the modern . . . form of losing The Problem in the problems." Indeed not.

The Problem is the lack of order in the world today, owing to technological change. Such a statement is neither original nor precise. But it indicates Mr. Ways's obsession with Order as the be-all and end-all of human existence, and it leads him to the conclusion that while modern technology destroys order it does not destroy the desire for order, which either America or the Communists will satisfy (especially in the backward countries). It is at this point that the issue of national purpose becomes urgent, for in Mr. Ways's view the vacuum left by modern technology in the soul of man must be filled by some purpose or another, ours or communism's.

The effects of having no national purpose are disastrous. It was because America had no national purpose, Mr. Ways tells us, that the representatives of the West bickered in China, failed to settle what the basic Western principles were, and therefore lost the country. "[Bertrand] Russell and (especially) John Dewey contradicted in China the teachings of Christian missionaries, who contradicted one another." John Dewey, it seems, not only ruined this country with his pragmatism, but other countries as well. Thus the failure of the West: "We stubbornly persist in trying to state the world conflict today in terms of 'the West' *vs.* some opponent, whether Communism or 'the East.' The fundamental action is inside the West itself, a conflict between its essential tradition and the modernist corruption thereof."

How is Mr. Ways's "Quest for Purpose" to be carried on? It cannot be carried on if false political ends are pursued. Survival is a false end. So is national interest. And the doctrine that Charles Burton Marshall has stated—that goals are easy, but getting to the goals is not—is false. Everything is false that does not revolve around national purpose. We are now at the crux of Mr. Ways's argument: there is a vast qualitative difference, he says, between national purpose and mere national policies. He says, speaking of Europe and Latin America, that "national interest . . . will tell us only that they have to be 'held.' The objective of establishing conditions that make for a more orderly and freer political life will give us a better idea of what we have to do in those areas."

Now the creation of a free and orderly political life in Europe was exactly the whole basis and purpose of the Marshall Plan, a masterpiece of national interest if there ever was one. Certainly no one—least of all Mr. Ways and Time, Inc.—would accuse Truman and Marshall of having had a national purpose. Yet a relatively simple and even obvious policy goal turned out to be the most significant act of American foreign policy since 1945, and it did just what Mr. Ways would like to achieve under the inspiration of a national purpose. So far all Mr. Ways has done is to convince us that Charles Burton Marshall was right.

Mr. Ways (and Mr. Luce for that matter) leaves us mystified as to what all the pother over national purpose is about. One is not encouraged when, after trying to prove Daniel J. Boorstin wrong about the uniqueness and incommunicability of American political life, he lamely concludes that "while it is easy to laugh at the 'incommunicable America' theory stated by Boorstin (and partly believed by millions of Americans), it is by no means easy to say what it is that we can and should communicate." And true enough, it proves to be very difficult indeed.

What are the principles Mr. Ways wants America to communicate? (1) Our political order is derived from the nature of man as derived from "Nature's God." (2) The national government is limited to the federal principle. (3) Judicial review limits the executive and legislature. (4) Natural law sets limits to political action and "enlightens the general direction of action," as well as establishing the obligation to obey. There are some other principles on this general order (ten in all), but they all come to much the same thing.

The trouble is, they don't really come to much. Mr. Ways tries to show that his principles are not high-flown phrases but practical guides to action, telling us what to do next. But he fails. Thus, assuming that one of our national principles is that "no democratic constitution makes sense except as it recognizes its dependence on a natural law," he attempts to show how that belief would dictate our behavior toward Ghana with its rather odd internal politics. His answer is: "Principle prevents us from washing our hands of Ghana's leaders because they may have violated an institution we rightly cherish. Principle also prevents us from accepting Ghana's leaders as they stand." In short, principle doesn't tell us very much.

Is this book a joke? No, *Beyond Survival* is not a joke. The discussion of national purpose it contains may appear to be a farce, but the book as a whole is a disturbing revelation of a set of political attitudes that are destructive of freedom and free government despite all the pious talk about judicial review, etc. The whole argument Mr. Ways gives for his concepts of national purpose leads straight to a larger pattern of national discipline which he would like to impose on America. His attitudes toward American politics, his envy of Communism as a more effective and purposeful system than the American, his suggestions about the necessity of bringing religion into politics, and his hatred of science, all add up to a threat to freedom. Let us be blunt. Who is Mr. Ways's and Mr. Luce's current hero? They never tell us his name, but he is easy to spot. Who else today represents national purpose so magnificently as Charles de Gaulle?

How, Mr. Ways asks, is the national purpose to be achieved? By a dialogue between the President and the public. Will Mr. Ways give Congress a role in that conversation? By no means. For Congress represents division, conflict, irresolution, the very opposites of national purpose. (It is not possible to describe what Mr. Ways thinks of American political parties because they are never discussed; obviously the subject is too painful.) Congress in Mr. Ways's eyes has about the same mean position in national life as the legislatures of France have in De Gaulle's eyes.

The two main formal elements of U.S. policy making are the Congress and the President. Legislatures are most prominent and useful in the formation of foreign policy where the underlying problem is one of composing into a whole separate regional or economic or other interests, each with a special stake in foreign policy. The House of Commons was the clearinghouse that struck the balance of commercial and strategic interests for Imperial Britain. This kind of problem has not much to do with the present-day policy formation by the United States because the total of the special interests and pressures is only a minute fraction of the total national foreign responsibility. Any defects in our policy are not likely to be caused by the old-fashioned kind of internally divided interests.[5]

Congress, it seems, is so impotent that it cannot even obstruct effectively. Mr. Ways's discussion of the American governmental system is really exhausted by his remark that since 1945 Congress has, "on the whole," been a "pitiable and somewhat repulsive object." But it can be ignored because the President now has a new way of getting in touch with the public. He is able to communicate with the American people by "acoustics."

"Acoustical" suggests the quality of the true public contribution to policy. Top political leaders cannot hear themselves, cannot develop either confidence or self-criticism except as they apprehend *what* effect their words and deeds have upon the public. A policy maker does not know quite what he has said at a press conference until he

[5] Max Ways, *Beyond Survival* (1959), p. 115.

reads the next morning's papers. Public relations, until recently a peripheral function of government, has now taken a much more central position; indeed, it sometimes appears to be the end product of government action even in the field of foreign policy. A leader who gets from the public the right resonance knows he is on the beam; one who does not will mumble and fumble.[6]

Mr. Ways either means Plebiscite Democracy by his fancy phrases or he means nothing.

But he is really less interested in systems of government than he is in metaphysics, and the particular form of metaphysics that grips Mr. Ways's soul is religion. Let there be no mistake: America does not just need religion in politics, it needs a particular religion, Christianity. It is because religion is so necessary to America that Mr. Ways gets angry at those who failed to see that Mr. Dulles really meant every bit of his invocations of God. "The idea of God has to be taken seriously in the politics of these Western societies." In what way? When put to the test, Mr. Ways wanders off again; religion, it seems, will fructify the politics of the United States by making "us convinced that the principles for which we stand are . . . derived from the idea of God." That may seem vague enough to be harmless, but not when it is taken in conjunction with Mr. Ways's praise of the medieval age: "Europe from Charlemagne to Robespierre was an experience of institutions working for order, the longest and most vigorous civilizational epoch of which we know, an age which owed much more to religion, ethics, metaphysics, and politics than it owed to economics or technology." One begins to have visions of a hierarchical society with Papa leading the parade to church. Since the question of national purpose is a moral one, and since, as Mr. Ways primly remarks, "churches are regularly concerned with ethics," the role of

[6] *Ibid.*, pp. 168-9.

churches at least is assured in the national-purpose society, even if nothing else is.

Mr. Ways's interest in religion is not only the result of his sorrowful discovery that the churches, even though their concern is with ethics, "are out of connection with the public philosophy," but also of his overwhelming disgust with the devil he sees everywhere around him. The devil is science and/ or positivism and, of course, the French Revolution.

We have not yet got our national purpose he thinks, because the very possibility of metaphysics has been destroyed by science. "The tendency to ignore all knowledge not formed by the methods of the physical sciences continues to be strong in our own day." The worst thing about science, according to Mr. Ways, is that "it cannot reintegrate knowledge but is potent enough to prevent its reintegration by any other principle or system." It flows naturally from these assumptions that science is the cause of all our troubles. Not economics ("which . . . never worked more successfully"), or weapons, or human greed, but science. The positivist is against faith, and he tries to establish a creed in which faith is unnecessary. Therefore he and his creed, science, destroy national faith. Comment on such gimcrack thinking is superfluous.

But Mr. Ways's book finds its climax in his discussion of communism and the Russian Communists. One is perhaps not surprised at his unhappiness over the failure of American society, but one is surprised that a man of his persuasions should say what he says in praise of communism. Considered functionally —and that is the main way he considers it—communism, we are told, "seems to be working better than our public philosophy." Certainly it works better than positivism and/or science, for "from top to bottom Marxism is pervaded by a sense of respect for the unity of truth, the idea that any two valid

propositions must be capable of some kind of harmony. [Evi]dently at Time, Inc., nothing *does* succeed like success. [The] efficacy of wholeness is what the Soviet Union has and [that] we, thanks to science, do not have. And above all and be[yond] all, Marxism prevents the Communist from losing The Prob[lem] in the problems!

The reason for all this praise is, of course, the need to expl[ain] how the Communist system works so well when, according [to] the capitalist creed, it should not work at all. "The evidence— especially the recent evidence—indicated that the capitalist institutions of the Soviet Union are working at a level of effi- ciency and a rate of progress comparable to that of the West. How explain the contradictory evidence?" The answer is clear. Just as Pope Pius X tried to inspire work with moral purpose, Mr. Ways says, so do the Communists. The difference is that the Communists are more successful. Their success extends to the whole realm of public order: Communism, thanks to its public philosophy, has developed "law of a sort, law that rests upon a Marxist ethic. . . ."

Enough. Mr. Ways has written and Mr. Luce has sponsored a book that is careless in its discussion and haphazard in its thought. No doubt Mr. Luce and Mr. Ways are serious in their intentions, but they have not been serious enough to think hard. But in the last analysis criticism is irrelevant, for these ideologues do not care whether their thought is slipshod or not. The end is all. And while the end that Mr. Ways and Mr. Luce postulate may be an impossible one in present-day America, and may therefore merely demonstrate the futility and irrele- vancy of Time, Inc., and its ideology, the matter is nevertheless important.

Their ideas are important, first, because all the talk about national purpose acts as a cover-up for the policy failures and

problems we face. It leads the American public—and Mr. Luce
—to ignore the concrete facts of our situation. Time, Inc., may
despise Eisenhower for his failures, but it must at the same
time protect him from the effects of his failures. Second, *Beyond Survival* reveals such an appalling bankruptcy of ideas
among the respectable American right wing that one is fearful
for a nation in which men of influence are so far out of touch
with reality and clear thinking. De Gaullism in America! Acoustical engineering in place of Congress! Plebiscite democracy
in place of political parties! Metaphysics instead of science!
And the imitation of communism as a method of politics and
strategy! (The way the French colonels did in Algeria, say?)

The question of national purpose might appear to be a real
issue. It is something, after all, that bothers many people who
wish to have no truck with Mr. Ways's metaphysics. One can
hardly be against purpose; obviously, purpose and a sense of
direction are essential to human existence and therefore, presumably, to the existence of a nation. But such truisms do not
dispose of the question. How can a nation have a purpose? It
may, with considerable effort, make decisions that become
policies. But this vague, long-term thing called a purpose! An
individual's purpose is cloudy, distant, abstract, and is often
neglected for long periods of time; one dreads to think what
would be the result of trying to fasten a purpose on a nation.
If it is difficult for an individual to keep his mind on his purpose
and keep his mind operative, then how much more so for
170,000,000 persons! And especially for a nation conceived in
liberty!

Leaving aside the possibility that America in fact does have
a national purpose based on the buying and selling of what
G. B. Shaw called "illth" and which has made Time, Inc., so
prosperous, one must look at the accusation that American politics, in both the domestic and foreign fields, is in a slough of

inaction. The point is, according to Time, Inc., and some national-purpose advocates, it is politics which is meaningless, not the wise boys of Mad. Av. It is necessary, therefore, to instill some backbone, some drive, some steam and push, some purpose into our disorderly political system. And, cries Mr. Ways, I have the way to do it!

The accusation claims nothing less than that the American political system is incapable of solving the problems we must face today because it cannot provide (Mr. Ways's version of) national purpose. When we consider the book as a whole, and Mr. Luce's specific rejection (in the foreword) of pluralism as a tolerable system for America, we can know what national purpose means today for those who would thrust it upon us. It means *One* Ideology. One ideology for the whole country. An ideological framework (or strait jacket) would firm up the American nation and give us a sense of drive, of movement.

But is One Big Ideology the only interpretation of national purpose that is possible? Perhaps there is another sense of national purpose, not quite so feverish and so destructive of American democracy and the American political system which that system can produce.

That America can make decisions without an ideology is demonstrated by the facts of such recent history as that of the years 1948-49, when the Marshall Plan and NATO came into being. They came into being not by ideology leading to consensus and then to action, but by argument leading to consensus and then to action. But who started the argument? The Executive. With whom did the Executive argue? Congress. But, the national-purpose boys cry, those were emergency years, and the problem is that America cannot act *today* in the emergency it faces because the American political system no longer works.

Is it true that what is needed today cannot be produced by

the American political system, but requires national purpose plus acoustical engineering and all that that implies? Mr. Ways never tells us what it is about the American political system that is blocking action. What has changed in the last decade to make the Eisenhowers the controllers of our fate? Certainly something has happened to make masterly inaction a policy of the American government. But that something is not to be cured by ideology. An emergency exists only when it is recognized; to paraphrase, a problem must not only exist but must be seen to exist. Does America face an emergency in regard to, say, India? American schools? Of course. But it will not become a public fact until it is made a public fact. There will be no recognition of crisis or emergency if the leaders of both parties refuse to drag problems into the light of day and examine them without regard to ideologies based on concepts of a fixed society.

Further, once the problem and its various answers are revealed, then somebody must make an issue out of them. When that is done, the national purpose that Mr. Ways so much desires will be formed in regard to at least one problem. There is no formation of national purpose (if you like) whenever America's problems do not exist as really live questions in the mind of the government, party leaders, and especially the executive branch of the government.

The American governmental system was not, therefore, being used under Eisenhower as it can and should be used. Liberal government in general, and the American government in particular, is a problem-solving device. But it is not an automatic problem-solving device, because no government is automatic. Even an electronic computer has to have the problem fed into it. Liberal government needs someone to bring up the issues. It needs more than that, but it needs at least that. It

388

has been pointed out by the Madison Avenue boys that the "New Ike" could get things done when he wanted to. Exactly. But he didn't seem to want to; or he preferred vetoes to Development Loan Funds. The executive branch of the government is potent. It does not need acoustical engineering, partly because it has it (the name of one acoustical engineer was James Hagerty), but mainly because acoustical engineering is of no use if all that comes from it is a petulant squeak now and then. ("Mr. Hagerty . . . said today that the President wanted him to repeat . . . that he was getting sick and tired of the steel strike.") The immense powers of the Executive do not need enumeration here. Those powers will shrivel, of course, if they are used to preach metaphysics. But if they are used to talk about schools, say, and the talk is followed by action, by a legislative program, then the President, the public, *and* Congress can indulge in debate. Then the old Republic would rock with clamor and the sounds of outrage and hosannas. An issue would have been raised, solutions would be in sight.

But the trouble is, who wants to raise an issue? Issues divide the nation. Everybody knows that. What we need is unity. Like the French today. But unfortunately for the advocates of One Ideology, the Republic is predicated on the assumption that issues will be raised. The tired old belief that issues are bad for the public health is hokum. Conflict is good for the public health. Lewis Coser has written as follows in his book *The Functions of Social Conflict*:

Internal social conflicts which concern goals, values or interests that do not contradict the basic assumptions upon which the relationship is founded tend to be positively functional for the social structure. . . . A flexible society benefits from conflict because such behavior, by helping to create and modify norms, assures its continuance under changed conditions. Such mechanism for readjustment of norms is hardly available to rigid systems: by suppressing conflict the latter smother a useful warning signal, thereby maximizing the danger of catastrophic breakdown.[7]

If ever a nation has needed a "readjustment of norms" it is America in 1959 and 1960.

The failures of the past decade have not come about because the machinery of liberal government is inadequate, but because it had nothing to work on. President Eisenhower, working closely with his colleague Lyndon Johnson, devoted his energies to blanketing the problems we face. Senator Johnson preferred to act as a shunter of bills; national needs were not for him. President Eisenhower saw financial orthodoxy as the purpose of his administration. But why blame individuals? Other nations in the West were (and are) on the same binge of unity-at-any price. The British have returned to their old weakness and voted for a figure straight out of Max Beerbohm. Who wants to argue when You Have Never Had It So Good? As for the French, they got unity-at-any-price, and what a price!

Does Mr. Ways wish to talk about the Problem? Very well. The problem is the failure of both parties to look at the problems that face America today. Is it necessary to destroy the American system of government and then erect national purpose on its ruins in order to get action today? If so, we are not swirling toward a dead end; we have reached it. But the contrary is true. One Ideology would smother the issues we face even more effectively than is being done today. For then debate would be at an end—for a long time. Belief in One Ideology is faith, something assumed to be always true of man; it is not the start of useful ideological debate on issues. That is why America has avoided it.

[7] Coser, *Functions of Social Conflict*, pp. 151, 154.

Hannah Arendt has this to say about the meaning of ideology:

In their claim to total explanation, ideologies have the tendency to explain not what is, but what becomes, what is born and passes away. . . . The claim to total explanation promises to explain all historical happenings, the total explanation of the past, the total knowledge of the present, and the reliable prediction of the future. . . . In this capacity ideological thinking becomes independent of all experience from which it cannot learn anything new even if it is just a question of something that has just come to pass. Ideological thinking orders facts into an absolutely logical procedure which starts from an axiomatically accepted premise, deducing everything else from it; that is, it proceeds with a consistency that exists nowhere in the realm of reality.[8]

Not all ideologies destroy experience, however. There are ideologies that improve one's sense of reality by giving a point of view, by avoiding chiliasm and commitment to One Ideology, and above all by recognizing that while men believe in an ideology and its values, they are also free—free even to repudiate their ideology and values. There can be a useful tension between an ideology and the facts of life; ideologies of some degree of firmness are a necessity of human existence, for otherwise human existence would have no meaning. But an ideology is useful only when it is one that recognizes that values are tentative, that change is inherent in society, that men are in constant movement from one stage of existence to another. An ideology is useful, in other words, only when it includes the fact that men are free and that they cannot be fixed within the confines of any Public Philosophy, Essence, or One Ideology.

[8] Hannah Arendt, *The Origins of Totalitarianism* (Second ed., 1958), p. 470.

That it is difficult for many people to create such an ideology in America today has been shown by the writers considered in this book. Some scramble in their panic to One Ideology; they ache for Essence. Others are discouraged and tired; they seek to avoid ideology altogether. Both are wrong.

What Mr. Ways and Mr. Luce have written is not only foolish; it is also incompatible with the American system of politics and government. Our government is one within which debate can and must take place. It exists to provide not a metaphysics, but the means for men to find agreement on specific issues when they initially have none. That is why we have all the paraphernalia of the Constitution; it assures the maximum amount of debate. Too much debate? At times, perhaps.

The common purpose that results from debate on specific problems is not an ideological commitment; One Ideology and the American governmental system are at opposite poles. The American governmental system produces something much less grandiose—agreement. Disgruntled agreement no doubt, but still agreement; we are dealing with men, not angels. The agreement is on issues, and the issues come either from the President or the force of circumstances or a variety of ideologies. Sometimes a clear-cut crisis exists and the machinery begins to grind. But need one wait? The President has an executive branch with eyes, ears, a mind; he has his own will to make decisions.

To ask for an end to issues is to wish to destroy the political and constitutional system of America. Since the avoidance of issues is what has been systematically pursued in the last eight years by the leadership of both parties and by such organs of public opinion as Time, Inc., it comes as a shock to be told we must now substitute national purpose for a political system our leaders neither understand nor—one fears—want to understand. The avoidance of concrete issues in *Beyond Survival* is no accident, for Time, Inc., are not really interested in issues at all, but simply in an abstraction which they call Order. If they have anything concrete to propose, let them propose it and then the debate can begin.

In fact, all the talk about national purpose is fantasy: do Time, Inc., and Mr. Luce really expect the American people to be badgered into One Ideology? But what can happen and has happened is that those who seek to avoid issues and conflict on the real problems we face can use their powerful influence to soothe and reassure the American public so that decisions will be ever more difficult to come by. The doctrine of national purpose is one more drug, following hard on the heels of the quiz shows.

Behind the ideal of One Ideology, behind the conviction that we must not lose The Problem in the problems, lies the old and futile desire to close off the future with all its unexpected dangers and contingencies by enclosing it, by fixing it, in One Ideology. Opposed to that aim is the American system of government, which is open to the conflicts of various beliefs and ideologies and is therefore also open to the future. It is a system that provides a method of debate as well as a means of decision on issues that are issues exactly because they are unexpected.

13. The Futilitarian Society

IN ORDER TO answer the first question posed at the beginning of this book—what is the nature of American conservatism?—it is necessary to consider the unique and peculiar quality of that conservatism. As we have seen, there are those who would deny that there is such a thing and who would claim instead either that America is liberal in the eighteenth-century sense of the word, or that it so ignores ideology that nothing resembling a conservative creed can be found here. Indeed, the conservatives themselves in their more despondent moments believe that they are a gallant few almost submerged by an America that refuses to base its political discussions on original sin. Yet, there are also the facts of American life, the reality of a society that preserves almost indefinitely its institutions—what other country has tolerated the stasis a House Rules Committee brings to Congress?—and is conservative in its conviction that its political framework has been created once and for all.

Americans perpetually confuse technological change and status movement with social change. Both, in fact, can lead to significant as distinct from insignificant change and both have done so. But they have often done so in the face of a refusal on the part of many Americans to admit that important social and

political change and innovation in our society is either necessary or desirable. Technological developments and status movement have created a kind of *sub-rosa* change in America, but
the idea that a different America might be made by innovation
has often met with deep resistance. In this sense Hartz and
Boorstin are true interpreters of the widespread and popular
assumption that America *is*. Americans will brag about technological change; they will explain that America is the most
mobile society in the world. But few will say that a new America is coming into existence, that it should come into existence,
that they hope it will come into existence, and that they have
been thinking about the form it will take. The idea of a new,
a *different* America, is not one to commend itself to them.

If ours is a sticky society it is not unique in this respect; it
simply shares with other societies a conservative instinct. It
may play with technological change and status movement but
at the same time it maintains the traditional form of the society that has come from the past. Its clinging to Lockian axioms
and its sense of givenness, which Hartz and Boorstin dwell on
so lovingly, are in themselves evidence of the profoundly conservative nature of American political and social thought. Certainly the deeply traditional quality of our politics and society
can no longer be open to question. Not after eight years of
political and social tail-chasing under the Eisenhower administration, a temporary and superficial phenomenon, but a significant one.

But where is the ideology of conservatism in America? The
political theorist sniffing the ground for a packaged set of ideas
widely retailed and labeled as conservative thinks he can find
no such ideology and concludes that there is none. Those who
think about the philosophy of politics often assume that the

attempt on the part of some writers, including many considered in this book, to create a conservative ideology in the U.S. is peripheral to the mainstream of American thought and that they are unrepresentative of anything but themselves, that they do not "count." The first mistake of this hypothesis is that even if it should be true it would not mean that there is no conservatism in the U.S. America may well be less ideological than many nations, something which in itself is no reason for either congratulation or despair. However, if one is to follow Boorstin, the discovery that there is no conservative ideology would mean that America is so deeply conservative that it need not talk about it and can take it as the quality of its "givenness." Thus even on its own ground the argument collapses.

But this book does not follow Boorstin. It does not because the second mistake of those who do not think conservatism counts in America is to misconceive the role of the ideologists of conservatism, to fail to see that they have considerable importance for the understanding of our political and social thought in general and of conservatism in particular. Messrs. Kirk, Chamberlin, Morley, Burnham, and Rossiter do not in any sense represent a political movement and they may not be widely read and conned by those who would be conservative. But can it be said that they stand outside of the stream of American political thought, various and shifting though that stream may be? To be sure, Kirk in particular has his wild fantasies of "ben-and-but" and Gothic romance; but every man should be allowed his private fantasies. Let us admit that Kirk and Co. do not have a wide influence today as such. But the significance of these ideologists is not dependent upon their direct influence. Rather it is dependent upon what they can tell us about those ideas that are widely accepted in America to-

day and about the common political and social assumptions of many or most of us. If Kirk and Co. do not have influence as such, their ideas nevertheless represent in highly organized and flamboyant form what many Americans think in bits and pieces.

The ideologists considered in these pages tell us what the conservative view is on man, society, and the state. Their ideas tell us what it is to be conservative, tell us how a conservative thinks. And if we compare what they think with what we have been told by Hartz is the common stock of ideas in America, with Lockian liberalism in its Horatio Alger synthesis, we shall find that the Alger-Locke syndrome is not liberal but conservative because it does not differ in its fundamental postulate from the ideologists considered here. One may grant that many Americans think in Algerian-Lockian terms—which is not to grant that strong dissent to it has not always been in evidence or that it has always and everywhere been dominant. But if such is the case, then America has an ideology that is indeed profoundly conservative both in its search for fixedness and essence instead of freedom and innovation, and in its constant fidelity to one set of values. We know that the Algerian-Lockian syndrome is conservative because we know that inherent in this particular offshoot of Lockian liberalism is a view of man, society, and law that is fundamentally at one with the view of those ideologists considered here. And we can know this because we know what conservatism in America has thought on those matters. The writers we have discussed may only be the tip of the iceberg but they indicate what lies beneath the placid waters.

No, Messrs. Kirk, Chamberlin, Morley, Burnham, Rossiter, and Lippmann are not a joke, although in their more *outré* moments they do their best to make us think so and although they have the quality all sectarians have of seeming to talk to themselves. What they say is what a conservative should say. The fact that some Americans do not say the same things indicates that they are not conservatives. The fact that some Americans say somewhat the same things but not all of them indicates that they are incomplete conservatives. And the fact that there are some Americans who say virtually the same things indicates that they are deeply conservative. These are conclusions we cannot reach until we know what the thoughts are of those who have tried to create a conservative ideology for America. Further, the fact that some of us refuse to acknowledge that there is a conservative ideology is simply a reflection of the refusal of many even to admit that there can be such ideas in America, or that they might be conservative. Such a refusal may, as we have seen, tell us a great deal about the instinctive conservatism of America.

Today there is again much talk about the possibilities of change, of moving forward, of innovation after an eight-year interregnum. There is even talk of relevant utopias and once again the American liberal of the twentieth century is beginning to poke his head out. But before he begins to allow his hopes to rise he should be aware that there is an enemy, that conservatism is a fact, and that there is a conservative temper in America that is not good-natured or confused Whiggism. He should also be aware that the attachment to that ideology goes deeper than affection for Eisenhower's personality. The years between 1952 and 1960 may stand as a symptom of the power of the conservative ideology in America, but they should not mislead anyone into thinking that with the disappearance of Eisenhower the attitudes that supported him—and he needed considerable support—will disappear. This book has tried to show some of the kinds of thinking that American conservatism displays. To assume that such thoughts are merely eccentric is to fall into the conservative trap, the belief that there is no important conflict in America but only a few mistakes that have been made along the path of our history.

Is the conservatism of today, which became so articulate and conscious of itself in the 1950's, the same as that which has existed in the past? Or is it a new kind? The possibility may even be raised that the conservatism of the 1950's was unique and unprecedented in American history. In the latter eventuality the Hartz thesis that America in the past has always been of one ideological mind might be considered to be a correct interpretation of the past even if it is not correct for this age. Although such questions lie outside of the formal terms of reference of this book, they are important because they enable the material presented here to be used to present a different way of looking at the history of American political and social ideas from that popularized by Hartz and Boorstin. They will also help dissolve some of the vast confusion about the term *liberal* and the place of liberalism in our thinking.

How does conservatism before 1950 compare with those ideas that have been described here as symptomatic of the 1950's? Undoubtedly the decade of the fifties saw a sharpening of the conservative consciousness and an attempt to distinguish conservatism more clearly from other ideas. But such a development does not necessarily mean that the conservatism of those years was thereby "new" or unique or distinctive. As we have seen, there is little significant difference between Old and New Conservatism; whatever differences exist lie mainly in the realm of greater or lesser articulation of premises. Conservatism, New or Old, is today mainly what it has always been in the U.S.—namely a set of ideas within the framework of traditional American thought.

To say that conservatism in America existed within eighteenth- and nineteenth-century liberalism is to say that it created its own significant, independent, and unique frame of reference within the common political and social assumptions of American thought. American as distinct from European conservatism is based on a bias inherent in American liberalism. Naturally that conservatism did not repudiate the basic unity of American thought any more than British conservatism repudiated the basic unity of British thought. If it had, either it or America would have disappeared. America has not disappeared, but there are many today—there were not in the past, it should be noted—who like to believe that conservatism either did disappear from our midst or failed to appear at all. The important feature of American conservatism, which it is vital to grasp, is that it represents one aspect of the bifurcation in American liberal thinking that stems from the eighteenth century. And it is equally important to realize that nineteenth-century liberalism is the form taken by conservatism in America then and now not just because it represented the privileges of the few in contrast with the lack of privileges of the many and therefore became a creed that maintained the power of those who already had power. Of far greater significance is the fact that many of the postulates that are fundamental to eighteenth- and nineteenth-century Lockian thought can be used for conservative ends. Lockianism and the ideas of Locke themselves, it must be emphasized, are not inherently conservative. Quite the contrary, Lockian categories could be and were used for explosive purposes both in Britain and America.[2] But granted that this is so, it is equally important to understand that not only is there nothing incompatible between conservatism, as it has been defined here, and Lockian thinking, but that many of the basic assumptions of the thought of Locke and his time are well fitted to sustain the conservative syndrome. Lockianism and the somewhat ambiguous thought of Locke himself could and did provide the basis for both radical and conservative traditions of thought.

The conservatives of the past and those of today talk about the freedom of man, but in fact aim to destroy the freedom of man by postulating a fixed society, a fixed quality of human existence and a fixed higher law. As we have seen, such postulates are the very nerve center of American conservatism. One

---

[2] Benjamin Wright's *American Interpretations of Natural Law* (1931) throws some light on the question of the use of natural-law concepts. He shows, of course, that use of the idea of natural law in America for radical purposes has been widespread; but the theme of his work is the variety of uses to which natural law has been put. Although he does not cast his analysis in the framework of a liberal-conservative dichotomy, his point is an important one, for he shows that natural-law thought has been interpreted in two main ways. One has been to look upon it as "scientific" laws of human behavior, as statements of laws of the universe; the other has been to look upon it as principles of right, "to designate principles of right and justice, either those which are incorporated in the laws and institutions of the time and place, or those which are not accepted but which ought to be made the basis of such laws." (See pp. 3, 331.) It is obvious that natural law of both types can be used for both the end of increasing freedom, and of establishing a fixed society, man, and law. (It is worth noting that Wright shows that twentieth-century reformers attacked the idea of natural law and that he says "we cannot escape the conclusion that for the defender of the established order . . . the natural and the customary are the same;" p. 338.) The use of natural-law thought as such will not tell us whether a thinker is a conservative or liberal (although in fact since the development of pragmatism and relativism in Progressive thought it will do so to some considerable degree); but it is important to understand that the conservative desire for a fixed society can be realized through the use of natural-law categories. Thus, there is nothing incompatible between the existence of natural law, or, if one prefers, Lockian thought, in America and conservatism in America. Quite the contrary, conservatism can find congenial ground in natural-law concepts. See also, Leo Strauss, *Natural Right and History*, (1953).

may assume that they are in any nation. But they take on a different form, find a different justification in different societies with their different unities of thought. In America they found their justification and their form in the categories of eighteenth-century thought as it was developed in the nineteenth century. It found that form and justification easily and without strain because much of the eighteenth- and nineteenth-century thought rested on a model of a fixed society, indeed, a fixed universe.

Naturally, a concept of fixed society, man, and law can be a radical way of thinking. It can be used to expand freedom, to thrust against the established way, to innovate. But it will be a means of expanding freedom and of innovation only if it is used to aim for freedom, if it is a statement that men should have more freedom, that they should be allowed to innovate, that change is a vital aspect of human life. To use the idea of higher law to increase freedom it is necessary, in other words, either to say that the higher law tells us that men are to be free on this earth, or that they will never quite realize a higher law and therefore must constantly change to come closer to it.[3] Thus used, belief in the higher law can be a most radical and even destructive doctrine. But, again, it will be such only if the essence of man is seen as freedom for a "long time" in this fallible existence, in this existence which never quite reaches the perfection of higher law, or if freedom is postulated as the goal of this existence.

Does the conservative conceive of higher law in that fashion?

[3] It could be argued, and this writer would so argue, that even given this radicalism there is an important vestige of conservatism within this doctrine, radical though it may be in practice, for it postulates an eventual rest and fixedness. It is not necessary to the theme of this book to make that point, but it should be mentioned as the source of that peculiar conservatism that always seems to be found at the heart of classical liberalism, radical though it was in historical fact.

He does not. He conceives of higher law instead as a means of stopping change and innovation, of binding the freedom of man. He looks to higher law to enclose the freedom of men, not to expand it.[4] And it is important to realize that he is not disappointed. It is important to realize that the concept of higher law can yield this conservative fruit. We have seen how it does so. We have seen how it is used to make men flee the freedom of human existence. What it is necessary to say now is that many of the essential postulates of Lockianism are capable of being used by the conservatives for their purpose of stopping change, innovation and freedom. To show this it will be useful to glance at some of the features of eighteenth-century Lockian thought, always remembering that those features can be used for radical as well as conservative ends. Having done so we will be able to understand how a conservative in America can talk Lockian talk and still be a real, an honest, conservative.

The eighteenth- and nineteenth-century Lockian model was based on a concept of society that postulated a fixed system of laws and interests that would work in perpetuity once the proper balance had been reached. This system, once established, responded so perfectly to the laws of nature that it need not be changed, could not be changed without disaster, without a return to the state of nature such as Locke foresaw would happen if the right of revolution was resorted to. The mundane societies of this world may or may not reach that blessed state,

[4] David Spitz, in an outstanding article, "Freedom, Virtue, and the New Scholasticism," *Commentary*, October, 1959, shows how the conservative puts freedom beneath virtue and subordinates it to restraint, or, more exactly, transforms freedom into restraint; as he says, to the conservatives freedom is "what you ought to do, what God (or nature) commands you to do . . ." (p. 314). He shows also how the conservatives think in terms of natural right and natural law and how such thought destroys freedom; he states their attitude thus: "man is part of the natural order of things; he occupies a place appropriate to his nature and must perform those duties necessary to maintain that system of order"; (p. 314).

but they could presumably (otherwise there would be no point to the whole idea) come very close to it. And once they did, change must of necessity be brought to an end. What rational man would disturb that which was perfect, in accord with the laws of nature, or almost so? As it was with the form of society so it was with the nature of man. *Tabula rasa* or not, it was man's obligation to conform to the laws of nature, to meet the demands of higher law. True, man was a changeable thing, and it might take him a long time to conform. But the idea that he should conform, should progress toward perfection in the sense of knowing what he should do and hence be, was the fundamental postulate of natural-law thought. Finally, underpinning both beliefs, was the belief in the laws of nature itself, belief in essence, in higher law. There was a law independent of man. Restraint would come not from men freely making up the rules they would use to restrain themselves. Rather it would come from finding out what nature intended for them. The very characteristic of civilization was to discover and unfold that law and then live by it. Man did not make his own laws; he obeyed the laws of nature.

Such was the fixed universe of Lockian thought. The nineteenth century may have corrupted those ideas, although it should be noted that the eighteenth century was an unhistorical century, one that searched for fixedness outside the flow of time. But nineteenth- and twentieth-century conservatism could find what it wanted in such thought by ignoring the radical impulse of the eighteenth century and by sticking close to its laws and concepts. The search of, say, Russell Kirk or Walter Lippmann for the higher law, essence, or The Public Philosophy would not have surprised John Locke. What would have surprised him was to find men assuming that there was no higher law, essence, or public philosophy.

But if the basic postulates of the ideas of the eighteenth

century concerning fixedness were accepted by latter-day conservatives, the content that was poured into the fixed vessels
was certainly changed. One need only point to one example,
the shift from the idea that man's fixed nature is rational and
good to the idea that man's fixed nature is irrational and sinful.
(It should be mentioned, however, that John Adams in the
eighteenth century and others like him indicate that that century was not of one mind about how to fill the fixed outlines of
man.) But whatever the specific content, and of course the
differences in content are of crucial importance, the idea of a
fixed society, of man as a fixed being, and of higher law, is the
very stuff of conservatism, and of eighteenth- and nineteenth-
century liberalism.

One can show the equivalence plainly and exactly. Fixed
law corresponds to the American belief in a fixed Constitution
and the fixed constitution we have always had; man as a fixed
quantity and essence corresponds to the belief in economic,
individualist man, man as a consumer go-getter, as well as
original-sin man; a fixed society corresponds to the *laissez-faire*
society that operates according to laws that balance effort and
reward, profits and loss, etc., etc., the perfectly self-perpetu-
ating society that never need be changed. But again, the equiv-
alences, the actual content, is less important than the assumption on which such a view of society, man, and law is based.
It is the assumption that man, society, and law *should* be fixed
and enclosed—the assumption of conservatism.

Although there may be no logical or necessary connection
between ideas of a fixed society, man, and law, on the one hand
and conservatism on the other,[5] in America in empirical fact

[5] For another example of the way natural law can be used for conservative
purposes see Gertrude Himmelfarb, "The Prophets of the New Conservatism,"
Commentary, January, 1950. She points out that Bertrand de Jouvenel's *On
Power* looks to natural law as the only way of finding the objective, eternal
standard beyond men by which to judge mundane reality.

the connection was close and intimate. The conservative in America, the man who sought for a position of fixity and for a society that would realize his dream of a fixed existence, had to use the rhetoric of the nation of which he was a part, in his case a liberal rhetoric. But in doing so he sought those ideas and concepts within eighteenth- and nineteenth-century Lockian thought that would answer to his need. He found them because that thought did provide in fact a basis for conservative beliefs.

The objection may be made that the eighteenth-century view of man, society, and law had a revolutionary effect in Europe when it came up against "feudalism." Undoubtedly it did, which only goes to prove what everyone should have known, that Europe and America differ. But whatever its effect in Europe (and once its revolutionary impulse was spent, it became the basis for a new conservatism) in America it became the means not by which change was prevented—one cannot prevent change no matter how hard one believes in Locke—but by which a certain view of social and political change was promulgated. Technological development was fine; developments that made possible money-making were fine, too. But neither should be allowed to cause those social changes that would disturb the established social and power hierarchy. Nor should they be allowed to cause political change, to make possible a different kind of state, one that might, for example, intervene in the economy. Man was economic man in the nineteenth century. That was a fixed datum from which to work. Society was *laissez-faire*. That was fixed too. And the constitution, the grand and glorious constitution, that was what it was and no tampering with it. Has any nation ever been *more* conservative?

Actually, of course, the social and economic and political life of America was not and could not be halted despite the groans and moans of American conservatives. But no one made them like it in the nineteenth century and no one can make them like it today. Although the conservatives of today, and those who have been considered in this book especially, are more subtle, more tortured, and more self-conscious both in their subtlety and in their torture, they are in a clear line of descent from the American conservatives of the past. They may have tried to fill the fixed vessels with a slightly different content, one which is more up-to-date and adapted to the particular fears of the 1950's, but they continue to postulate what American conservatives have always postulated. The American conservative of the 1950's has fastened as his ancestors did on those features of Lockian eighteenth-century liberalism that appeal to his conservative instincts.

To understand the distinction between this American conservatism, which uses eighteenth-century liberal concepts, and the American liberalism of the twentieth century, it is necessary to understand the impact of social Darwinism on the two groups. Social Darwinism, with its emphasis on change is, of course, at odds with any kind of concept of a fixed society, fixed man, fixed law. Yet the conservative, brought face to face with this new idea, absorbed it into his beliefs with hardly a waver. He did it by equating the concept of natural selection and the survival of the fittest with his concept of a fixed society, the *laissez-faire* society. Social Darwinism became simply another form of the endless round of competition which the fixed society had always been, simply another arrangement of the perfectly balanced society. Hence the conservatives' marvelous sleight of hand; one must not attempt to change the nature of society, or to change the law, or to change human nature, because if one did one would disturb the natural balance of a self-regulated society, a society that regulated itself by the cut and thrust of killing off the weak. Social Darwinism became simply the newest form of social law, which the conservative erected to fix man in an eternal essence under an eternal law. It did not, in short, change the conservatives' assumptions about essence and a fixed universe; it merely confirmed them.

But twentieth-century liberalism in response to social Darwinism, and other influences, created a different view of man, society, and law. Undoubtedly this view again owed much to Locke. But it was Locke with a difference, for twentieth-century liberalism followed the path of pragmatism, a philosophy that does not assume fixed man, society, and law but assumes the exact opposite. It postulates instead a perpetually changing man, society, and law; it postulates that change comes about because men have chosen to make it. It postulates freedom since it destroys the idea that anything is fixed and destroys even the hope for a fixed man, society, and law. The pragmatic belief in *any possibility* and in the need for man to make up his own mind about what he wants to do and not to wait for the higher law to tell him, is the root characteristic of twentieth-century liberalism and that which distinguishes it sharply from any vestige of conservatism. One can even say that if an American conservative and an American liberal (of today) should agree, say, on the need for a welfare state, a most unlikely contingency, they would agree for different reasons—reasons that are important, since one would look to the welfare state to tie man down and the other to increase his freedom. It would not, thus and despite surface appearances, be the same social phenomenon, a fact that would soon appear in the actual administration of such a state. The main contributions of the pragmatic liberal of the twentieth century, the relativist, is to free men from the idea that there is a fixed universe. He tells men instead that there is only a free universe.

This hypothesis, that a common Lockian, eighteenth-century inheritance yielded both a conservatism and a liberalism which resulted in a conflict of ideas in America rather than the elimination of that conflict, explains dissension within the unity of America. To talk only about the liberal unity of America is to miss the point that there has also been a disunity—a conflict between liberalism and conservatism no matter how the labels may have been confused—and that the cause of the disunity was a conflict between those who saw man as fixed and enclosed and those who saw him as free.

We have answered the first question with which this book began: what is the nature of conservatism? Let us now try to answer the second question: what is the use of conservatism? To do so we must examine the nature of the futilitarian society.

What is the futilitarian society? It is a society that will not attempt to solve the problems it faces and often refuses even to face its problems because it fears freedom. Because it fears freedom it will not allow the experimentation, change, discovery, and adventure that are necessary to the solution of its problems. Thus it avoids the possibilities before it by refusing to acknowledge the only way any problem can be solved or anything new can be brought into the world, by refusing to acknowledge change and the freedom that makes change possible. Instead it attempts to limit man to what he has always been, to what his eternal essence tells him to be.

The futilitarian society is the conservative society because conservatism is dedicated to the proposition that society, law, and man should be fixed. Conservatism fears not just modern society, but all societies in which change is both frequent and valued,[6] in which freedom to change is both widespread and valued. The conservative may talk of freedom or, as he likes to call it, liberty, but he is antifreedom because he strives above all to confine man. Freedom may or may not be a by-product of his endeavors in actual daily fact, but it is not his aim, it is not his supreme value, and therefore it will not be cherished and extended. It is secondary to the task of fixing man in his essence. For the conservative, existence truly does not and should not precede essence but essence should dominate and crush existence. Freedom thus for the conservative is what is left over after man has been put in his place. The conservative faces the problem of order *vs.* freedom by avoiding freedom, by searching for the best way of hemming man in, of confining him, of bringing to a stop his incurable desire for freedom, his radicalism. Thus, to a conservative what is good and proper about classical liberalism is not its sense of man's freedom, but its eighteenth-century assumption that society, law, and man are fixed, that they obey certain laws, and can arrive at a final and complete position of stasis. The conservatism of the American, therefore, does not lie in his feudal ancestry or anything so esoteric. It lies instead in the way he uses the liberal institutions of America to tie man down, to prevent freedom, in the way he uses those institutions and the concepts they embody as a means of fixing man in a certain pattern of social behavior, in the way he uses them to destroy man's freedom to create another way of life. Liberal government in this view is a perpetual round of the same thing. The

* See, for example, the statement of Samuel P. Huntington in his "Conservatism as an Ideology," *The American Political Science Review*, June 1957, p. 461; "conservatism is not just the absence of change. It is the articulate, systematic, theoretical resistance to change." It is because it is systematic resistance to change that Huntington wishes the liberals to become conservatives today, thus adopting the Viereck line.

conservative does not ask whether or not it is sufficient to the needs of the time because the question might open up new and strange possibilities. He prefers instead the futilitarian society.

Today it is necessary to rescue liberal and constitutional government from the hands of the conservative, and to make it an instrument for freedom instead of a bind for stasis. It is a system of government admirably suited to freedom and change, but not when run by a conservative. It is necessary to do other things, too. It must be said that if man is cantankerous and apathetic today, that is not because he has too much freedom as the conservative would tell us, but because he has not enough freedom, has not been given the chance to use himself in experimentation, but instead must simply seek the fruitless excitement of a street gang,[7] or the idiot box. Man will not be tied down, and the attempt to tie him down forces him to seek destructive and meaningless forms of change. The man in subtopia seeking his futile achievement and the youth slouching on a street corner are in the same terrible dilemma.

Today it is also necessary to say that conservatism is dead set against innovation, that it is the philosophy of the futilitarian society because innovation has no place and can have no place in its system. Now, more than ever, new and unique acts are required if American society is to deal with not merely a threat from without but with fatigue and despair and apathy from within, with the hopeless sense that there is nothing that can be done about what ails us. America must deal with its problems by creative acts, by invention. It must be jerked around to look at what is coming toward it and to look to where

[7] See Paul Goodman's *Growing Up Absurd* (1960). See also W. W. Rostow, *The United States in the World Arena* (1960) for specific descriptions of the type of innovation both necessary and possible for America in the 1960's.

it is going. But no one can do this for America, no one man, no one threat. It can only do it for itself, and it can only do it if it rejects the postulates of conservative thought and, instead of running away from innovation, seeks innovation. If it does not, it will become a futilitarian society with all the frightful consequences that futility carries with it.

Conservatism and the futilitarian society aim to strip men of their possibilities, and society of the alternatives which lie before it. The conservative is the philosopher of the futilitarian society precisely because he wants to destroy possibilities, because he cannot face the costs of freedom. He cannot help us because he cannot see that the only limit on man which is viable is that which man creates for himself, and that man can only create such limits if he is given the freedom to do so, is given the freedom to limit himself. There is no other way. The effort to limit him from the outside by the concept of essence is simply the most futile of the assumptions of conservatism. Yet to enbalm man in essence is what the conservative aims to do in America today. It may be true that conservatism will not succeed in bringing freedom to an end, because man is free whether he likes it or not. But the desire and the attempt to avoid the fact of freedom will both harm America and make each of us that much less of a human being, for if man cannot loses his freedom he can choose to shrink or extend the area and amount of his freedom.

It is necessary, therefore, to proclaim once again that man is not conservative but radical, not fixed but free.